THE LIBERAL TRADITION

FROM FOX TO KEYNES

EDITED BY

ALAN BULLOCK

CENSOR OF ST. CATHERINE'S SOCIETY, OXFORD

AND

MAURICE SHOCK

FELLOW OF UNIVERSITY COLLEGE, OXFORD

NEW YORK UNIVERSITY PRESS

Washington Square

GENERAL PREFACE

ONE of the unique contributions the English people have made to civilisation has been the discussion of political issues which has been going on in Britain continuously since the 16th century. It is a discussion which has ranged over the whole field of political thought and experience. It began with the relation of the State to the individual in religious matters; for the last half century it has been increasingly pre-occupied with the relation of the State to the individual in economic matters. The strength of the tradition, the right of rebellion; the demand for equality, the rights of property; the place of justice and morality in foreign policy, the relations between Britain and her overseas territories; the claims of minorities, the value of civil and religious freedom; the rule of law, the Rule of the Saints; the rights of the individual, the claims of the State—all these have been the subject of passionate and incessant argument among Englishmen since the time of the Reformation.

This debate has never been of an academic character. There are, it is true, masterpieces of political philosophy in the English language: Hobbes' *Leviathan* is an obvious example. But the true character of this debate has been empirical: the discussion of particular and practical issues, in the course of which a clash of principle and attitude is brought out, but in which the element of abstract thought is always kept in relation to an immediate and actual situation. The riches of British political thought are to be found less in the philosophers' discussions of terms 'like 'The State', 'freedom' and 'obligation'—important though these are—than in the writings and speeches on contemporary political issues of men like Lilburne, Locke, Bolingbroke, Burke, Tom Paine, Fox, the Mills, Cobden, Disraeli, Gladstone and the Fabians. No other literature in the world is so rich in political pamphlets as English, and the pages of *Hansard* are a mine not only for the historian of political events but also for the historian of political ideas. It is in the discussions provoked by the major crises in British history—the Civil War, the Revolt of the American Colonies, the Reform Bills of the 19th century—that our political ideas have been hammered out.

One unfortunate result of this is that much of the material which anyone interested in English political ideas needs to read is inaccessible. Pamphlets and speeches are often only to be found in contemporary publications hidden away on the more obscure shelves of the big libraries. Even when the reader has secured a volume of 17th-century pamphlets or of Gladstone's speeches, he may well be deterred by the large amount of now irrelevant detail or polemic through which he has to make his way before striking the characteristic ideas and assumptions of the writer or speaker. It is to meet the need of the reader who is interested in English political ideas but has neither the time, the patience, nor perhaps the opportunity, to read through a library of books to find the material he is looking for that this present series of books is designed. Its aim is to present from sources of the most varied kind, books, pamphlets, speeches, letters, newspapers, a selection of original material illustrating the different facets of Englishmen's discussion of politics. Each volume will include an introductory essay by the editor together with sufficient explanation of the circumstances to make each extract intelligible. In some cases it has seemed best to make a particular crisis the focus of the discussion: this has been done with Mr. Beloff's volume, *The Debate on the American Revolution*, and with Dr. Cobban's *The Debate on the French Revolution*. In other cases the development of a particular view has been traced over a long period of years: this is the case, for instance, with the volumes on the Conservative, the Liberal, and the Radical Traditions. In a third case, that of the volume on 'Britain and Europe', our idea has been to single out a recurrent problem in English politics and trace its discussion from Pitt's day to our own.

To begin with, we have concentrated our attention on the period between the Revolt of the American Colonies and the Great War of 1914. When that has been covered we hope to treat the earlier period in the same way, notably the political discussions of the 17th century.

We do not believe that any one of these facets can be singled out and labelled as in some particular way more characteristic than others of the British Political Tradition: the rebels have as great a part in our political tradition as those who have argued the case for the claims of prescription and established authority. The wealth of that tradition is that it includes Lilburne, Tom Paine, Richard Cobden and the Early English Socialists as well as Locke, Burke and Disraeli.

We have tried to hold the balance even. In no sense do we wish to act as propagandists or advocates. While each editor has been given complete freedom to present his material as he wishes, we have been concerned as general editors to see that equal representation is given to different views in the series as a whole. Only in this way, we believe, is it possible to display the British Political Tradition in its unequalled richness, as built up out of a variety of political opinions and out of the clash between them, as the great and continuous debate of the nation to which, in its very nature, there can be no end.

ALAN BULLOCK
F. W. DEAKIN

Oxford

CONTENTS

4. THE GOVERNMENT AND THE NATIONAL ECONOMY

5. IMPERIALISM AND THE BOER WAR

6. ARMAMENTS

7. FOREIGN POLICY

ACKNOWLEDGEMENTS

WE would thank the following authors and owners of copyright material for their kind permission to use extracts from these works:

Messrs George Allen & Unwin Ltd (*Imperialism* by J. A. Hobson; *Speeches on Foreign Affairs* by Sir Edward Grey edited by P. Knaplund; *The Liberal Way*).

Messrs Ernest Benn Ltd (*Britain's Industrial Future*: The Report of the Liberal Industrial Enquiry).

Sir Felix Brunner, Bt (speech by Sir John Brunner, Bt).

Mrs Mary Carnegie (speeches by Mr Joseph Chamberlain published in *The Radical Platform*).

Messrs Constable & Co. Ltd (*The Life of Sir William Harcourt* by A. G. Gardiner).

Mrs L. Barbara Hammond (contribution by J. L. Hammond to *Liberalism and the Empire*).

Messrs Rupert Hart-Davis Ltd (*Essays in Persuasion* by J. M. Keynes).

The Executors of the late Earl Lloyd George of Dwyfor (speeches and *Better Times*).

Trustees of the XIth Marquess of Lothian (*The Outlawry of War* by Philip Kerr, XIth Marquess of Lothian).

Messrs Macmillan & Co. Ltd (*The Economic Consequences of the Peace* by J. M. Keynes).

The Manchester Guardian (leading articles).

Messrs Frederick Muller Ltd (*The Making of the Manchester Guardian* by C. P. Scott).

Dr Gilbert Murray, O.M. and Oxford University Press (*The League of Nations and the Democratic Idea*).

New Statesman and Nation (summary of *Full Employment in a Free Society* by Lord Beveridge).

Messrs Odhams Press Ltd (*Liberalism and the Social Problem* by Sir Winston Churchill).

The Executors of the late Earl of Oxford and Asquith (speeches).

Oxford University Press (*Liberalism* by L. T. Hobhouse; *The League of Nations* by Viscount Grey).

The Rt Hon. the Earl of Rosebery (speech by the late Earl of Rosebery).

The Rt Hon. the Viscount Samuel and Messrs Curtis Brown Ltd (*Liberalism*).

H.M.S.O., The Publishers of *Hansard* (speeches by W. P. Byles, Sir Edward Grey, J. M. Robertson, A. Ponsonby, J. Wedgwood, and J. G. S. MacNeill).

The Times (speeches by Sir Henry Campbell-Bannerman).

Should any extracts from works still in copyright be included inadvertently without acknowledgement the publishers should be notified so that such acknowledgement may be made in future editions.

A. B.
M. S.

NOTE

WITH one exception, none of the extracts printed in this volume is later in date than 1934. It would certainly have been possible to have included material from the period after 1934, but it has been our purpose to illustrate the historical development of the Liberal tradition and for this reason it seemed better to stop before the Second World War and not to engage in political controversy about the future of Liberalism or of the Liberal Party.

THE LIBERAL TRADITION

INTRODUCTION

I

AT first sight, the most striking thing about the Liberal
tradition is its intellectual incoherence. No one would
reasonably deny the name of 'Liberal' to any of the men
represented in this book, yet each of them—Fox and
Bentham, Richard Cobden and Lord John Russell, Macaulay
and Acton, Herbert Spencer and T. H. Green, Gladstone
and Lloyd George, Mill and Keynes—held views widely
different in some respect from those of the others. And these
differences are differences not only of policy and programme
—those are more easily explained—but also of principle, for
example on the role of the State, the vexed question of
laissez-faire.

This is the strongest argument in favour of treating
Liberalism historically. For it is only when they are seen as
part of a developing, and therefore changing, historical
tradition that the differences fall into place and the contradictions are reduced to manageable proportions. They can
never be eliminated, and it would be a distortion of the
Liberal tradition to try to gloss over its inconsistencies. For
that tradition has drawn on many different streams of
experience and thought. It owes much to the Dissenters
with their strong belief in individualism, the place of conscience in politics and their democratic tradition of self-
government, but something also to the Whigs with their
aristocratic tradition of civil and religious liberty and their
dislike of arbitrary government. It inherits a belief in natural
law and natural rights only to see these scornfully repudiated
by Bentham and the Philosophical Radicals in favour of the
principle of utility. From the Classical Economists and the
Manchester School it derives the orthodoxy of free trade
and *laissez-faire*, yet at the end of the 19th century embraces

the heretical view of working-class radicalism that something ought to be done for the poor.

This catholicity of origins is reflected in the divisions of opinion which have always characterised English Liberalism, but it has its compensation in the richness of the English tradition by comparison with the more doctrinaire views of continental liberalism.

II

English Liberalism was born out of the 17th-century struggle for freedom of conscience and the resistance of Parliament to the arbitrary authority of the King. By the end of the 18th century, the period at which this book begins, half the things for which Continental Liberalism had still to fight in the 19th century, were well established in England. The principles of civil and religious liberty, the rule of law and the freedom of the press, the institutions of parliamentary government, limited monarchy and an independent judiciary had made the English Constitution the cynosure of 18th-century Liberals like Montesquieu and Voltaire.

The hereditary guardians of this Liberal tradition were the Whigs, and the Whig defence of Wilkes and their opposition during the American War of Independence showed that 'the principles of 1688' had not lost their vitality.[1] But it had become in the hands of the Whigs, a tradition of *aristocratic* Liberalism, a tradition to be maintained rather than extended, and its limitations were shown by the equivocal attitude of the Whig leaders towards proposals for parliamentary reform. The issue of the French Revolution made even clearer the extent to which the Whigs had become conservative.[2] Edmund Burke, the greatest of 18th-century Whig writers, damned the Revolution and all its works, and a majority of the Whigs followed Portland in joining Pitt and supporting the war with France. Indeed Burke and the Portland Whigs appear to have suffered particularly severely from the panic fears which affected the English ruling class

---

[1] See *The Debate on the American Revolution*, edited by Max Beloff, in this series.
[2] See *The Debate on the French Revolution*, edited by Alfred Cobban, in this series.

at the news from France. It was left to the handful of Whigs
who remained faithful to Fox—Grey, Erskine, Sheridan—
and above all to Charles James Fox himself to defend the
liberties of the subject, freedom of the press and of public
meeting against the encroachments of a panicky Government. Fox was almost certainly wrong in his estimate of the
danger from France, especially after Napoleon's *coup d'état*,
and Whig opposition to the war had a tendency to degenerate into factiousness, but his defence of liberty was a vindica-
tion both of his own courage and of the Liberal tradition.[1]

The growth of that tradition up to the end of the 18th
century lies outside the scope of this book. But to include its
restatement by Fox in a book concerned with the development of Liberalism after 1800 serves two purposes: it
establishes the continuity between 19th-century Liberalism
and that older tradition which reaches back to Milton and
Locke, and it underlines the point after which the Whigs,
confronted with the issue of revolution in France, had either
openly to turn conservative like Burke or be prepared to
extend 'the principles of 1688'. The split between Fox and
Burke in 1791 thus forms one of the starting-points for the
development which culminated in the second half of the
19th century in the creation of a Liberal Party out of the old
Whig Party.

While the war with France and the fight for office absorbed
the attentions of the political world between 1793 and 1815,
great changes had been taking place in the economic and
social structure of the country, especially in those parts north
of Birmingham which were least known and least visited
by 18th-century politicians. The axis of English history,
which had hitherto lain along a line running from London
along the Thames Valley to Oxford and projected westwards
to the Bristol Channel, was shifting to the line London-
Birmingham-Manchester.

These changes provide the second starting-point for the
modern history of English Liberalism. They may be briefly

[1] It is interesting to find Richard Cobden, who was highly critical of the
aristocratic liberalism of the Whig tradition, looking back to Fox and claiming
the authority of his opposition to the French War when he was himself fighting
against interventionist policies in the 1850's. See Richard Cobden, *1793 and
1853, in Three Letters* (1853).

described as growth in trade, growth in industry and growth in population.

The greater part of English history since has been a commentary on these changes. Two immediate consequences were the bewilderment of the Government, confronted with problems for which there were no precedents, and the growth of a middle-class opinion impatient and critical of the Government's aristocratic incompetence.

Disraeli has well described the state of mind of Lord Liverpool's Ministry at the end of the war with Napoleon: 'The peace came . . . the people found themselves without guides. They went to the ministry; they asked to be guided, they asked to be governed. Commerce requested a code; trade required a currency; the unfranchised subject solicited his equal privilege; suffering labour clamoured for its rights; a new race demanded education. What did the ministry do? They fell into a panic. Having fulfilled during their lives the duties of administration, they were frightened because they were called upon, for the first time, to perform the functions of government. Like all weak men, they had recourse to what they called strong measures. They determined to put down the multitude. They thought they were imitating Mr. Pitt, because they mistook disorganisation for sedition.'[1]

While Government fumbled with the problems of the new society growing up in England, there began to emerge among the new middle class of manufacturers and merchants, bankers and business men, a number of ideas which, many of them became convinced, would lead to the solution of all social and economic problems. The intellectual parentage of these ideas can be traced to two remarkable groups of writers, closely linked and in part identical. The first was the Political Economists: the most famous name, that of Adam Smith (who belongs to an earlier generation than the others), followed by Malthus, Ricardo, James Mill, McCulloch, Nassau William Senior and J. S. Mill. The second was the Benthamites, known sometimes as the Philosophical Radicals: Bentham himself, who died in 1832, James Mill, Grote, Romilly, Place, Bowring, Molesworth and Joseph Hume.

[1] Disraeli, *Coningsby*.

III

There was nothing very original in these ideas. Most of them are to be found in the 18th century, if not earlier.[1] What was new was the extraordinary authority which they now acquired and the way in which they fitted like a glove the needs, the interests and the prejudices of that new middle class which was elbowing itself into power.

What were the characteristics of this phase of Liberal thought?

It was intensely individualist. 'The community', Bentham wrote, 'is a fictitious body, composed of the individual persons who are considered as constituting, as it were, its members.'[2] It was taken for granted that all social progress depended upon the unhampered initiative of individuals and a prudent self-interest was regarded as the predominant motive in human nature. But, in economics at least, there was no need to anticipate any contradiction between the individual's selfish pursuit of his own ends and the interest of the community. Bentham added to the passage just quoted the further sentence: 'The interest of the community then is, what?—the sum of interests of the several members who compose it.' It was as simple as that: there was no problem to be solved.

For those who still had doubts there was Adam Smith's comfortable assurance that while each individual 'intends only his own gain, he is in this, as in many other cases, led by an invisible hand to promote an end which was no part of his intentions.'

The conclusion was obvious. It was the height of folly on the part of Governments to attempt to interfere with the processes of this 'natural' order which, *of its own accord*, worked to produce a spontaneous increase in wealth and social improvement. 'The general rule is', Bentham wrote, 'that nothing ought to be done or attempted by government. The motto, or watchword of government, on these occasions,

[1] See Leslie Stephens, *The English Utilitarians*, 3 v. (1900) ; Elie Halevy, *The Growth of Philosophic Radicalism* (1928) ; J. P. Plamenatz, *The English Utilitarians* (1949).

[2] Bentham, *Introduction to the Principles of Morals and Legislation* (ed. W. Harrison, 1948), p. 126.

ought to be—*Be quiet.* . . . The art (of government) therefore, is reduced within a small compass. . . . The request
which agriculture, manufactures and commerce present to
governments, is as modest and reasonable as that which
Diogenes made to Alexander: Stand out of my sunshine.'[1]

This conclusion the Economists reinforced by the further
argument that, even if (as Malthus and Ricardo thought)
the prospects of human society were gloomier than Adam
Smith had foreseen, it was still useless for governments to
meddle or for the unfortunate to complain, since the world
is governed by certain immutable economic laws which are
not susceptible to human regulation. 'There are miseries in
the social state', Ricardo wrote, 'which legislation cannot
relieve.' Hence the futility of poor relief, and of attempting
to raise wages by combining in trade unions. 'They might
as well attempt', Cobden remarked, 'to regulate the tides by
force, or change the course of the seasons, or subvert any of
the other laws of nature—for the wages of labour depend
upon laws as unerring and as much above our coercive power
as any other operations of nature.'

But most important of all was to stop the State meddling
with the flow of foreign trade, to remove the hundred and
one obstacles placed in the way of imports and exports and
to establish freedom of trade. It was Cobden who made
Free Trade the Ark of the Liberal covenant, but it was
common doctrine to the Classical Economists and Philosophical Radicals long before the Anti-Corn Law League was
formed and, as the Petition of the Merchants of 1820 shows,
once the Napoleonic Wars were over, it was rapidly put in
the forefront of their demands by the merchants and
industrialists. Much the same is true of that dislike of colonies
and imperialism which was closely connected with the
advocacy of Free Trade. Some of the most famous pages in
Adam Smith deal with the evils of the Old Colonial System,
while long before he took up radical politics Bentham wrote
*Emancipate your colonies! addressed to the National Convention of
France, Anno* 1793. *Shewing the uselessness and mischievousness of
distant dependencies to an European State.* Here, as in the case

[1] Bentham, *Manual of Political Economy*, Works, ed. Bowring (1843), iii, pp.
33-5.

of Free Trade, there is a line of development which runs
through English Liberal thought from Adam Smith to the
1906 Government of Campbell-Bannerman and beyond.

IV

An inveterate distrust of the power of the State was
characteristic of 19th century Liberalism up to the last
decades of the century, from Bentham to Acton. But there
was a difference between the Liberal attitude towards the
State in economics and in politics. The principle of a *natural*
identity of interests which, in the economic sphere, meant
laissez-faire, did not extend to the political sphere. As the
Abbé Morellet wrote to Lord Shelburne: 'Since liberty is a
natural state and restrictions are, on the contrary, the state
of compulsion, by giving back liberty, everything resumes
its own place, and everything is in peace, *provided only that
thieves and murderers continue to be caught.*'[1] Governments were
necessary, therefore, if only to make such provision; their
job was to provide the framework of security within which
the principle of the natural identity of interests could then
come into play. 'The essential business of government', says
Nassau Senior, 'is to afford defence; to protect the community against foreign and domestic violence and fraud.
Unfortunately, however, governments have generally supposed it to be their duty, not merely to give *security*, but
wealth; not merely to enable their subjects to produce and
enjoy in safety, but to teach them what to produce and how
to enjoy.'[2]

The first task of reform, therefore, was to curb the pretensions of Governments and to confine them to that sphere
which, even on the strictest *laissez-faire* views, was legitimate
for them. The second was to provide security against the
abuse of power in their private interest by those who controlled the Government. 'All the difficult questions of
Government', James Mill writes, 'relate to the means of
restraining those, in whose hands are lodged the powers

---

[1] *Lettres de l'Abbé Morellet à Lord Shelburne*, p. 102, quoted by Halevy, *op. cit.*
p. 116.

[2] Nassau William Senior, *Political Economy*, 2nd ed. 1850, p. 176.

necessary for the protection of all, from making a bad use of it.'[1] In practical terms this meant measures against Bentham's two Sinister Interests, the Monarchical and the Aristocratic. The Whigs, conscious of the dangers from the first of these, though not from the second, relied on the mixed nature of the constitution to preserve a balance. Bentham had nothing but contempt for such a view. 'Talk of balance: never will it do: leave that to Mother Goose and Mother Blackstone.' As he went on to point out, it did not provide —indeed, it was not intended to provide—any guarantee against a cardinal feature of the unreformed political system, corruption and the abuse of power not by the Monarchical but by the Aristocratic Interest. For this the only remedy was a drastic reform of the parliamentary system which would safeguard the interests of all by the representation of all: in short by universal suffrage and the ballot.

Thus, in economics (which was the business of the middle class) the principle of utility pointed to *laissez-faire* and trust in the natural play of forces to produce the greatest happiness of the greatest number. In politics, however (which was still the business of the aristocracy and not of the middle class), the principle of utility pointed in the opposite direction —'Minimise confidence'. In an iconoclastic frame of mind which was totally indifferent to Burke's argument of prescription, the Philosophical Radicals demanded the submission of all institutions—legal, constitutional, ecclesiastical— to the rationalist criterion of utility. Utility meant the greatest happiness of the greatest number, interpreted in turn to mean the greatest happiness of the greatest number of individuals all pursuing their own enlightened self interest. 'I asked myself', Bentham records, '*how* this or that institution contributed to the greatest happiness?—*Did* it contribute?—If not, what institution *would* contribute to it?'[2] It was this frame of mind which made Benthamite ideas the impetus behind the greater part of the reforming activity for which the years from 1815 to 1870 are remarkable. Yet all the time the Liberalism of these years looked on reform, not as the imposition of a blue-print upon society, but as the

---

[1] James Mill, *Essay on Government*, ed. Ernest Barker, Cambridge, 1937, p. 6.
[2] Bentham, *Works*, ed. Bowring, x, p. 581.

reverse of planning, as the liberation of natural, spontaneous forces in society which would *of their own accord* promote social improvement.

Any account of the influence of the Philosophical Radicals and the Classical Economists on English liberal thought needs careful qualification. The Benthamites and the Economists never founded a party of their own; their angular orthodoxies were too rigid for English politics. They exercised their influence through the permeation of both the existing parties with their ideas. In certain directions—an obvious example is commercial policy—that influence was very great, but it was never, even in its hey day between 1830 and 1870, the sole influence shaping the Liberal tradition, and it encountered considerable opposition inside the Whig as well as inside the Tory Party. A good instance of this is Macaulay. For Macaulay was certainly very much influenced by the ideas of the utilitarians and the political economists, but at times he was hotly critical of them and quite capable of taking an independent line of his own, as he did in his defence of the Ten Hours Bill in the teeth of *laissez-faire* prejudice, and again in his views on education.[1]

Moreover, in the last quarter of the 19th century the authority of these ideas, especially in relation to social problems, was badly shaken. To many Liberals the influence of *laissez-faire* economics and a doctrinaire Benthamite distrust of intervention by the State came to appear as a dead hand crippling the attempt to revise drastically the social and economic assumptions of Liberalism. From this point of view the influence of these ideas distorted the development of the English Liberal tradition, and from John Stuart Mill to Keynes the history of English Liberalism is principally concerned with the effort to shake itself free from the preconceptions of the early 19th century.

To identify the Liberal tradition with the views of the Utilitarians, the Classical Economists and the Manchester School is therefore to ignore its historical development. It is equally unhistorical, however, to underestimate the extraordinary influence which those ideas had up to 1870 and their persistence long afterwards. Possibly no other set of

[1] See nos. 38 and 41, below.

ideas has ever enjoyed such authority in England. In Keynes'
phrase, this was the true Church of England for a great part
of the 19th century and later deviations into heresy have not
yet obliterated all traces of the original orthodoxy.

v

The impact of these ideas on both parties was disruptive.
The first to attempt to come to terms with them were the
Tories. In the 1820's it was a group of Tory ministers
—Huskisson, Robinson, Wallace—who were impressed by
the Economists' arguments and took the first steps towards
Free Trade; it was another Tory, Robert Peel, who began
the reform of the English law which Bentham had long
demanded. But Liberal Toryism was crippled by its own
contradictions. Any attempt to put into effect, even partially,
the views of Ricardo and Bentham must sooner or later run
up against the demand for the repeal of the Corn Laws and
for the reform of Parliament. No Tory minister, however
liberal his sympathies, could entertain either of these
demands without splitting the party. Liberal Toryism led
down a blind alley at the end of which was a wall too high
for any leader to get his party over intact. With Canning's
succession as Prime Minister in 1827 the split in the Tory
Party became open: three years later the Tories' long
monopoly of office came to an end.

From the election of 1784 to the election of 1830 the Whigs
had been continuously out of power, with the brief exception
of a share in the Ministry of All the Talents. By 1818 they
had brought their strength up to 173 seats in the Commons,
but they lacked leaders and were divided by faction. Nevertheless, it was something to have an Opposition at all, something to have even a handful of men in Parliament who
would defend civil liberty in the black years of distress after
the war, as Fox had done in the 1790's.

Nor was Whig criticism of the Government limited to
home affairs and the panic legislation of 1817 and 1819, any
more than Fox's had been. Sharply critical of the Vienna
Settlement and of the measures taken by the restored
Governments in Europe after 1815, they were hostile to

Metternich's Congress system and outspoken in their sympathy for the national and liberal movement in Greece, in Italy, in Spain and South America. It was from this sympathy with the *Liberales* of Spain that the word 'Liberal' as a party label came into English politics in the years after 1815. For this was the age of Byron as well as of Bentham, of the Romantics no less than of the Utilitarians, and Byron's poems in praise of freedom—even more perhaps his death at Missolonghi—played a part in forming one of the most persistent traditions of English Liberalism, sympathy with peoples struggling to be free. It is a sympathy which has been arbitrary in its operation, more often than not misinformed, muddle-headed and unpractical, even more often raising hopes it was bound to disillusion, yet always generous in its nature and characteristic of English Liberalism from the Peninsular War of Napoleon's time to the Spanish Civil War of our own.

The Whigs, however, were as much entangled in contradictions as the Tories. Although they sympathised with Spanish *Liberales* and Italian *carbonari*, they were certainly not prepared to go to war on their behalf. Although they had traditional ties with the commercial interest, they were much slower than the Tories to adopt Free Trade and the new ideas of the Economists. Although they had been playing with the idea of parliamentary reform since the 1780's, they were distrusted by every reformer for the luke-warmness and fickleness of their support. Radical opinion was well summed up by Francis Place when he wrote: 'There is no real difference between the Whig and Tory factions, except the difference which always existed: namely, that the Tories would exalt the kingly power that it might trample upon the aristocracy and the people, while the Whigs would establish an aristocratical oligarchy to trample on the King and the people.'[1]

The Whigs still saw politics in terms of an hereditary governing class, the handful of great families who constituted the Whig connection. They were as reluctant as the Tories to recognise that the social changes which had taken place in the fifty years—1780–1830—made political and economic

[1] From *A Reply to Lord Erskine by an Elector of Westminster*, 1819.

reform imperative. Yet in the end, screwed up to the sticking point by spending most of those fifty years out of office, the Whigs made their bid for an alliance with middle-class Liberalism and passed the Reform Act of 1832. Forty years afterwards, the logic of Fox's split from Burke in 1791 had worked itself out: the Whig connection and 'the principles of 1688' had been extended to include the middle class, and the unimpeachably middle-class Macaulay joined the unimpeachably aristocratic Russell to defend the first triumph of the new Whigs.

It was an uneasy combination with much recrimination on both sides. Roebuck expressed a view common enough among middle-class Radicals when he wrote: 'The Whigs have ever been an exclusive and aristocratic faction, though at times employing democratic principles and phrases. . . . When out of office they were demagogues, in power they became exclusive oligarchs.'[1] It was the Tories who had initiated the economic reforms of the 1820's and a Tory Prime Minister, Peel, who repealed the Corn Laws in 1846. At that time Cobden urged Peel to come out and lead a new Liberal Party—'You represent the IDEA of the age, and it has no other representative amongst statesmen.'[2]

A little earlier he had written to his friend George Combe: 'The Whig leader (*i.e.* Russell) is great upon questions of a constitutional character, and has a hereditary leaning towards a popular and liberal interpretation of the Constitution. But his mind is less adapted for the mastery of economical questions, and he attaches an inferior importance to them. . . . He breathes the atmosphere of a privileged clique. His sympathies are aristocratic. He is sometimes thinking of the House of Russell, whilst Peel is occupied upon Manchester. They are in a false position; Peel ought to be the leader of the middle class.'[3]

But Peel declined Cobden's advice and although Peel's Liberal Toryism contributed Gladstone to the Liberal Party, that party when it was finally born in the 1860's was a reconstituted Whig Party. Another forty years after 1832,

[1] J. A. Roebuck, *History of the Whig Ministry of 1830* (1862), ii, 405-6.
[2] Cobden's letter of June 23, 1846, and Peel's reply, in Morley, *Life of Richard Cobden*, vol. i., ch. xvii.
[3] *Ibid.* i, p. 366.

the Whig Party of Fox and Grey and Russell had become the party of middle-class Liberalism. By the 1880's it was Whigs like the Duke of Argyll and Lord Hartington who were defending the pure orthodoxy of *laissez-faire* against Radicals like Chamberlain who were abandoning it.

VI

Much the most effective political expression of middle-class Liberalism, before Gladstone created the Liberal Party, was the Anti-Corn Law League of the 1840's. 'I believe this', John Bright said, 'to be a movement of the commercial and industrial classes against the lords and great proprietors of the soil', and his and Cobden's speeches make clear how much both sides felt the issue of the Corn Laws to be the symbol of a deeper conflict. It was a conflict between two ways of life, two different views of the future of England. On the one hand was the landed class, accustomed to a monopoly of political power and social influence, especially locally. Heirs to a traditional set of values, they regarded land as the paramount interest in the country and were contemptuous of the Manchester 'bagman's millenium', with buying in the cheapest market and selling in the dearest as the height of its social philosophy. On the other hand, as Cobden saw, was engaged the manufacturers' pride as an order, the pride as well as the interests of a stubborn, hard-headed class of men. Bred in the values of the world of business and the Chapel, the manufacturers in their turn were contemptuous of the landlords as a parasitic class; they were hostile to both the virtues and the vices of the aristo-cratic ideal, narrow-minded, aggressive, but immensely self-confident that the future of the country lay with them and the industry of the North and the Midlands.

Cobden, however, was a good deal more than the success-ful organiser of a manufacturers' pressure group. Out of the League grew the Manchester School and its attempt to build upon the principle of Free Trade a whole new system of policy appropriate to a country whose greatness was bound up with her commerce. Cobden was always attracted by the United States and he preferred the commercially-minded policies of the U.S.A. to the policies of the balance of power and Palmerstonian diplomacy pursued by England.' He looked on trade as an activity which drew peoples together, which gave them a common interest in overcoming the barriers of race, language and religion; peace therefore was the natural corollary of trade. What threatened trade and peace alike was the intervention of Governments and the governing class which controlled them, insular, annexationist, aggressive, thinking only in terms of power and prestige, mercantilist in their politics as much as in their economics, believing that one nation could only gain at the expense of another. Cobden and Bright attacked such a policy on the grounds that it conceived of the relations between independent nations purely in terms of force, ultimately of war, and of the relations between England and her colonies purely in terms of supremacy and exploitation.

Cobden's non-intervention was the policy of *laissez-faire* applied to international relations, and it rested on the same belief in a natural harmony of interests—if only governments would observe Bentham's maxim, *Be quiet*. On the one side it shows the same distrust of government and the activity of the State, on the other the same hostility to the English ruling class with its traditional interest in foreign policy and diplomacy.

Neither Cobden nor Bright had the least sympathy with the extension of British rule over other peoples, but they were insistent on the obligations which an empire imposed on the metropolitan country. 'I do not now', Bright said in 1858, 'make any comment upon the mode in which this country has been put into possession of India. I accept that possession as a fact. There we are; we do not know how to leave it, and therefore let us see if we know how to govern it. It is a problem such as, perhaps, no other nation has had to solve. Let us see whether there is enough of intelligence and virtue in England to solve the difficulty.'[1] Bright approached the problems of Ireland in the same spirit. If it was Gladstone who made a settlement with Ireland the touchstone of English Liberalism, it was Bright who, long before Gladstone,

[1] See no. 54 and nos. 57-8, below.

pointed to the disgrace which the condition of Ireland
represented to the good name of Britain and who, a quarter
of a century before the Conservative Party was converted to
land-purchase as the solution of the Irish problem, cam-
paigned for the removal of every obstacle to the free sale of
land in Ireland.

Cobden and Bright, however, commanded less and less
support in the 1850's. Middle-class Liberal England preferred
Palmerston's views on foreign policy. Time and again he
beat them on their own ground in an appeal to the middle-
class electorate; in the election of 1857 Cobden was defeated
at Huddersfield and Bright in Manchester itself.

Palmerston was Palmerston. To call him a Whig or even
a Canningite does less than justice to that extraordinary
personality. To call him a Liberal sounds odder still. Yet in
his support for Italian independence, in his generous, offhand
encouragement to the Liberal cause in Europe, his dislike
of tyranny, Palmerston did represent a side of the Liberal
tradition. His Liberalism was unsystematic, a matter of
temperament rather than principle, yet a part of the tradition which has to go in along with the Benthamites and
the Manchester School.

The truth was that the middle classes had 'arrived' and
in the process were shedding their radicalism. They were
becoming respectable. 'The result [Cobden wrote] has been
to make a large increase in the number of Tories, and to cool
down to a genteel tone the politics of the Whigs, until at
last the majority find an earnest Radical not sufficiently
genteel for their taste.' If Liberalism was to develop further,
it had to find wider support than in the middle-class electorate enfranchised by the 1832 Reform Act.

That meant a further extension of the franchise, and in
1858 Bright, transferring his seat from Manchester to the
more democratic Birmingham, opened the campaign which
was to bear fruit nine years later in the second Reform Act.
For a long time Bright had to conduct this campaign single-
handed: the official Liberal Party, still led by Palmerston,
would have nothing to do with it. Not until 1865 did he
find powerful support in the newly-converted Gladstone who
declared in characteristic fashion to the crowded Free Trade

Hall in Manchester, 'At last my friends I am come among you, and I am come among you unmuzzled'.

It was a momentous conversion. In the same year Palmerston died and, after a brief interlude under Russell, Gladstone succeeded to the leadership of the Liberal Party. At the first election fought on the extended franchise, Gladstone won a clear majority and formed a cabinet which (with John Bright at the Board of Trade) was representative for the first time of all sections of Liberal opinion. With the controversial issue of the franchise removed, the conflicting elements in the Liberal tradition were brought into temporary equipoise and found in Gladstone a leader capable of uniting them in the most effective Liberal ministry of the century.

VII

To create an effective Liberal Party it was necessary, as Bright saw, to put it on a broader basis than that of a middle class which, once its interests had been recognised, was ceasing to be radical. A similar development was taking place in Liberal ideas.

Had English Liberalism remained what it was at the beginning of the 1850's, a reflection of Peacock's 'steam intellect mind' on the eve of the Great Exhibition, it would have been a more consistent but much poorer and less interesting view of politics than it became. In the first phase of its development, up to the 1850's, Liberalism had expressed the needs, the interests, the prejudices and the beliefs of the manufacturing and commercial middle class which had been enfranchised in 1832 and made its power felt in the repeal of the Corn Laws in 1846. In the second phase of its development, however, Liberalism loses a good deal of this narrow character and turns into a social philosophy in its own right, a set of ideas no longer dependent for their validity or acceptance upon the extent to which they reflect the interests of a single class.

A few months after John Bright began his campaign for an extension of the franchise, John Stuart Mill published his essay *On Liberty*. Mill had been brought up as the child and heir of Benthamite Liberalism. He repaid the debt by producing in his *Utilitarianism* and in his *Principles of Political Economy* the most finished exposition of the system of ideas derived from that source. But, even at that early stage of his life, he was already in revolt against the narrowness of utilitarian thought and driven by his own honesty to make a series of damning concessions. In his later work the transformation is complete. To turn from James Mill's essay *On Government* to his son's *On Liberty* is to enter a different intellectual climate.

In his *On Liberty* (1859) and in his *Representative Government* (1861) Mill produces formal arguments which are designed to show that liberty, in particular liberty of thought and expression, is necessary for the development of human society. Progress, he argues, depends upon the freedom of individuals to innovate and experiment; conformity inevitably produces stagnation. This is the utilitarian basis of his argument against fully fledged democracy, that it is likely to produce a tyranny of the majority which will stifle those individual forces in society which give it life and meaning. For James Mill democracy had been a weapon to destroy the power of the 'sinister interest'; for his son it was a potential threat to liberty and social diversity, the mainsprings of human progress.

But the heart of Mill's argument for the cause of Liberty transcends the utilitarian. In pages which are the classical expression of English Liberal thought he argues the case for liberty and for representative institutions on the grounds that these are essential to that full and rich development of human individuality which he obviously values as an end in itself. When he quotes with approval von Humboldt's remark, 'It really is of importance not only what men do but also what manner of men they are that do it', or states that, 'If all mankind minus one were of one opinion, and only one person were of the contrary opinion, mankind would be no more justified in silencing that one person than he, if he had the power, would be justified in silencing mankind', Mill is, in the first instance, arguing for a theory of self-realisation and, in the second, saying that freedom of thought has a value in itself which is superior to Benthamite considerations of the greatest good of the greatest number.

It is this belief, crystallised in his demand for 'a social support, a *point d'appui* for individual resistance to the ruling power; a protection, a rallying point, for opinions and interests which the ascendant public opinion views with disfavour' that led Mill to hold back from any scheme which involved the granting of sovereign power to a democratically elected legislature except under special conditions designed to guarantee the over-representation of minority groups.

Acton faced the same problem from a different standpoint. For him, too, 'Liberty is not a means to a higher political end. It is itself the highest political end'. But he concentrated his attack on the dangers inherent in the doctrine of equality, which he regarded as totally incompatible with liberty. Forced as an historian to admit the faults of the old order which was passing away, Acton could not regard a too rapid advance towards democracy with anything but distrust.

In his essay *On Compromise* (1874), John Morley, the most brilliant of the young Liberal intellectuals in the Gladstonian era, attempted to provide a practical political answer to these fears. *On Compromise* is really an exposition of the technique of gradualism. Small reforms are the key to ordered political progress, minimising at all times the dangers which arise when political parties move too far apart. Morley, therefore, is able to argue that 'a right conception of political method . . . leads the wise conservative to accept the small change, lest a worse thing befall him, and the wise innovator to seize the chance of a small improvement, while incessantly working in the direction of great ones'. If no one reads Morley today, he showed real insight in pointing to the path which British politics have followed during the age of democracy.

In this middle period of Liberalism, then, not only has the argument for liberty taken a different form from the brash and aggressive utilitarian theory of Bentham and James Mill; it has become a defence of intellectual and moral freedom, valued for its own sake, against the dangers inherent in democracy. It is a striking fact that these dangers should have been recognised at a time when Liberals were coming to accept the necessity of a further advance towards democracy in the second Reform Act. It was in no easy spirit of optimism but with a clear understanding of the risks involved that men like Gladstone and Mill accepted such a step as necessary and right.

VIII

Matthew Arnold, in his famous essay *Culture and Anarchy* (1869), criticised the Philistinism and provincialism of English Nonconformist Liberalism and ascribed these qualities to the Hebraic inspiration of Nonconformity and its neglect of the Hellenic tradition of humanism. 'Their idea of human perfection', he wrote, 'is narrow and inadequate; the Dissidence of Dissent and the Protestantism of the Protestant religion will never bring humanity to its true goal.' The Philosophical Radicalism of Bentham and James Mill, another of the sources from which Liberalism had drawn inspiration, was open to the same sort of criticism. The liberalism of Mill's essay *On Liberty* on the other hand represents an emancipation from influences to which the Liberal tradition owed much of its strength but also a certain narrow-mindedness in its earlier phase. This emancipation finds its clearest expression in Gladstone.

For Gladstone, as J. L. Hammond points out,[1] combined the religious feeling of a Wilberforce or a Shaftesbury with a passion for the classical civilisation of Greece and Rome. His Christianity was illuminated by his love of Homer and Aristotle, Augustine and Dante. These, together with Bishop Butler and Burke, were the influences which had the deepest effect on him and gave him an intellectual approach to Liberalism wholly different from that of a man like Bright.

On one side of his complex personality Gladstone was an orthodox Liberal and it was this side which was uppermost in his career until his first retirement in 1874. Had Gladstone died then at the age of sixty-five he would have appeared as the man who had put into effect (as Chancellor of the Exchequer from 1859 to 1865 and as Prime Minister from 1868 to 1874) the programme of Liberal reforms which Cobden had once called on Peel, Gladstone's master, to carry out.[2]

[1] J. L. Hammond, *Gladstone and the Irish Nation*, p. 60.   [2] See above, p. xxx.

Free trade, a commercial treaty with France, the abolition of the paper duties, the reduction of expenditure and taxation, the disestablishment of the Irish Church, the Education Act of 1870, the Ballot Act, the opening of the Universities to Nonconformists and of the Civil Service to competitive examination, Cardwell's Army reforms, the Alabama arbitration and neutrality in the Franco-Prussian War—it was an impressive record, but all well within the canon of accepted Liberal ideas.

Where Gladstone made his own individual contribution and enlarged the Liberal tradition was in the two crusades which brought him back into politics after 1874: foreign policy and the Irish question. On both issues his attitude gave expression to the vivid conception of the place of the moral law in the relations between nations which made him the most controversial figure of his age.

Gladstone's ideas on foreign policy were not those of Cobden and Bright. Far from advocating non-intervention, he insisted (for example, in the Eastern crisis of 1875–8) on England's duty to intervene and to pursue an active policy. Where he differed from Palmerston and Disraeli was on the grounds of intervention and the objectives of an active foreign policy.

Although there are many anticipations of his views on earlier occasions, they find their clearest expression in the sustained attack which he made on Disraeli's foreign policy in the 1870's and which reached its climax in the Midlothian campaign of 1879–80.

Gladstone took as his starting-point the principle that foreign policy ought to be conducted in accordance with the demands of justice, not of expediency or power. He condemned 'a vigorous, that is to say, a narrow, restless, blustering and self-asserting foreign policy . . . appealing to the self-love and pride of the community' and setting up national interests selfishly conceived ('a new and base idolatry') as its sole objective. 'I appeal to an established tradition, older, wiser, nobler far—a tradition not which disregards British interests, but which teaches you to seek the promotion of those interests in obeying the dictates of honour and of justice.'[1]

[1] See no. 76, below.

A policy based upon such principles, Gladstone believed, would always find support in 'the general sentiment of the civilised world' to which the statesman must appeal for those 'moral supports which the general and fixed convictions of mankind afford'. But even if such a policy was backed by the moral force of public opinion, how was it to be put into effect? Gladstone answered: by the Concert of Europe, by the European Powers engaging in joint intervention to see that justice was done. Common action alone, he argued, would unite the Great Powers for the common good and at the same time would 'neutralise and fetter the selfish aims of each'.

Gladstone believed that there had been a good prospect of such joint intervention by the Powers in the Balkans in 1876 and that this had been destroyed by Disraeli's determination to pursue a unilateral policy and break up the Concert of Powers—with the result that Russia too broke away and proceeded to intervene on her own in pursuit of her national, and not the common, interest.

Disraeli's action angered Gladstone the more because he believed that it was the special role of Britain, as the one disinterested Great Power on the European scene, to take the lead in organising the Concert of Europe. This was her mission, to press for common action in the interests of justice and the common good, but it was a part which she could only play if she remained free from all taint of seeking material gain, a position destroyed in this case by the annexation of Cyprus.

Throughout his life Gladstone felt a passionate sympathy for peoples struggling to achieve national independence. This provides the other foundation of his views on foreign policy. 'The powers of self-government', this was his answer alike to the problems of the Balkans and those of Ireland. 'Give those people freedom and the benefits of freedom', he said of Turkey's Christian subjects in 1880, 'that is the way to make a barrier against despotism. Fortresses may be levelled to the ground; treaties may be trodden under foot— the true barrier against despotism is in the human heart and the human mind.'

From this sympathy it followed for Gladstone that all nations should enjoy equality of rights. 'To claim anything more than equality of rights in the moral and political intercourse of the world is not the way to make England great, but to make it both morally and materially little.' From this in turn sprang his condemnation of imperialism which proclaimed supremacy, not equality, and in its eagerness for aggrandisement brushed aside the rights of other nations to bring them under alien rule.

Back in office after 1880, Gladstone failed to put these principles into practice. The occupation of Egypt accorded ill with the spirit of the Midlothian campaign and his views on foreign policy proved less and less applicable to the rivalries of the Great Powers as the 19th century drew to its close. But the ideas to which he gave currency, far from losing their hold upon the Liberal imagination, have gained in strength since 1914. In the hopes placed in the League of Nations and the United Nations, in the attempt to organise collective security and the disappointed but constantly renewed appeals to world opinion against injustice and aggression, in the demand of the peoples of Asia, Africa and the Middle East for self-government, Gladstone's beliefs have found a frustrated but passionate confirmation.

It was in his campaign for Irish Home Rule that Gladstone himself tried most tenaciously to carry out his ideas. He came to see the Irish question, not as a domestic problem of law and order—any more than the American question had been in the 1770's—but as the claim of a nation to self-government, as much deserving of sympathy as the claims of the Italians, the Greeks and the Bulgars. Gladstone's determination to satisfy this claim deeply affected the fortunes of Liberalism for years to come. It split the Liberal Party, put back the cause of social reform for a generation, necessitated a dangerous alliance with the Irish Nationalists, and, because of its unpopularity in England, was electorally disastrous. In spite of all this Gladstone and his followers were convinced that justice for Ireland was the great culminating work of the Liberal tradition. Ireland was the touchstone of that sympathy which Liberal England had shown so generously in the case of others: was it now to be overridden by self-interest when it was a question of Britain's own empire?

Self-government had already been granted to Canada and the other colonies with the most felicitous results. No more was being asked for Ireland where, by contrast, 'the first conditions of civil life—the free course of law, the liberty of every individual in the exercise of every legal right, the confidence of the people in the law and their sympathy with the law' were entirely absent. It was only in Ireland that the sovereign Liberal remedy of freedom had not been tried. Elsewhere it had never failed and the settlement of Ireland, the thorniest question in British politics, would be its supreme justification.

IX

Gladstone had resumed the leadership of the Liberal Party after his retirement in 1874 with the limited objectives, first of challenging Disraeli's foreign policy and later of achieving a settlement with Ireland. On the other issues, however, which were to play so great a part in the politics of the next half century, social reform and the condition of the working classes, he offered no lead at all. His preoccupation with Ireland heavily handicapped the efforts of those who were becoming alive to the need to question and revise orthodox Liberalism's approach to social problems.

The Liberals of the Manchester School had assumed that with the destruction of the 'sinister interests' which stood in the way of the free development of social and economic forces, a natural harmony of interests would emerge of its own accord. This dream of a self-regulating society reduced to a minimum the role of the State. All the State had to do was to 'hold the ring', to ensure the conditions in which economic and political interests could have free play. Dissatisfied with this view, John Stuart Mill attempted to provide a new criterion for the intervention of the State by drawing a sharp distinction between 'self-regarding' and 'other-regarding' actions. 'The only part of the conduct of anyone for which he is amenable to society', Mill wrote, 'is that which concerns others. In the part which merely concerns himself, his independence is, of right, absolute'. But Mill's criticism did not go far enough. The distinction on which he sought to base his social philosophy proved untenable and was repudiated by the next generation of Liberal thinkers. The last quarter of the 19th century in fact produced a new philosophy of Liberalism and a new programme of radical legislation.

The old positions, built around the individual and his interests, were not given up without a fight, characteristically described by Herbert Spencer in the title he gave to a volume of his essays *Man versus The State*.[1] In the political world resistance was much greater. Even when discredited intellectually, the orthodoxy of *laissez-faire* kept its hold on a large section of the Liberal Party, crippling its effectiveness as a vehicle of social reform. None the less, the new attitude to be found in the writings of T. H. Green, D. G. Ritchie, J. A. Hobson and Leonard Hobhouse marks a turning-point in the development of British Liberalism, leading half a century later to the 'New Deal' of Keynes and the Liberal Yellow Book.

The stumbling-block which Mill had been unable to overcome was the hackneyed antithesis between the individual and society which dominated Liberal thought for the greater part of the 19th century. To prophets of the New Liberalism it was the first idol to be abandoned. 'Underlying all these traditions and prejudices', wrote D. G. Ritchie in 1891, 'there is a particular metaphysical theory—a metaphysical theory which takes hold of those persons especially who are fondest of abjuring all metaphysics. . . . The chief symptom of this metaphysical complaint is the belief in the abstract individual. The individual is thought of as if he had a meaning and significance apart from his surroundings and apart from his relations to the community of which he is a member. It may be quite true that the significance of the individual is not exhausted by his relations to any given set of surroundings; but apart from all these he is a mere abstraction, a logical ghost, a metaphysical spectre. . . . Now, along with this negative and abstract view of the individual there goes, as counterpart, the way of looking at the State as an opposing element to the individual. . . . Their relation is regarded as one merely of antithesis. . . . Such a conception is quite inadequate as a basis for any profitable discussion of the duties of Government.'[2]

[1] See no. 87, below.   [2] See no. 88, below.

With this stumbling-block removed, the way was open to a more positive view of freedom, something more (to quote T. H. Green) than 'the mere removal of compulsion, the mere enabling a man to do as he likes'. 'When we speak of freedom as something to be so highly prized, we mean a positive power or capacity of doing or enjoying something worth doing or enjoying, and that, too, something that we do or enjoy in common with others.'[1]

The task of the State was to provide the conditions in which this sort of freedom could be pursued and, by the beginning of the 20th century, it had become a commonplace to describe the means as the provision of 'equality of opportunity'. It was clear, too, that within the framework of a deeply rooted social hierarchy and a developed capitalist system such freedom, 'the presence of opportunity', could only be achieved by state interference. Freedom had emerged as a social conception, not one which involved the individual alone. Green did not claim that legislation could in itself promote moral goodness; his argument was that, in many situations, legislative intervention alone could bring into existence conditions in which men could exercise freely their faculties of moral judgment, enlarging, as it did so, the area of 'positive freedom'.

The emphasis in Liberal thought remained, as it had always done, upon the individual, but he was now a social individual, and the aim of political activity was to enlarge the area within which he might enjoy an ever widening degree of freedom. 'The sphere of liberty', wrote Leonard Hobhouse, 'is the sphere of growth itself.' Such growth could only be ensured by State intervention, for every act of liberation involved for some individual or group a corresponding act of restraint.

Yet this was not a betrayal of Liberalism, as Spencer and other opponents suggested. The *laissez-faire* doctrine had, in its time, successfully transformed the social and economic system, but the development of capitalism and the move towards democracy now, in their turn, made necessary a new interpretation of the fundamental Liberal belief in liberty. Its evolution was a sign of intellectual strength, of a

[1] See no. 86, below.

capacity to take account of changing circumstances. The new view of freedom, based upon the provision of opportunity for all, was essentially wider in scope and more humane than the narrow outlook of earlier generations. Liberalism had acquired a social as well as an intellectual conscience. Freedom, like Liberalism itself, had moved down the social scale.

X

The change in the philosophical assumptions of Liberalism was only part of a much wider process. The Radical wing of the Liberal Party was reaching similar conclusions at the level of party policy. The Reform Acts of 1867 and 1884 destroyed the electoral monopoly which the middle and upper classes had enjoyed since 1832. With the extension of the franchise to almost universal male suffrage, political success came to depend upon the ability to appeal to a predominantly working-class electorate. Such an appeal could, in the long run, only be based on a radical programme of social reform.

The older Liberalism, represented both by the Whigs and the heirs of the Manchester School, was hostile to any such programme. It preached self-help and *laissez-faire* as the answer to distress, stubbornly insisting that nothing could be done to relieve an industrialised nation's problems of poverty and exploitation other than to leave their solution to the spontaneous action of those economic forces which had created them.

This view, or rather a watered-down version of it, continued until almost the end of the 19th century to colour the outlook of Gladstone and other Liberal leaders in Parliament. But, in the country, the younger generation of Liberals was quick to realise the implications of the Reform Acts and to take advantage of the opportunity which it gave them of implementing a programme of increased State and municipal intervention.

The first demonstration of what could be done was given in Birmingham in the 1870's where, under the leadership of Joseph Chamberlain and the inspiration of an able group of Nonconformist Ministers, Dale, Crosskey and Dawson, the city was transformed by the technique of 'municipal socialism'. It was in Birmingham and the other cities where Liberal Radicals gained control that public ownership and social welfare were first explored in miniature at the municipal level.

But the Radicals were not content to exercise their talents locally. Their success in Birmingham led them to take the initiative in the formation of the National Liberal Federation in 1877, an organisation which was designed to shake the hold of the Whigs both on the leadership of the party and on its parliamentary policy. Led by Chamberlain, Dilke and Morley, the Radicals engaged in a running fight which culminated in the Unauthorised Programme of 1885.[1]

The political arguments in favour of a programme which would appeal to a working-class electorate were reinforced by other considerations. The Golden Age of Victorian capitalism, the twenty years following the Great Exhibition of 1851, had ended. The depressions of the 1870's and 1880's removed the economic justification for the old untroubled confidence in the competitive system. The social investigations of men like Charles Booth and Seebohm Rowntree shattered complacency about its social consequences. The absolute faith in free competition which had marked earlier generations of Liberals was being eroded by harsh economic facts.

In any case, as that acute observer, J. A. Hobson, pointed out, the actual structure of the industrial and commercial system of the country at the end of the 19th century no longer corresponded to models derived from the classical economists. An economy which was increasingly dominated by the power of trusts, combines and the financial strength of the City of London could no longer be adequately diagnosed with the tools of Ricardian economics.

The trend towards collectivism, of course, extended far beyond the Liberal Party. It found expression in the Conservative Party as well as the Liberal, in the trade union movement as well as in the administrative practice of the Government, in the spread of socialist propaganda and in the foundation of the Fabian Society. For the Liberal Party,

[1] See nos. 96 and 97, below.

however, long identified with economic individualism and *laissez-faire*, it posed problems of peculiar difficulty. Could those who believed in the New Liberalism carry the party with them? Could they do it in time and with sufficient conviction to hold or win back working-class support? The Liberal Party was steadily losing to the Tories much of the support it had once been able to count on from the manufacturing and commercial classes as well as from the Whig connection. In 1888 Gladstone could say: 'I do not disguise from myself the strength of the combination that is against us. . . . They have nearly the whole wealth of the country; they have the whole of the men of social station in the country; they have a vast preponderance in social strength.' At the close of the century the Liberal Party, outside the Celtic fringe, was organised on a much narrower class basis than thirty years before. With the Tories re-establishing themselves as the party of property, the Liberals' future had come to depend on success or failure in winning the working-class vote in the industrial constituencies of the Midlands and the North.

There is an obvious case for arguing that, once the franchise was widely extended, politics must inevitably come to reflect more and more the division between the satisfied and the dissatisfied classes and that this must eventually prove fatal to the Liberal Party. What chance had the Radicals of averting this by capturing the party and swinging it to the left? On a dispassionate estimate, this cannot be rated high at any time. Their best chance was in the 1880's, but this was spoiled by the return of Gladstone to the leadership of the party.

Gladstone was the despair of the Radicals. As his Midlothian campaign showed, he could arouse Radical and working-class enthusiasm in a way that only Bright had equalled. In his attitude to imperialism and to the Irish question he was in advance of Radical opinion. But on social and economic issues his views remained those of the orthodox Chancellor of the Exchequer whose name has become synonymous with the strictest economy in public expenditure. Gladstone had little sympathy with the radicalism of the Unauthorised Programme. The passion and imagination of which he was capable when roused by the wrongs of the Christian peoples of the Balkans or of Ireland were wholly untouched by the 'condition of the people' question. Yet so long as he remained in politics, he dominated the Liberal Party and absorbed its energies in the single issue of Ireland.

In 1886 Gladstone's determination to carry Irish Home Rule drove Chamberlain, the one man with the ability to put a Radical programme into effect, out of the party. Not until 1894—and then against his will—was Gladstone forced to abandon his attempt to pass a Home Rule Bill and to lay down the leadership which he had first resigned twenty years before, leaving behind him a divided party without a policy. Those twenty years remain the most controversial episode in the most controversial career of the 19th century, a career which illustrates as no other the contradictions of the Liberal tradition, its greatness and its shortcomings.

Was the price which the Liberal Party paid for Gladstone's crusades the loss of the opportunity to turn itself into a Radical Party? There were certainly Radicals at the time who believed this and it has often been repeated since. But it is also necessary to ask whether, even if Gladstone had remained in retirement after 1874, the Liberal Party—given its character and traditions—could have turned itself into a Radical Party. For our part, we are inclined to think that in answering this further question, too much importance has been attached to Gladstone, too little to the stubborn resistance which Chamberlain and the Radicals met in the party apart from Gladstone. If Chamberlain had secured the succession to the leadership in the 1880's it could only have been at the price of an even deeper split in the party and one may well ask how long the working-class electorate would have remained content with the radicalism of the Unauthorised Programme.

At first sight the Liberal victory of 1906 seems to have offered the Radicals a second chance with a new leader in Lloyd George. 'British Liberalism', Lloyd George declared, 'is not going to repeat the fate of Continental Liberalism. The fate of Continental Liberalism should warn us of that danger. It has been swept on one side before it had well begun its work, because it refused to adapt itself to new conditions.'

Yet there are solid reasons for doubting whether the prospects of Radicalism in 1906 were as brilliant as they have sometimes been made to appear. The pressure for direct working-class representation was growing and had already led to the formation of the Labour Representation Committee to be followed in 1906 by the foundation of the Labour Party. If the Labour Party failed to make much headway before the war, this was less because of working-class loyalty to the Liberal Party than because even an independent Labour Party failed to satisfy the growing impatience of the rank-and-file trade unionist, especially in the years 1911–14.

The Radicals succeeded in carrying a number of important measures between 1906 and 1911, but the politically conscious section of the working class was asking for something more than a programme of social reform by 1914; it wanted fundamental changes in the economic social system. Lloyd George's identification of the landowner as the enemy might win support in rural districts or in Wales and Scotland but it aroused little enthusiasm in the industrial areas where the working class saw their enemy in the employer and the capitalist. In any case the most influential section of the Liberal Party remained unconverted to the Radicals' bid for working-class support or only accepted it reluctantly without conviction.

As the fight over the powers of the House of Lords showed, a Liberal Government could still draw strength from and add to its past achievements. But the Parliament Act of 1911 was the logical conclusion to the extension of political democracy which the Liberal Party had championed in the 19th century; it did not prove the capacity of the party to meet the demands of social democracy in the 20th. Lloyd George's Insurance Act pointed the way, but an impression of reluctance and hesitation remained which, after the war, was to be reflected in the Liberals' steady loss of radical votes to the Labour Party. For, if the consequences of this were blurred at the time by other issues—the House of Lords, Ireland and the outbreak of war—after 1918 it became only too clear that the Liberal Party had been replaced by the Labour

Party as the hope of those who sought for radical solutions to problems now pushed into the forefront of politics by the stagnation of trade and mass unemployment.

This is not the end of the story, however. The paradox of British Liberalism in the 20th century is that, while the Liberal Party has dwindled in strength, the Liberal tradition has in large part been taken over by one or other of the competing parties, each of which claims with some justification to be the heir of different parts of that tradition. More than that: Liberalism, as a distinctive political philosophy, has shown itself capable of an original approach to the problems which defeated every party between the wars. John Maynard Keynes, working, as he believed, within the framework of the Liberal tradition, went further than any other man towards resolving what many had come to believe were the incompatibilities of a free society and a relatively stable economy. Just before the publication in 1936 of the *General Theory of Employment, Interest and Money* he wrote to George Bernard Shaw: 'To understand my state of mind you have to know that I believe myself to be writing a book on economic theory which will largely revolutionise—not, I suppose, at once but in the course of the next ten years—the way the world thinks about economic problems.'[1]

Long before the theoretical refinement of his views, Keynes hammered away at their practical application during the 1920's. In a series of articles, pamphlets and lectures, he argued the necessity for thinking out the *Agenda* of Government anew, the irrelevance of economic and political attitudes which still had their roots in the 19th century, the possibility of utilising resources which were running to waste in the misery of unemployment. The policy which he and a group that included Walter Layton, Hubert Henderson, Philip Kerr and Seebohm Rowntree, produced between 1926 and 1927 under the leadership of Lloyd George was, in effect, a comprehensive New Deal for Britain. But the Liberal Yellow Book represented a policy which, at that time, was altogether too bold for 'the old gentlemen tightly buttoned-up in their frock coats'—in all parties.

[1] R. F. Harrod, *The Life of John Maynard Keynes*, p. 462. (Macmillan).

With the publication of his *General Theory*, Keynes moved from the field of practical remedies into an area where his views were, in the words of his letter to Bernard Shaw, to change the way the world thinks about economic problems.

Keynes' refusal to accept the antithesis between socialism and capitalism which had marked almost all previous thought on the subject carried a stage further the rejection of the antithesis between the individual and the State by the New Liberalism fifty years before. Like that, it marked not the abandonment but the enlargement of the fundamental Liberal conception of liberty. In working out this theme in the technical analysis of the *General Theory* (a book, Keynes wrote, 'chiefly addressed to my fellow economists'), he set the climate of Liberal thought in the mid-20th century as certainly as did the Classical Economists in the 19th, and brilliantly vindicated the vitality of the Liberal tradition in the changed conditions of a mass society and a controlled economy.

XI

The course of events outside Great Britain after 1870 confronted Liberalism with a challenge no less sharp and problems no less difficult than those raised by the course of domestic change. The relations of the Great Powers with each other, and with smaller, weaker peoples, were dominated by a crude and intensified struggle for power, prestige and profits, finding expression in the contest for colonies and spheres of influence, in the struggle for markets and the erection of tariff-barriers, in armaments races and the shrill aggressive nationalism which politicians and press alike found to be very much to the taste of the new electorate.

Imperialism split the Liberal Party in the 1890's and produced a Liberal version in Lord Rosebery and the Liberal Leaguers, Haldane, Grey and Asquith. The outbreak of the Boer War sharpened the divisions in the party. The traditional Liberal opposition to imperialism, represented by Harcourt and Morley, was restated in more trenchant terms by writers like J. A. Hobson (whose *Imperialism* was to prove one of the most influential books of the century) and by

Radical politicians like David Lloyd George. It was not, however, until the course of the war spread disillusionment that Campbell-Bannerman succeeded in reuniting the party. The split was finally healed by the attack which Chamberlain, in logical extension of his imperialist principles, launched on free trade.

Free trade was still the first article in every Liberal's creed, whatever their other differences, and Chamberlain could have picked no issue more favourable to Liberal unity. In the Parliament of 1906, with its unprecedented Liberal majority, Campbell-Bannerman was able to put the seal on the Liberal repudiation of Chamberlain's South African policy by the grant of self-government to the Transvaal and Orange River Colony, the essential foundation of the Union of 1909.

Balfour denounced Campbell-Bannerman's South African settlement as 'the most reckless experiment ever tried in the development of a great colonial policy'. The development of that policy in the 20th century has proved Balfour wrong. It has been the grant of self-government, first to the white Dominions, then to India, Pakistan, Ceylon, finally to African territories like Nigeria and to Malaya which alone has held the Commonwealth together. Indeed there is a good case to be argued for the view that the modern British Commonwealth, with its conception of a community of independent, self-governing nations, is one of the most spectacular triumphs of the Liberal tradition—its contradictions and inconsistencies included.

The fundamental problem of external policy remained the relations of the Great Powers, of which colonial rivalry was one, but only one, expression. Up to 1914, Liberals were still active in championing the Gladstonian cause of downtrodden peoples: Armenia, Macedonia, Persia. They welcomed the settlement with France but were decidedly critical of closer relations with Tsarist Russia. For the rest such attention as they paid to foreign affairs was strongly coloured by ideas inherited from Cobden and Bright: free trade, nonintervention, freedom from entanglements, distrust of the Balance of Power, and the reduction of expenditure on armaments.

Grey, however, faced with the responsibilities of office, could not afford to take so simple a view. The concealed premises on which the orthodox Liberal attitude rested were a stable balance of power in Europe and a naval supremacy which together guaranteed the invulnerability of these islands. But if these were threatened, as Grey came to believe they were by the growth of German power, then a Liberal Government, however reluctantly, must resist the demand of its supporters for the reduction of armaments and exert its power to correct the threatened balance.

Only once in these years was this issue threshed out, in the debate following the Agadir crisis of 1911 which roused Grey's Radical critics with the revelation of how close Britain had been to war with Germany at the side of France. This was one of the rare occasions on which Grey defended his policy in public.

'The ideal of splendid isolation', he told the House of Commons, 'contemplated a balance of power in Europe to which we were not to be a party, and from which we were to be able to stand aside in the happy position of having no obligations and being able to take advantage of any difficulties which arose in Europe from friction between opposing Powers. That policy is not a possible one now. . . . It is the negation of a policy, and if it were accompanied, as I suppose it would be accompanied, with constant criticisms about the internal affairs and proceedings of other Governments, constant pressure . . . to interfere and make representations . . . then I say that the disastrous consequences of such an attitude of mingled interferences and drift would soon become apparent in an expenditure on armaments even greater than the present, and sooner or later the very peace that people desired to preserve would topple over.'[1]

Grey's critics failed to answer him but he did not press the issue between them and their concern died away, partly distracted by domestic and Irish affairs, partly lulled by renewed efforts to reach an understanding with Germany and by Grey's success in making the Concert of Europe a reality at the time of the Balkan wars. When war came it caught the Liberal Party, as distinct from the Liberal foreign

[1] See no. 119, below.

minister, unprepared and the instinctive reaction of Liberal opinion as represented by the *Manchester Guardian* under the editorship of C. P. Scott was to call for a policy of neutrality and to hold aloof from the European conflict.

The war sharpened Liberal dissatisfaction with the traditional methods of conducting foreign policy. In retrospect they became far more critical of Grey and the 'secret diplomacy' of the Foreign Office than they had been at the time. They found in President Wilson a man after their own hearts. His views and theirs coincided at many points: a just peace without annexations or indemnities; the map of Europe redrawn on the principle of self-determination; 'open covenants openly arrived at', arbitration and the rule of law; disarmament and the replacing of exclusive alliances by a League of Nations; above all, a devotion to the ideal of the brotherhood of man.

In the 1920's Liberals were among the sharpest critics of the peace treaties, calling for their revison, for the strengthening of the League, disarmament and the outlawry of war. In common with the Labour Party they found themselves entangled in the contradiction of purposes involved in the simultaneous demands for disarmament and collective security and in the 1930's discovered no more effective answer than anyone else to the dictators' blackmail than the reluctant employment of the force they abhorred.

The Liberals' search for an alternative means of conducting the relations between nations other than by force and the threat of force ended in frustration. Yet from Fox in the 1790's to the League of Nations Union and the Peace Ballot there is nothing more characteristic of the Liberal tradition. Nor in a world still living under the threat of war is there any part of that tradition which finds so anxious an echo in the fears of ordinary men and women.

XII

The Liberal Party lasted as an effective political force for not more than seventy years. It can scarcely be said to have existed before Gladstone joined Palmerston's government in 1859 and after 1931 it was reduced to a handful of members in the House of Commons. The Liberal tradition has had a longer history and a more lasting influence.

The permanent achievements of that tradition are embodied in the British Constitution; it is still to be found at work in both the other parties, Labour and Conservative. Outside party politics it has deeply affected education (especially in the universities) and the administration of the law. It has remained the strongest element in the philosophy of government evolved by the civil service and by local authorities. It has inspired the transformation of a colonial empire into a commonwealth of nations. There is not a single institution in the country which has not felt the impact of these ideas while at the deeper level of instinctive feeling they have become a part of the national character, finding expression in the tradition of 'fair play'.

In the pages which follow two ideas recur again and again. The first is a belief in the value of freedom, freedom of the individual, freedom of minorities, freedom of peoples. The scope of freedom has required continual and sometimes drastic re-defining, as in the abandonment of *laissez-faire* or in the extension of self-government to the peoples of Asia and Africa. But each re-definition has represented a deepening and strengthening, not an attenuation, of the original faith in freedom.

The second is the belief that principle ought to count far more than power or expediency, that moral issues cannot be excluded from politics. Liberal attempts to translate moral principles into political action have rarely been successful and neglect of the factor of power is one of the most obvious criticisms of Liberal thinking about politics, especially international relations. But neglect of the factor of conscience, which is a much more likely error, is equally disastrous in the long run. The historical role of Liberalism in British history has been to prevent this, and again and again to modify policies and the exercise of power by protests in the name of conscience.

We began this introduction by underlining the intellectual incoherence of the Liberal tradition unless it is seen as an historical development. We end it by pointing to the belief in freedom and the belief in conscience as the twin foundations of Liberal philosophy and the element of continuity in its historical development. Politics can never be conducted by the light of these two principles alone, but without them human society is reduced to servitude and the naked rule of force. This is the truth which the Liberal tradition has maintained from Fox to Keynes—and which still needs to be maintained in our own time.

ALAN BULLOCK
MAURICE SHOCK

Oxford, 1956

PART I

FOX AND THE WHIG TRADITION

1. CHARLES JAMES FOX: Speech in the House
of Commons, 13 December 1792

But what, Sir, are the doctrines that they desire to set up by this insinuation of gloom and dejection? That Englishmen are not to dare to have any genuine feelings of their own; that they must not rejoice but by rule; that they must not think but by order; that no man shall dare to exercise his faculties in contemplating the objects that surround him, nor give way to the indulgence of his joy or grief in the emotions that they excite, but according to the instructions that he shall receive. That, in observing the events that happen to surrounding and neutral nations, he shall not dare to think whether they are favourable to the principles that contribute to the happiness of man, or the contrary; and that he must take, not merely his opinions, but his sensations, from his majesty's ministers and their satellites for the time being! Sir, whenever the time shall come that the character and spirits of Englishmen are so subdued; when they shall consent to believe that everything which happens around is indifferent both to their understandings and their hearts; and when they shall be brought to rejoice and grieve just as it shall suit the taste, the caprice, or the ends of ministers, then I pronounce the constitution of this country to be extinct. . . . See to what lengths they carry this system of intellectual oppression! 'On various pretexts there have been tumults and disorders, but the true design was the destruction of our happy constitution.' So says the speech; and mark the illustration of the right honourable magistrate: 'There have been various societies established in the city of London, instituted for the plausible purpose of merely discussing constitutional questions, but which were really designed to propagate seditious doctrines.' So, then, by this new scheme of tyranny, we are not to judge of the conduct of men by their overt acts, but are to arrogate to ourselves at once the province and the power of the Deity: we are to arraign a man for his secret thoughts, and to punish him because we choose to believe him guilty! 'You tell me, indeed,' says one of these municipal inquisitors, 'that you meet for an honest purpose, but I know better: your plausible pretext shall not impose upon me: I know your seditious design: I will brand you for a traitor by my own proper authority.' What innocence can be safe against such a power? What inquisitor of Spain, of ancient or of modern tyranny, can hold so lofty a tone? Well and nobly and seasonably has the noble earl said . . . 'There are speculative people in this country who disapprove of the system of our government, and there must be such men as long as the land is free; for it is of the very essence of freedom for men to differ upon speculative points.' Is it possible to conceive that it should enter into the imaginations of free men to doubt this truth? The instant that the general sense of the people shall question this truth, and that opinion shall be held dependent on the will of ministers and magistrates, from that moment I date the extinction of our liberties as a people. . . .

Now this, Sir, is the crisis which I think so truly alarming. We are come to the moment when the question is whether we shall give to the king, that is, to the executive government, complete power over our thoughts: whether we are to resign the exercise of our natural faculties to the ministers for the time being, or whether we shall maintain that in England no man is criminal but by the commission of overt acts forbidden by the law. . . .

A noble lord (Fielding), for whom I have a high respect, says he will move for a suspension of the Habeas Corpus Act. I hope not. I have a high respect for the noble lord; but no motive of personal respect shall make me inattentive to my duty. Come from whom it may, I will with my most determined powers oppose so dreadful a measure.

But, it may be asked, what would I propose to do in times of agitation like the present? I will answer openly. If there is a tendency in the dissenters to discontent, because they conceive themselves to be unjustly suspected and cruelly calumniated, what would I do?—I would instantly repeal the Test and Corporation Acts, and take from them, by such a step, all cause of complaint. If there were any persons tinctured with a republican spirit, because they thought that the representative government was more perfect in a republic, I would endeavour to amend the representation of the Commons, and to show that the House of Commons, though not chosen by all, should have no other interest than to prove itself the representative of all. If there were men dissatisfied in Scotland or Ireland, or elsewhere, on account of disabilities and exemptions, of unjust prejudices, and of cruel restrictions, I would repeal the penal statutes, which are a disgrace to our law books. If there were other complaints of grievances, I would redress them where they were really proved; but above all I would constantly, cheerfully, patiently listen. I would make it known that if any man felt, or thought he felt, a grievance, he might come freely to the bar of this House and bring his proofs: and it should be made manifest to all the world that where they did exist they would be redressed; where they did not, that it should be made evident. If I were to issue a proclamation, this should be my proclamation: 'If any man has a grievance, let him bring it to the bar of the Commons' House of Parliament with the firm persuasion of having it honestly investigated.' These are the subsidies that I would grant to government.

Charles James Fox, *Speeches during the French Revolution*, pp. 6-17.

2. CHARLES JAMES FOX: Speech in the House of Commons, 13 May 1794

Were the House aware of the extent of this measure? It was no less than giving to the executive authority absolute power over the personal liberty of every individual in the kingdom. It might be said that ministers would not abuse that power. He must own for his part that he did not feel himself very comfortable under that reflection; every man who talked freely; every man who detested, as he did from his heart, this war, might be, and would be, in the hands and at the mercy of ministers. Living under such a government, and being subject to insurrection, comparing the two evils, he confessed he thought the evil they were pretending to remedy was less than the one they were going to inflict by the remedy itself. . . .

To deny to the people the right of discussion because upon some occasions that right had been exercised by indiscreet or bad men, was what he could not subscribe to. The right of popular discussion was a salutary and an essential privilege of the subject. He would not answer long for the conduct of parliament if it were not subject to the jealousy of the people. They all entertained becoming respect for the executive government, that was, for the chief magistrate of the kingdom, but their respect for the king did not supersede the vigilance of parliament. In his opinion, the best security for the due maintenance of the constitution was in the strict and incessant vigilance of the people over parliament itself. Meetings of the people, therefore, for the discussion of public objects were not merely legal, but laudable; and unless it was to be contended that there was some magic in the word 'convention' which brought with it disorder, anarchy, and ruin, he could perceive no just ground for demolishing the constitution of England merely because it was intended to hold a meeting for the purpose of obtaining a parliamentary reform.

Ibid. pp. 187 and 199.

3. R. B. SHERIDAN: Speech on the Standing Order for the Exclusion of Strangers, House of Commons, 6 February 1810

His right hon. friend had, by implication, questioned the use of the liberty of the press. Give me, said Mr. Sheridan, but the liberty of the press, and I will give to the minister a venal House of Commons—I will give him the full swing of the patronage of office—I will give him the whole host of ministerial influence—I will give him all the power that place can confer upon him to purchase up submission and overawe resistance; and yet armed with liberty of the press, I will go forth to meet him undismayed; I will attack the mighty fabric he has reared with that mightier engine; I will shake down from its height corruption and bury it beneath the ruins of the abuses it was meant to shelter. . . .

What was it that had caused the downfall of all the nations of Europe? Was it the liberty of the press? No: it was the want of that salutary control upon their governments, that animating source of public spirit and national exertion. If the liberty of the press had existed in France before or since the Revolution—if it had existed in Austria —if in Prussia—if in Spain, Bonaparte would not now find himself in the situation to dictate to Europe.

Cobbett's Parliamentary Debates,
vol. xv, cols. 341-3.

4. EARL GREY: Speech in the House of Lords, 23 November 1819

[The Speech from the Throne at the opening of the session of 1819–20 called for strong measures against the seditious spirit shown in the manufacturing districts. Earl Grey moved an amendment in the Lords, calling for an enquiry into the events of 16 August, in order to maintain 'that confidence in the public institutions of the country, which constitutes the best safeguard of all law and government.' The following extracts are from Earl Grey's speech on 23 November 1819: his amendment, supported by the Whig peers, was defeated by 159 votes to 34.]

The noble lord who moved the address had, in the course of his speech, warned the House not to let an anxiety for liberty lead to a compromise of the safety of the state. He, for his part, could not separate those things. The safety of the state could only be found in the protection of the liberties of the people. Whatever was destructive of the latter also destroyed the former. . . .

The discontent existing in the country had been insisted

on as a ground for the adoption of some measures. . . . But there was another axiom no less true—that there never was an extensive discontent without great misgovernment. . . . When no attention was paid to the calls of the people for relief, when their petitions were rejected and their sufferings aggravated, was it wonderful that at last public discontents should assume a formidable aspect? . . .

Their lordships had some experience in that House two years ago, when restrictive laws were passed and when the Habeas Corpus Act was suspended, of the effect which such measures were likely to produce. The same complaints were then made of the existence of disaffection and discontent, and the same means of resorting to force were suggested. Did these measures produce the effects which were promised? . . .

The effect of these measures was, in his opinion, the cause of a great portion of the discontent which now prevailed. After all the experience which they had had, there was no attempt at conciliation, no concession to the people; nothing was alluded to but a resort to coercion. . . . The natural consequence of such a system, when once begun, was that it could not be stopped: discontents begot the necessity of force; the employment of force increased discontents: these would demand the exercise of new powers, till by degrees they would depart from all the principles of the constitution. . . .

Such was the order of things which prevailed in Ireland previous to the rebellion, and which ended in the destruction of the independent legislature of that country. He knew not whether it was intended to adopt the same measures with regard to this country as had been adopted in Ireland, where the sword had been substituted for persuasion. . . . Could government rest with confidence upon the sword for security? It was impossible that a government of such a nature could exist in England. . . . Without that spirit which the knowledge of the advantages they enjoyed under their constitution infused, all their energies would flag, and all their feelings by which their glory as a nation had been established, would be utterly dissipated.

Parliamentary Debates, vol. xli, pp. 7-19.

5. LORD JOHN RUSSELL: *An Essay on the History of the English Government and Constitution from the Reign of Henry VII to the Present Time*

(1821)

There is another circumstance with respect to public opinion, which is of more importance than any. It is, that opinion has become much more sensitive, and men are more disposed to go to extremes than they were before. Since the beginning of the present reign, a popular party has appeared, which professes itself dissatisfied with the measure of liberty secured to us at the Revolution. Others have followed them, who, generally perhaps without any serious intention, have found pleasure in trying how far violence of language would be permitted. There has naturally arisen in the opposite quarter of the heavens, another party, who cling to ease and quiet, and would fain see political discussion silenced altogether. In times of great ferment, the dissensions of these parties become highly dangerous to all regular and sober freedom. Thus, at the beginning of the French Revolution, Mr. Burke having got a hold of the public mind, raised a spirit of the most bitter persecution against all who did not approve of the policy of the war. The extreme nervousness of the nation made it unsafe to indulge any honest differences in politics. The minister, by instituting trials for treason, gave in to and promoted the popular fury; and had it not been for Mr. Erskine's eloquence, it is impossible to say whether the lives of Mr. Fox and all the chief of his party might not have been sacrificed to the rage and fear of the alarmists. The demagogues of the day, on the other hand, lose no opportunity of exciting the people, in times of distress, to acts of outrage and rebellion. The quiet and well-disposed, and indeed all persons of property, naturally take the alarm. The panic is increased by miserable wretches, who imitate the language of demagogues, in order to inspire terror into the community, and strengthen the ministers of the day. The evil of violent language and blasphemous publications, however, admits of an easy remedy. We have laws sufficiently strong against sedition and tumult;

it is only necessary to put them in force. Instead of this, two other methods have been taken; both, in my mind, injudicious, and one extremely dangerous. The first is the suspension of the Habeas Corpus Act. Now this is a very proper precaution, when a conspiracy is carried on by a few principal leaders whose imprisonment puts an end to the plot. But it is no remedy at all, when the evil consists in the discontent of some thousands of unemployed manufacturers. . . . The other remedy consists in new laws, restraining the right of speaking and writing. Acts of this kind interpose obstacles to public meetings and public newspapers, and serve to discountenance, for a time, by the authority of Parliament, the abuses of liberty which have prevailed. But it is manifest, that it is impossible to prevent sedition and blasphemy, unless all freedom of speech and the liberty of the press be extinguished. It is impossible to provide beforehand, by Act of Parliament, that all speeches and writings shall keep within the bounds of loyalty and moderation. Therefore, the restraining laws are, except for the moment, inefficient. They are also pernicious; for they admit a principle, which, if pushed to its full extent, authorises a censorship of the press. They are, therefore, in direct opposition to the maxims of the Revolution, which allowed any man to do freely, that which in itself was harmless. . . .

It would seem, that we have now gone as far as it is possible to go safely upon the system of restraint. If blasphemy and sedition again alarm the timid, they must be suppressed by the ordinary laws: otherwise we must either admit a censorship, or surrender the present mode of trial by jury.

It is to be hoped, that, rather than adopt either of these tyranical expedients, England would impeach the minister, who gave such atrocious advice to his sovereign.

Lord John Russell, Essay . . . (1821),
pp. 287-91.

6. LORD JOHN RUSSELL: Speech in the House of Commons, 26 February 1828

[Lord John Russell was proposing a motion for the repeal of the Test and Corporation Acts. It was carried by 237 to 193.]

I now come to the great principle involved in the numerous petitions before the House; petitions signed by the noble body of Dissenters, by Roman Catholics, and by many members of the established Church. That principle is, that every man ought to be allowed to form his religious opinions by the impressions on his own mind, and that, when so formed, he should be at liberty to worship God according to the dictates of his conscience, without being subjected to any penalty or disqualification whatever; that every restraint or restriction imposed on any man on account of his religious creed is in the nature of persecution and is at once an offence to God and an injury to man. This is the just and noble principle on which the Dissenters claim the repeal of the Test Act.

. . . It may be asked, if I remove these securities, what other tests would I propose? My answer is, that I am opposed to religious tests of every kind. . . . I would wish to see applied to persons taking seats in parliament, and all the offices of government or corporations, a simple provision, that they should be called upon only to swear allegiance to the king.

Parliamentary Debates, N.S. xviii, pp. 678-9.

2. OPPOSITION TO THE WAR AGAINST REVOLUTIONARY FRANCE

7. CHARLES JAMES FOX: Speech in the House of Commons, 1 February 1793

None of the professed causes were grounds for going to war. What, then, remained but the internal government of France, always disavowed, but ever kept in mind, and

constantly mentioned? . . . Such would be the real cause
of the war, if war we were to have—a war which he trusted
he should soon see as generally execrated as it was now
thought to be popular. He knew that for this wish he should
be represented as holding up the internal government of
France as an object for imitation. He thought the present
state of government in France anything rather than an
object of imitation; but he maintained as a principle inviolable that the government of every independent state was
to be settled by those who were to live under it, and not
by foreign force. The conduct of the French in the Netherlands was the same with such a war as he was now
deprecating, and might be an omen of its success. It was
a war of pikes and bayonets against opinions; it was
the tyranny of giving liberty by compulsion; it was an
attempt to introduce a system among a people by force,
which the more it was forced upon them the more they
abhorred. . . .

To those who proposed repelling opinions by force, the
example of the French in the Netherlands might teach the
impotence of power to repel or to introduce. But how was
a war to operate in keeping opinions supposed dangerous
out of this country? It was not surely meant to beat the
French out of their own opinions; and opinions were not
like commodities, the importation of which from France
war would prevent.

Charles James Fox, <i>Speeches during the French Revolution</i>,
pp. 67-70.

8. CHARLES JAMES FOX: Speech in the House of Commons, 17 April 1794

Certainly, he thought the war on our part to be both
just and necessary, provided it was impossible to obtain,
in the first instance, satisfaction and security by negotiation;
but he could never agree that we should continue the war
for the purpose of imposing a form of government on
France. He certainly thought that, even though the
government of France was an unjust or wicked government,

it was in direct contradiction of the first principles of an independent state, and of the sovereignty of nations, to interfere with its formation. If a people, in the formation of their government, have been ill-advised, if they have fallen into error, if they have acted iniquitously and unjustly towards each other, God was their only judge; it was not the province of other nations to chastise their folly, or punish their wickedness, by choosing who should rule over them, or in what manner and form they should be governed.

Ibid. p. 156.

9. CHARLES JAMES FOX: Speech in the House of Commons, 3 February 1800

One campaign is successful to you—another to them; and in this way, animated by the vindictive passions of revenge, hatred, and rancour, which are infinitely more flagitious even than those of ambition and the thirst of power, you may go on for ever; as, with such black incentives, I see no end to human misery. And all this without an intelligible motive—all this because you may gain a better peace a year or two hence! So that we are called upon to go on merely as a speculation—we must keep Bonaparte for some time longer at war, as a state of probation. Gracious God, Sir! Is war a state of probation? Is peace a rash system? Is it dangerous for nations to live in amity with each other? Is your vigilance, your policy, your common powers of observation, to be extinguished by putting an end to the horrors of war? Cannot this state of probation be as well undergone without adding to the catalogue of human sufferings? 'But we must *pause*!'. . .

If a man were present now at a field of slaughter, and were to inquire for what they were fighting: 'Fighting!' would be the answer; 'they are not fighting, they are *pausing*.' 'Why is that man expiring? Why is that other writhing with agony? What means this implacable fury?' The answer must be: 'You are quite wrong, Sir, you deceive yourself.—They are not fighting.—Do not disturb them—

they are merely pausing!—This man is not expiring with agony—that man is not dead—he is only pausing! Lord help you, Sir! they are not angry with one another; they have now no cause of quarrel—but their country thinks that there should be a pause. All that you see, Sir, is nothing like fighting—there is no harm, nor cruelty, nor bloodshed in it whatever—it is nothing more than a political pause!—it is merely to try an experiment—to see whether Bonaparte will not behave himself better than heretofore; and in the meantime we have agreed to a pause, in pure friendship!' And is this the way, Sir, that you are to show yourselves the advocates of order? . . .

Sir, I have done. I have told you my opinion. I think you ought to have given a civil, clear, and explicit answer to the overture which was fairly and handsomely made you. If you were desirous that the negotiation should have included all your allies, as the means of bringing about a general peace, you should have told Bonaparte so; but I believe you were afraid of his agreeing to the proposal. You took that method before. 'Ay, but,' you say, 'the people were anxious for peace in 1797.' I say they are friends to peace now; and I am confident that you will one day own it. Believe me, they are friends to peace; although, by the laws which you have made, restraining the expression of the sense of the people, public opinion cannot now be heard as loudly and unequivocally as heretofore. But I will not go into the internal state of this country. It is too afflicting to the heart to see the strides which have been made, by means of, and under the miserable pretext of this war, against liberty of every kind, both of speech and of writing; and to observe in another kingdom the rapid approaches to that military despotism which we affect to make an argument against peace. I know, Sir, that public opinion, if it could be collected, would be for peace, as much now as in 1797, and I know that it is only by public opinion—not by the inclination of their minds—that ministers will be brought, if ever, to give us peace.

Ibid. pp. 413-15.

3. FOREIGN POLICY AND THE STRUGGLE FOR FREEDOM ABROAD

10. EARL GREY: Speech in the House of Lords, 19 February 1821

[Grey was speaking in the debate on Naples. After the revolution in Naples in July 1820 the protocol which affirmed the right of the European Alliance to interfere to crush dangerous internal revolutions had been issued at the Congress of Troppau, October 1820.]

The claim set up was nothing less than the right of a general superintendence of the states of Europe, and of the suppression of all changes in their internal government, if those changes should be hostile to what the Holy Alliance called the legitimate principles of government. . . .

Every reform of abuses, every improvement in government, which did not originate with a sovereign, of his own free will, was to be prevented. Were this principle to be successfully maintained, the triumph of tyranny would be complete, and the chains of mankind would be riveted for ever. . . . Hopeless, indeed, was the condition of the human race, if they were to obtain no political rights except such as spring from the benevolence of sovereigns—of the monarchs who composed the Holy Alliance.

[After criticising the Government for breaking off relations with the constitutional government established in Naples, Earl Grey continued:]

Their lordships had seen free constitutions overthrown by armies in concert with kings, and yet no such consequence as the interruption of friendly relations had followed. . . . Their lordships well knew that the constitution of Spain was overthrown by an army under the direction of the king, and yet they had seen no such consequence as had occurred with respect to Naples. Amicable relations were without scruple continued with the court of Spain after Ferdinand had subverted that constitution which this country was bound to support. There was no accounting for this distinction but upon the supposition that ministers had one rule for revolutions in favour of liberty, and another for revolutions in favour of despotism. The latter were by every means to be encouraged, and the former discountenanced, and if possible punished. When what had passed was impartially looked at, the inference drawn must be this—that the objection to the Neapolitan revolution was the characteristics of freedom which belonged to it, and that, being a revolution the object of which was to limit, not to create arbitrary power, it was therefore to be severely condemned. . . .

We were told that there was a sect or party at Naples which had occasioned the revolution, and that this sect was called the Carbonari; but if the fact of the revolution being occasioned by a sect gave a right of interference, such a right might be claimed in every revolution. . . . He was one of those old-fashioned politicians who thought that every great political change might be traced to previous misgovernment. In such a situation, sects could be formed, and leaders would always be found, for effecting a revolution; and it would be very unjust to accuse those as being the causes of it who were only the instruments, and to punish them for taking the only means of effecting their objects. Let their lordships look to the revolution of 1688, and then he would ask them, if it could have been carried into effect without the combinations of those great men, who restored and secured our religion, our laws, and our liberties, and without such mutual communications among them as would bring them under the description of a sect or party? . . .

They were told, however, that the Neapolitan revolution had not only been the work of a sect, but that they had employed the army as the instrument in effecting their purpose. He did not see any more strength in this objection than in the former. If they were to have armies, they must reconcile themselves to the idea, that when a soldier enlisted into them he did not surrender the feelings of a man; that he remained a citizen when under arms, and must sympathise with his countrymen. In a revolution the army must always take one side or the other; it must support the sovereign against the people, or aid the people in demanding their rights of the sovereign. God forbid that it should always, and in all circumstances, take the side of arbitrary power! God forbid that tyranny, however monstrous or oppressive, should always be defended by the army! He rejoiced to consider that soldiers when enlisted did not cease to be men, and that sovereigns were sometimes taught by their taking an opposite side, that their best guards and protection were the confidence and love of the people. . . .

Divesting the principles promulgated in the circular, and the conduct of the allies, of all pretexts, what language did they hold but the following, to the people of Naples? 'You shall have no liberty but what is agreeable to our will; we cannot permit it to be enjoyed in our states, nor will we allow it in you: as we are resolved not to give freedom our-selves, we will not have free neighbours; freedom at Naples might encourage the people of Germany, and the people in the north of Italy, to demand a similar boon. It might incite the inhabitants of Breslau, or of the banks of the Rhine, to seek for those constitutions which have been long promised and always delayed; nay, it might even penetrate into the frosts of Russia and elicit a new spark in the breasts of those who expelled Bonaparte from their inhospitable wilds. Expect not, therefore, that we can permit you to improve the system of your government. Overthrow the constitution you have established, or prepare for the full infliction of our wrath.' Such was the language held by the assembled sovereigns to the people of Naples. . . .

When he looked around, and saw that no changes were to be permitted but those which were inconsistent with the independence of states and the rights of mankind; when he saw Austria, because she had dominions in Italy, declaring that no part of Italy should enjoy freedom, lest that freedom should become contagious, he could scarcely restrain his indignation. Of what nature was the government of Austria in Italy? It was the government of strangers in that country; it was founded on recent conquest, and had for its principle that everything was to be done there for the benefit of Austria, and not for that of Italy. If any new law was to be enacted, it was, to secure the interests of Austria; if any tax was to be levied, it was for Austria; if any conscription was to be raised, it was for defending the rights of Austria, and not of Italy. Agriculture, manufactures, and commerce, languished on account of the power exercised by Austria;

even literature and the arts had felt the influence of foreign dominion. No improvement could be expected in a state so governed; and was Naples to be restrained from attaining her rights, or establishing her freedom, because the dominion of the Emperor of Austria might be rendered less secure in the north of Italy by an improvement in the south?

Parliamentary Debates, N.S. iv, pp. 744-59.

11. MARQUIS OF LANSDOWNE: Speech in the House of Lords, 2 March 1821

[Lansdowne was also speaking in the debate on Naples.]

Was it probable that a new order of things, never attempted to be established before, could now be reared and permanently established? If such a state of things in Europe had heretofore been attempted, would Holland have obtained what she had achieved? Would Switzerland? Would the United States? Would Spain or Portugal? They never could have changed their situations had the principles of this alliance of sovereigns been heretofore promulgated. . . . It was against such a system that England had repeatedly acted both in ancient and modern times, so late as at the breaking out of the war when Bonaparte was first consul. . . . At that time reasons were not wanting for France to have said of Switzerland as Austria now did of Naples, that her proceedings were calculated to inflame contiguous states. But no such plea was thought of by England; the act of France was justly complained of, because it was an act inconsistent with the independence of nations, and particularly in that most essential part, the right of a free people to choose their own form of government. In former times Great Britain had acquired deserved glory by the policy she adopted, as the fosterer of every nascent spark of liberty which was struck out of any of the nations in the world. The moment that spark arose, it was considered by England as an acquisition to be cherished, not extinguished. The greatest man who had ever written upon the policy of an empire, or who had enlightened any age by his wisdom, the great Lord Bacon, when justly praising the principles that governed the counsels of Queen Elizabeth in her intercourse with foreign states, after reviewing the various merits which he justly ascribed to that policy, fixed for the highest theme of his panegyric upon that part of Elizabeth's conduct, where, to use his own words, 'she cultivated and encouraged the liberties of other nations on the continent of Europe.'. . .

He knew it had been said, that all interference would be now useless; that the die was cast, and it was now too late to interfere in the hope of promoting any practical good. He was not of that opinion; he did not despair, even now, if England properly interposed. But even were he satisfied that the people of Naples were over-run by their assailants, and every foot of land there in the firm occupation of German soldiers, still he should say it was not too late for that House to disclaim the principle upon which the congress at Troppau were now acting, and to save Europe from the eventual calamities which such a principle was but too well calculated to produce.

Ibid. pp. 1047-9.

12. EARL BYRON: *Sonnet on Chillon*
(1816)

Eternal Spirit of the chainless Mind!
    Brightest in dungeons, Liberty! thou art:
    For there thy habitation is the heart—
The heart which love of thee alone can bind;
And when thy sons to fetters are consigned—
    To fetters, and the damp vault's dayless gloom,
    Their country conquers with their martyrdom,
And Freedom's fame finds wings on every wind.
Chillon! thy prison is a holy place,
    And thy sad floor an altar—for 'twas trod,
Until his very steps have left a trace
    Worn, as if thy cold pavement were a sod,
By Bonivard![1]—May none those marks efface!
    For the appeal from tyranny to God.

BYRON.

[1] See Note on Bonivard, p. 18.

13. EARL BYRON: *Childe Harold*
(1817)

Yet, Freedom! yet thy banner, torn, but flying,
Streams like the thunder-storm *against* the wind;
Thy trumpet voice, though broken now and dying,
The loudest still the Tempest leaves behind;
Thy tree hath lost its blossoms, and the rind,
Chopped by the axe, looks rough and little worth,
But the sap lasts,—and still the seed we find,
Sown deep, even in the bosom of the North;
So shall a better spring less bitter fruit bring forth.

Childe Harold, Canto IV, xcviii.

14. EARL BYRON: *Marino Faliero*
(1821)

[From Act II, Scene ii, of Byron's historical drama of 14th-century Venice, *Marino Faliero*. It was written in 1820 and produced at Drury Lane in 1821.]

ISRAEL BERTUCCIO: They never fail who die
In a great cause: the block may soak their gore:
Their heads may sodden in the sun; their limbs
Be strung to city gates and castle walls—
But still their spirit walks abroad. Though years
Elapse, and others share as dark a doom.
They but augment the deep and sweeping thoughts
Which overpower all others, and conduct
The world at last to Freedom. What were we,
If Brutus had not lived? He died in giving
Rome liberty, but left a deathless lesson—
A name which is a virtue, and a soul
Which multiplies itself throughout all time,

François Bonivard, born in 1493, was one of the leaders of the Genevese in their attempt to throw off the yoke of the House of Savoy and convert their city into a republic. He was arrested and imprisoned by the Duke of Savoy, on the second occasion spending six years in the Chateau de Chillon. He was released by the Bernese in 1536. Byron and Shelley visited Chillon together in June 1816.

When wicked men wax mighty, and a state
Turns servile. He and his high friends were styled
'The last of Romans.' Let us be the first
Of true Venetians, sprung from Roman sires.

4. PARLIAMENTARY REFORM

15. LORD JOHN RUSSELL: Speech in the House of Commons, 25 April 1822

[Lord John Russell's speech introducing the motion 'That the present state of the representation of the People in Parliament requires the most serious consideration of this House.' The motion was lost by 269 votes to 164.]

At the present period, the ministers of the Crown possess the confidence of the House of Commons, but the House of Commons does not possess the esteem and reverence of the people. . . . We have seen discontent breaking into outrage in various quarters—we have seen alarm universally prevailing among the upper classes and disaffection among the lower—we have seen the ministers of the Crown seek a remedy for these evils in a system of severe coercion—in restrictive laws—in large standing armies—in enormous barracks, and in every other resource that belongs to a government which is not founded on the hearts of its subjects. . . . It is my persuasion that the liberties of Englishmen, being founded upon the general consent of all, must remain upon that basis, or must altogether cease to have any existence. We cannot confine liberty in this country to one class of men: we cannot erect here a senate of Venice, by which a small part of the community is enabled to lord it over the majority; we cannot in this land and at this time make liberty the inheritance of a caste. . . . I speak according to the spirit of our constitution when I say, that the liberty of England abhors the unnatural protection of a standing army; she abjures the countenance of fortresses and barracks; nor can those institutions ever be maintained by force and terror that were founded upon mildness and affection.

If we ask the causes, why a system of government, so contrary to the spirit of our laws, so obnoxious to the feelings of our people, so ominous to the future prospects of the country has been adopted, we shall find the root of the evil to lie in the defective state of our representation. The votes of the House of Commons no longer imply the general assent of the realm; they no longer carry with them the sympathies and understandings of the nation. The ministers of the Crown, after obtaining triumphant majorities in this House, are obliged to have recourse to other means than those of persuasion, reverence for authority, and voluntary respect, to procure the adherence of the country. They are obliged to enforce, by arms, obedience to acts of this House —which, according to every just theory, are supposed to emanate from the people themselves.

Parliamentary Debates, N.S. vii, p. 73.

16. LORD MELBOURNE: Speech in the House of Lords, 4 October 1831

[This speech was made on the occasion of the second reading of the Reform Bill in 1831.]

But all experience proves, when the wishes of the people are founded on reason and justice and when they are consistent with the fundamental principles of the constitution, that there must come a time when both the legislative and executive powers must yield to the popular voice or be annihilated. . . . When your lordships see, that on every occasion of public calamity and distress, from whatever cause arising, the people call for an alteration in the representation, and that the call is accompanied with a deep, rankling sense of injustice suffered, and of rights withheld, can your lordships suppose that an opinion so continually revived has not some deep-seated foundation, and can you be insensible to the danger of continuing a permanent cause for angry and discontented feelings to be revived and renewed at every period of public distress and public calamity.

Ibid. p. 1179.

17. THOMAS BABINGTON MACAULAY: Speech in the House of Commons, 2 March 1831

[Macaulay was speaking in the debate on the First Reform Bill.]

I support this bill because it will improve our institutions; but I support it also because it tends to preserve them. That we may exclude those whom it is necessary to exclude, we must admit those whom it may be safe to admit. At present we oppose the schemes of revolutions with only one half, with only one quarter of our proper force. We say, and we say justly, that it is not by mere numbers, but by property and intelligence, that the nation ought to be governed. Yet, saying this, we exclude from all share in the government great masses of property and intelligence, great numbers of those who are most interested in preserving tranquillity, and who know best how to preserve it. We do more. We drive over to the side of revolution those whom we shut out from power. . . .

This is not government by property. It is government by certain detached portions and fragments of property, selected from the rest, and preferred to the rest, on no rational principle whatever. . . .

All history is full of revolutions, produced by causes similar to those which are now operating in England. A portion of the community which had been of no account expands and becomes strong. It demands a place in the system, suited, not to its former weakness, but to its present power. If this is granted, all is well. If this is refused, then comes the struggle between the young energy of one class and the ancient privileges of another. Such was the struggle between the plebeians and the patricians of Rome. Such was the struggle of the Italian allies for admission to the full rights of Roman citizens. Such was the struggle of our North American colonies against the mother country. Such was the struggle which the Third Estate of France maintained against the aristocracy of birth. Such was the struggle which the Roman Catholics of Ireland maintained against the aristocracy of creed. Such is the struggle which the free people of colour in Jamaica are now maintaining against the aristocracy of skin. Such, finally, is the struggle which the middle classes in England are maintaining against an aristocracy of mere locality, against an aristocracy the principle of which is to invest a hundred drunken pot-wallopers in one place, or the owner of a ruined hovel in another, with powers which are withheld from cities renowned to the furthest ends of the earth, for the marvels of their wealth and their industry. . . .

The question of Parliamentary Reform is still behind. But signs, of which it is impossible to misconceive the import, do most clearly indicate that, unless that question also be speedily settled, property, and order, and all the institutions of this great monarchy, will be exposed to fearful peril. Is it possible that gentlemen long versed in high political affairs cannot read these signs? Is it possible that they can really believe that the Representative system of England, such as it now is, will last to the year 1860? If not, for what would they have us wait? Would they have us wait, merely that we may show to the world how little we have profited by our own recent experience? Would they have us wait, that we may once again hit the exact point where we can neither refuse with authority, nor concede with grace? Would they have us wait, that the numbers of the discontented party may become larger, its demands higher, its feelings more acrimonious, its organisation more complete? Would they have us wait till the whole tragicomedy of 1827 has been acted over again? till they have been brought into office by a cry of 'No Reform', to be reformers, as they were once brought into office by a cry of 'No Popery', to be emancipators? Have they obliterated from their minds—gladly, perhaps, would some among them obliterate from their minds—the transactions of that year? And have they forgotten all the transactions of the succeeding year? Have they forgotten how the spirit of liberty in Ireland, debarred from its natural outlet, found a vent by forbidden passages? Have they forgotten how we were forced to indulge the Catholics in all the license of rebels, merely because we chose to withhold from them the liberties of subjects? Do they wait for associations more formidable than that of the

Corn Exchange, for contributions larger than the Rent, for agitators more violent than those who, three years ago, divided with the King and the Parliament the sovereignty of Ireland? Do they wait for that last and most dreadful paroxysm of popular rage, for that last and most cruel test of military fidelity? Let them wait, if their past experience shall induce them to think that any high honour or any exquisite pleasure is to be obtained by a policy like this. Let them wait, if this strange and fearful infatuation be indeed upon them, that they should not see with their eyes, or hear with their ears, or understand with their heart. But let us know our interest and our duty better. Turn where we may, within, around, the voice of great events is proclaiming to us, Reform, that you may preserve. Now, therefore, while everything at home and abroad forebodes ruin to those who persist in a hopeless struggle against the spirit of the age, now, while the crash of the proudest throne of the Continent is still resounding in our ears, now, while the roof of a British palace affords an ignominious shelter to the exiled heir of forty kings, now, while we see on every side ancient institutions subverted, and great societies dissolved, now, while the heart of England is still sound, now, while old feelings and old associations retain a power and a charm which may too soon pass away, now, in this your accepted time, now, in this your day of salvation, take counsel, not of prejudice, not of party spirit, not of the ignominious pride of a fatal consistency, but of history, of reason, of the ages which are past, of the signs of this most portentous time. Pronounce in a manner worthy of the expectation with which this great debate has been anticipated, and of the long remembrance which it will leave behind. Renew the youth of the State. Save property, divided against itself. Save the multitude, endangered by its own ungovernable passions. Save the aristocracy, endangered by its own unpopular power. Save the greatest, and fairest, and most highly civilised community that ever existed, from calamities which may in a few days sweep away all the rich heritage of so many ages of wisdom and glory. The danger is terrible. The time is short. If this bill should be rejected, I pray to God that none of those who concur in rejecting it may ever remember their votes with unavailing remorse, amidst the wreck of laws, the confusion of ranks, the spoliation of property, and the dissolution of the social order.

Miscellaneous Writings and Speeches of Lord Macaulay
(1882), pp. 484-92.

PART II

THE BENTHAMITES AND THE POLITICAL ECONOMISTS, 1776-1830

18. ADAM SMITH: *The Wealth of Nations*
(1776)

Every individual is continually exerting himself to find out the most advantageous employment for whatever capital he can command. It is his own advantage, indeed, and not that of the society, which he has in view. But the study of his own advantage naturally, or rather necessarily, leads him to prefer that employment which is most advantageous to the society.

... As every individual, therefore, endeavours as much as he can both to employ his capital in the support of domestic industry and so to direct that industry that its produce may be of the greatest value, every individual necessarily labours to render the annual revenue of the society as great as he can. He generally indeed, neither intends to promote the public interest nor knows how much he is promoting it. By preferring the support of domestic to that of foreign industry, he intends only his own security; and by directing that industry in such a manner as its produce may be of the greatest value, he intends only his own gain, and he is in this, as in many other cases, led by an invisible hand to promote an end which was no part of his intention. Nor is it always the worse for the society that it was no part of it. By pursuing his own interest he frequently promotes that of the society more effectually than when he really intends to promote it. I have never known much good done by those who affected to trade for the public good. It is an affectation, indeed, not very common among merchants, and very few words need be employed in dissuading them from it.

Adam Smith, *The Wealth of Nations* (Everyman edn.), vol. i, pp. 398-400.

19. ADAM SMITH: *The Wealth of Nations* (1776)

(A)

Though the profusion of government must, undoubtedly, have retarded the natural progress of England towards wealth and improvement, it has not been able to stop it. The annual produce of its land and labour is, undoubtedly, much greater at present than it was either at the restoration or at the revolution. The capital, therefore, annually employed in cultivating this land, and in maintaining this labour, must likewise be much greater. In the midst of all the exactions of government, this capital has been silently and gradually accumulated by the private frugality and good conduct of individuals, by their universal, continual, and uninterrupted effort to better their own condition. It is this effort, protected by law and allowed by liberty to exert itself in the manner that is most advantageous, which has maintained the progress of England towards opulence and improvement in almost all former times, and which, it is to be hoped, will do so in all future times. England, however, as it has never been blessed with a very parsimonious government, so parsimony has at no time been the characterised virtue of its inhabitants. It is the highest impertinence and presumption, therefore, in kings and ministers, to pretend to watch over the economy of private people, and to restrain their expense, either by sumptuary laws, or by prohibiting the importation of foreign luxuries. They are themselves always, and without any exception, the greatest spendthrifts in the society. Let them look well after their own expense, and they may safely trust private people with theirs. If their own extravagance does not ruin the state, that of their subjects never will.

(B)

It is thus that every system which endeavours, either by extraordinary encouragements to draw towards a particular species of industry a greater share of the capital of the society than would naturally go to it, or, by extraordinary restraints, force from a particular species of industry some share of the capital which would otherwise be employed in it, is in reality subversive to the great purpose which it means to promote. It retards, instead of accelerating, the progress of the society towards real wealth and greatness; and diminishes, instead of increasing, the real value of the annual produce of its land and labour.

All systems either of preference or of restraint, therefore, being thus completely taken away, the obvious and simple system of natural liberty establishes itself of its own accord. Every man, as long as he does not violate the laws of justice, is left perfectly free to pursue his own interest his own way, and to bring both his industry and capital into competition with those of any other man, or order of men. The sovereign is completely discharged from a duty, in the attempting to perform which he must always be exposed to innumerable delusions, and for the proper performance of which no human wisdom or knowledge could ever be sufficient; the duty of superintending the industry of private people, and of directing it towards the employments most suitable to the interest of the society. According to the system of natural liberty, the sovereign has only three duties to attend to; three duties of great importance, indeed, but plain and intelligible to common understandings: first, the duty of protecting the society from the violence and invasion of other independent societies: secondly, the duty of protecting, as far as possible, every member of the society from the injustice or oppression of every other member of it, or the duty of establishing an exact administration of justice; and, thirdly, the duty of erecting and maintaining certain public works and certain public institutions which it can never be for the interest of any individual, or small number of individuals, to erect and maintain; because the profit could never repay the expense to any individual or small number of individuals, though it may frequently do much more than repay it to a great society.

Ibid. (A), vol. i, pp. 309-10; (B), vol. ii, pp. 180-1.

20. JEREMY BENTHAM: *A Manual of Political Economy* (1798)

The practical questions, therefore, are . . . how far the end in view is best promoted by individuals acting for themselves? and in what cases these ends may be promoted by the hands of government?

With the view of causing an increase to take place in the mass of national wealth, or with a view to increase of the means either of subsistence or enjoyment, without some special reason, the general rule is, that nothing ought to be done or attempted by government. The motto, or watchword of government, on these occasions, ought to be—Be quiet.

For this quietism there are two main reasons: 1. Generally speaking, any interference for this purpose on the part of government is needless. The wealth of the whole community is composed of the wealth of the several individuals belonging to it taken together. But to increase his particular portion is, generally speaking, among the constant objects of each individual's exertions and care. Generally speaking, there is no one who knows what is for your interest so well as yourself— no one who is disposed with so much ardour and constancy to pursue it.

2. Generally speaking, it is moreover likely to be pernicious, viz. by being unconducive, or even obstructive, with reference to the attainment of the end in view. Each individual bestowing more time and attention upon the means of preserving and increasing his portion of wealth, than is or can be bestowed by government, is likely to take a more effectual course than what, in his instance and on his behalf, would be taken by government.

It is, moreover, universally and constantly pernicious in another way, by the restraint or constraint imposed on the free agency of the individual. . . .

. . . With few exceptions, and those not very considerable

ones, the attainment of the maximum of enjoyment will be most effectually secured by leaving each individual to pursue his own maximum of enjoyment, in proportion as he is in possession of the means. Inclination in this respect will not be wanting on the part of any one. Power, the species of power applicable to this case—viz. wealth, pecuniary power— could not be given by the hand of government to one, without being taken from another; so that by such interference there would not be any gain of power upon the whole.

The gain to be produced in this article by the interposition of government, respects principally the head of knowledge. There are cases in which, for the benefit of the public at large, it may be in the power of government to cause this or that portion of knowledge to be produced and diffused, which, without the demand for it produced by government, would either not have been produced, or would not have been diffused.

We have seen above the grounds on which the general rule in this behalf—Be quiet—rests. Whatever measures, therefore, cannot be justified as exceptions to that rule, may be considered as *non agenda* on the part of government. The art, therefore, is reduced within a small compass: security and freedom are all that industry requires. The request which agriculture, manufactures and commerce present to governments, is modest and reasonable as that which Diogenes made to Alexander: 'Stand out of my sunshine.' We have no need of favour—we require only a secure and open path.

Bentham's Works, ed. Bowring (Edinburgh, 1843),
vol. iii, pp. 33-5.

2. NATURAL LAWS AND THE IMPOSSIBILITY OF INTERFERENCE

21. THOMAS ROBERT MALTHUS: *Essay on Population* (1798)

(A)

. . . There is one right, which man has generally been thought to possess, which I am confident he neither does, nor can, possess, a right to subsistence when his labour will not fairly purchase it. Our laws indeed say that he has this right, and bind the society to furnish employment and food to those who cannot get them in the regular market; but in so doing, they attempt to reverse the laws of nature. . . .

A man who is born into a world already possessed, if he cannot get subsistence from his parents on whom he has a just demand, and if the society do not want his labour, has no claim of *right* to the smallest portion of food, and in fact, has no business to be where he is. At nature's mighty feast there is no vacant cover for him. . . .

The Abbé Raynal has said, that: 'Avant toutes les loix sociales l'homme avoit le droit de subsister.' He might with just as much propriety have said, that before the institution of social laws, every man had a right to live a hundred years. Undoubtedly he had then, and has still, a good right, to live a hundred years, nay, a thousand, *if he can* . . . but the affair, in both cases, is principally an affair of power, not of right. . . .

The poor are by no means inclined to be visionary. Their distresses are always real, though they are not attributed to the real causes. If these real causes were properly explained to them, and they were taught to know how small a part of their present distress was attributable to government, and how great a part to causes totally unconnected with it, discontent and irritation among the lower classes of people would show themselves much less frequently than at present.

(B)

Almost everything that has been hitherto done for the poor, has tended, as if with solicitous care, to throw a veil of obscurity over this subject and to hide from them the true cause of their poverty. When the wages of labour are hardly sufficient to maintain two children, a man marries and has five or six. He of course finds himself miserably distressed. . . . He accuses his parish. . . . He accuses the avarice of the rich. . . . He accuses the partial and unjust institutions of society. . . . In searching for objects of accusation, he never adverts to the quarter from which all his misfortunes originate. The last person that he would think of accusing is himself. . . .

We cannot justly accuse them (the common people) of improvidence and want of industry, till they act as they do now after it has been brought home to their comprehensions, that they are themselves the cause of their own poverty; that the means of redress are in their own hands, and in the hands of no other persons whatever; that the society in which they live and the government which presides over it, are totally without power in this respect; and however ardently they may desire to relieve them, and whatever attempts they may make to do so, they are really and truly unable to execute what they benevolently wish, but unjustly promise.

Malthus, *Essay on the Principle of Population*
(2nd edn. 1803), (A), pp. 531-5; (B), pp. 506-7.

22. DAVID RICARDO: *The Principles of Political Economy and Taxation*
(1819)

Labour, like all other things which are purchased and sold . . . has its natural and its market price. The natural price of labour is that price which is necessary to enable the labourers, one with another, to subsist and to perpetuate their race, without either increase or diminution. . . .

The market price of labour is the price which is really paid for it, from the natural operation of the proportion of the supply to the demand. . . .

It is when the market price of labour exceeds its natural price, that the condition of the labourer is flourishing and happy, that he has it in his power to command a greater proportion of the necessaries and enjoyments of life, and therefore to rear a healthy and numerous family. When, however, by the encouragement which high wages give to the increase of population, the number of labourers is increased, wages again fall to their natural price, and indeed from a reaction sometimes fall below it.

When the market price of labour is below its natural price, the condition of the labourers is most wretched: then poverty deprives them of those comforts which custom renders absolute necessaries. It is only after their privations have reduced their number, or the demand for labour has increased, that the market price of labour will rise to its natural price, and that the labourer will have the moderate comforts which the natural price of wages will afford. . . .

These then are the laws by which wages are regulated, and by which the happiness of far the greatest part of every community is governed. Like all other contracts, wages should be left to the fair and free competition of the market and should never be controlled by the interference of the legislature.

The clear and direct tendency of the poor laws, is in direct opposition to these obvious principles: it is not, as the legislature benevolently intended, to amend the condition of the poor, but to deteriorate the condition of both poor and rich; instead of making the poor rich, they are calculated to make the rich poor; and while the present laws are in force, it is quite in the natural order of things that the fund for the maintenance of the poor should progressively increase, till it has absorbed all the net revenue of the country, or at least so much of it as the state shall leave us, after satisfying its own never failing demands for the public expenditure. . . .

It is a truth which admits not a doubt, that the comforts and well-being of the poor cannot be permanently secured without some regard on their part, or some effort on the part of the legislature, to regulate the increase of their numbers, and to render less frequent among them early and improvident marriages. . . .

The nature of evil points out the remedy. By gradually contracting the sphere of the poor laws, by impressing on the poor the value of independence, by teaching them that they must look not to systematic or casual charity but to their own exertions for support, that prudence and forethought are neither unnecessary nor unprofitable virtues, we shall by degrees approach a sounder and more healthful state.

No scheme for the amendment of the poor laws merits the least attention, which has not their abolition for its ultimate object, and he is the best friend to the poor and to the cause of humanity who can point out how this end can be attained with the most security, and at the same time with the least violence. . . .

If by law every human being wanting support could be sure to obtain it, and obtain it in such a degree as to make life tolerably comfortable, theory would lead us to expect that all other taxes would be light compared with the single one of poor rates. The principle of gravitation is not more certain than the tendency of such laws to change wealth and power into misery and weakness; to call away the exertions of labour from every object except that of providing more subsistence; to confound all intellectual distinction; to busy the mind continually in supplying the body's wants; until at last all classes should be infected with the plague of universal poverty.

David Ricardo, *The Principles of Political Economy and Taxation* (2nd edn., London, 1819), ch. v, 'On Wages' *passim*.

3. FREE TRADE

23. ADAM SMITH: *The Wealth of Nations* (1776)

(A)

If a foreign country can supply us with a commodity cheaper than we ourselves can make it, better buy it of them with some part of the produce of our own industry employed in a way in which we have some advantage. The general industry of the country, being always in proportion to the capital which employs it, will not thereby be diminished; but only left to find out the way in which it can be employed with the greatest advantage. It is certainly not employed to the greatest advantage when it is thus directed towards an object which it can buy cheaper than it can make. The value of its annual produce is certainly more or less diminished when it is thus turned away from producing commodities evidently of more value than the commodity which it is directed to produce. According to the supposition, that a commodity could be purchased from foreign countries cheaper than it can be made at home, it could, therefore, have been purchased with a part only of the commodities, or, what is the same thing, with a part only of the price of the commodities, which the industry employed by an equal capital would have produced at home, had it been left to follow its natural course. The industry of the country, therefore, is thus turned away from a more to a less advantageous employment, and the exchangeable value of its annual produce, instead of being increased, according to the intention of the lawgiver, must necessarily be diminished by every such regulation.

(B)

The Portuguese, it is said, indeed, are better customers for our manufactures than the French, and should therefore be encouraged in preference to them. As they give us their custom, it is pretended, we should give them ours. The sneaking arts of underling tradesmen are thus erected into political maxims for the conduct of a great empire: for it is the most underling tradesmen only who make it a rule to employ chiefly their own customers. A great trader purchases his goods always where they are cheapest and best, without regard to any little interest of this kind.

By such maxims as these, however, nations have been taught that their interest consisted in beggaring all their neighbours. Each nation has been made to look with an invidious eye upon the prosperity of all the nations with which it trades, and to consider their gain as its own loss. Commerce, which ought naturally to be, among nations, as among individuals, a bond of union and friendship, has become the most fertile source of discord and animosity. The capricious ambition of kings and ministers has not, during the present and the preceding century, been more fatal to the repose of Europe than the impertinent jealousy of merchants and manufacturers. The violence and injustice of the rulers of mankind is an ancient evil, for which, I am afraid, the nature of human affairs can scarce admit of a remedy. But the mean rapacity, the monopolising spirit of manufacturers, who neither are, nor ought to be, the rulers of mankind, though it cannot perhaps be corrected, may very easily be prevented from disturbing the tranquillity of anybody but themselves.

That it was the spirit of monopoly which originally both invented and propagated this doctrine cannot be doubted; and they who first taught it were by no means such fools as they who believed it. In every country it always is and must be the interest of the great body of the people to buy whatever they want of those who sell it cheapest. The proposition is so very manifest that it seems ridiculous to take any pains to prove it; nor could it ever have been called in question had not the interested sophistry of merchants and manufacturers confounded the common sense of mankind. Their interest is, in this respect, directly opposite to that of the great body of the people. As it is the interest of the freemen of a corporation to hinder the rest of the inhabitants from employing any workmen but themselves, so it is the interest of the merchants and manufacturers of every country to secure to themselves the monopoly of the home market. Hence in Great Britain, and in most other European countries, the extraordinary duties upon almost all goods imported by alien merchants. Hence the high duties and prohibitions upon all those foreign manufactures which can come into competition with our own. Hence, too, the extraordinary restraints upon the importation of almost all sorts of goods from those countries with which the balance of trade is supposed to be disadvantageous; that is, from those against whom national animosity happens to be most violently inflamed. The wealth of a neighbouring nation, however, though dangerous in war and politics, is certainly advantageous in trade. . . .

The modern maxims of foreign commerce, by aiming at the impoverishment of all our neighbours, so far as they are capable of producing their intended effect, tend to render that very commerce insignificant and contemptible. It is in consequence of these maxims that the

commerce between France and England has in both countries been subjected to so many discouragements and
restraints. If those two countries, however, were to consider
their real interest, without either mercantile jealousy or
national animosity, the commerce of France might be more
advantageous to Great Britain than that of any other
country, and for the same reason that of Great Britain to
France. . . .

France could afford a market at least eight times more
extensive, and, on account of the superior frequency of the
returns, four-and-twenty times more advantageous than
that which our North American colonies ever afforded.
The trade of Great Britain would be just as advantageous
to France, and, in proportion to the wealth, population,
and proximity of the respective countries, would have the
same superiority over that which France carries on with
her own colonies. Such is the very great difference between
that trade, which the wisdom of both nations has thought
proper to discourage, and that which it has favoured the
most.

Adam Smith, *The Wealth of Nations* (Everyman edn.),
vol. ii, (A), pp. 401-2; (B), pp. 436-40.

24. DAVID RICARDO: *The Principles of Political Economy and Taxation*
(1819)

Under a system of perfectly free commerce, each country
naturally devotes its capital and labour to such employments
as are most beneficial to each. This pursuit of individual
advantage is admirably connected with the universal good
of the whole. By stimulating industry, by rewarding ingenuity, and by using most efficaciously the peculiar powers
bestowed by nature, it distributes labour most effectively
and most economically: while, by increasing the general
mass of productions, it diffuses general benefits, and binds
together by one common tie of interest and intercourse, the
universal society of nations throughout the civilised world.
It is this principle which determines that wine shall be made

in France and Portugal, that corn shall be grown in America and Poland, and that hardware and other goods shall be manufactured in England.

> David Ricardo, *The Principles of Political Economy and Taxation* (2nd edn., 1819), p. 144.

25. *Petition of the London Merchants*, 1820

[Drafted by Thomas Tooke and supported by the Edinburgh and Manchester Chambers of Commerce.]

To the Honourable the Commons of Great Britain and Ireland:—

The Petition of, etc.

Humbly showeth,

That foreign commerce is eminently conducive to the wealth and prosperity of a country, by enabling it to import the commodities for the production of which the soil, climate, capital, and industry of other countries are best calculated, and to export in payment those articles for which its own situation is better adapted.

That freedom from restraint is calculated to give the utmost extension to foreign trade, and the best direction to the capital and industry of the country.

That the maxim of buying in the cheapest market and selling in the dearest, which regulates every merchant in his individual dealings, is strictly applicable as the best rule for the trade of the whole nation.

That a policy founded on these principles would render the commerce of the world an interchange of mutual advantages, and diffuse an increase of wealth and enjoyments among the inhabitants of each State. . . .

Your petitioners therefore humbly pray that your honourable house will be pleased to take the subject into consideration, and to adopt such measures as may be calculated to give greater freedom to foreign commerce, and thereby to increase the resources of the State.

> F. W. Hirst, *Free Trade and Other Fundamental Doctrines of the Manchester School* (London, 1903), pp. 118-21.

4. COLONIES

26. ADAM SMITH: *The Wealth of Nations*
(1776)

The maintenance of this monopoly has hitherto been the principal, or more properly perhaps the sole end and purpose of the dominion which Great Britain assumes over her colonies. In the exclusive trade, it is supposed, consists the great advantage of provinces, which have never yet afforded either revenue or military force for the support of the civil government, or the defence of the mother country. The monopoly is the principal badge of their dependency, and it is the sole fruit which has hitherto been gathered from that dependency. Whatever expense Great Britain has hitherto laid out in maintaining this dependency has really been laid out in order to support this monopoly. . . .

Under the present system of management, Great Britain derives nothing but loss from the dominion which she assumes over her colonies.

To propose that Great Britain should voluntarily give up all authority over her colonies, and leave them to elect their own magistrates, to enact their own laws, and to make peace and war as they might think proper, would be to propose such a measure as never was, and never will be adopted, by any nation in the world. No nation ever voluntarily gave up the dominion of any province, how troublesome soever it might be to govern it, and how small soever the revenue which it afforded might be in proportion to the expense which it occasioned. Such sacrifices, though they might frequently be agreeable to the interest, are always mortifying to the pride of every nation, and what is perhaps of still greater consequence, they are always contrary to the private interest of the governing part of it, who would thereby be deprived of the disposal of many places of trust and profit, of many opportunities of acquiring wealth and distinction, which the possession of the most turbulent, and, to the great body of the people, the most unprofitable province seldom fails to afford. The most visionary enthusiast would scarce be capable of proposing such a measure with any serious hopes at least of its ever being adopted. If it was adopted, however, Great Britain would not only be immediately freed from the whole annual expense of the peace establishment of the colonies, but might settle with them such a treaty of commerce as could effectually secure to her a free trade, more advantageous to the great body of the people, though less so to the merchants, than the monopoly which she at present enjoys. By thus parting good friends, the natural affection of the colonies to the mother country which, perhaps, our late dissensions have well nigh extinguished, would quickly revive. It might dispose them not only to respect, for whole centuries together, that treaty of commerce which they had concluded with us at parting, but to favour us in war as well as in trade, and, instead of turbulent and factious subjects, to become our most faithful, affectionate, and generous allies; and the same sort of parental affection on the one side, and filial respect on the other, might revive between Great Britain and her colonies, which used to subsist between those of ancient Greece and the mother city from which they descended.

Adam Smith, *The Wealth of Nations* (Everyman edn.), vol. ii, pp. 111-13.

5. REFORM

27. JEREMY BENTHAM: *Plan of Parliamentary Reform in the Form of a Catechism, with an Introduction showing the Necessity of Radical, and the Inadequacy of Moderate Reform*

(1817)

Money, power, factitious dignity—these as it is the interest, so has it ever been the study—as it has been the study, so has it been the endeavour—of the monarch—as it has been so will it, and where the monarch is a human being, so must it be everywhere—to draw to himself in the greatest quantity possible. And then we have one *partial*, one *separate*, one *sinister* interest, the monarchical—the interest of the ruling *one*—with which the *universal*, the *democratical* interest has to antagonize. . . .

Meantime the money, which, in an endless and boundless stream, is thus to keep flowing into the monarchical coffers —this one thing needful cannot find its way into those sacred receptacles without instruments and conduit pipes. Upon and out of the pockets of the people it cannot be raised, but through the forms of parliament . . . nor therefore without the concurrence of the richest men in the country—in the situation of peers, great landholding commoners styled country gentlemen—and others. In those men is the chief *property* of the country and with it—(for in the language of the aristocratic school, *property* and *virtue* are synonymous)—the *virtue* of the country. And then we have another partial, separate and sinister influence—the *aristocratical* interest . . . —another overbearing, and essentially and immutably hostile interest—against which and under which, the universal interest has to struggle, and as far as possible defend itself.

. . . Waste begets corruption; corruption, waste. For through the already enumerated drains—viz, useless places, needless places, overpay of needful places, groundless pensions, and sinecures . . . these together with peerages and baronetages and ribbons—for peerage-hunters, baronetage-hunters, and ribbon-hunters—these, by their bare existence, and without need of their being either asked or offered—always with the fullest effect, never with the personal danger, or so much as the imputation, attached to the word *bribery*—operate in the character, and produce the effect, of *matter of corruptive influence*. . . . What the real, the sensible mischief consists in is—the sacrifice made of the interest and comfort of the *subject many* to the overgrown felicity of the *ruling few*. . . .

Such being the disease, behold now the remedy—the only remedy. . . . This remedy—two words, viz., *democratical ascendancy*, will, in principle, suffice for the expression of it. Taking this for the general description of the *end, parliamentary reform*, will next make its appearance in the character of *means* . . . *radical* parliamentary reform as the only means.

Without any outward and visible change in the forms of
the constitution—though waste already committed cannot
be caused not to have been committed—though past misrule
cannot be caused not to have reigned—yet may the plague
be stayed. To the democratical, to the universal interest,
give—one might almost say, restore—that ascendency which
by the confederated, partial, and sinister interest has been
so deplorably abused, and so long as it continues, will
continue to be abused:—thus you have the remedy. . . .

At present, the cause of the misrule is this: viz., the rule
is completely in the hands of those whose interest it is—
their interest, and thence of necessity their desire, and, as
far as depends upon them, the determination—that the
misrule should continue:—the thing required is—leaving
the executive part of the government where it is—so to
order matters, that the controlling part of the government
shall be in the hands of those whose interest it is that good
government shall take the place of misrule: of misrule in every
shape, and more particularly in the two most intimately
connected and mutually fostering shapes—waste and corruption, corruption and waste. . . .

Ascendancy? Yes; ascendancy it must be: nothing less
will serve.

Talk of mixture: yes, this may serve, and must serve:
but then, the intrinsically noxious ingredients—the ingredients which must be kept in, though for no better reason
than that we are used to them—and being so used to them,
could not bear—(for who is there that could bear?)—to
part with them—these ingredients, of which the greatest
praise would be that they were inoperative, must not be in
any such proportion of force, as to destroy, or materially to
impair, the efficiency of the only essentially useful one.

Talk of balance: never will it do: leave that to Mother
Goose and Mother Blackstone. Balance! balance! Politicians
upon roses—to whom, to save the toil of thinking—on
questions most wide in extent, and most high in importance
—an allusion—an emblem—an anything—so as it has been
accepted by others, is accepted as conclusive evidence—
what mean ye by this your balance? Know ye not, that in a
machine of any kind, when forces balance each other, the

machine is at a stand? Well, and in the machine of government, immobility—the perpetual absence of all motion—is that the thing which is wanted? Know ye not that—since an emblem you must have—since you can neither talk, nor attempt to think, but in hieroglyphics—know you not that, as in the case of the body natural, so in the case of the body politic, when motion ceases, the body dies?

So much for the balance: now for the mixture—the mixture to which, as such, such virtue is wont to be ascribed. Here is a form of government, in which the power is divided among three interests:—the interest of the great body of the people—of the many;—and two separate interests—the interest of the one and the interest of the few—both of which are adverse to it:—two separate and narrow interests, neither of which is kept on foot—but at the expense, to the loss, and by the sacrifice, of the broader interest. This form of government (say you) has its advantages. Its advantages? —compared with what?—compared with those forms of government, in which the people have no power at all, or in which, if they have any, they have not so much? Oh yes: with any such form of government for an object of comparison, its excellence is unquestionable. But, compare it with a form of government in which the interest of the people is the only interest that is looked to—in which neither a single man, with a separate and adverse interest of his own, nor a knot of men with a separate and adverse interest of their own, are to be found—where no interest is kept up at the expense, to the loss, by the sacrifice, of the universal interest to it,—where is then the excellence?

Bentham's Works, ed. Bowring (Edinburgh, 1843), vol. iii, pp. 440-50.

28. DAVID RICARDO: *Observations on Parliamentary Reform (The Scotsman, 24 April 1824)*

The last point for consideration is the supposed disposition of the people to interfere with the rights of property. So essential does it appear to me, to the cause of good government, that the rights of property should be held sacred, that I would agree to deprive those of the elective franchise against whom it could justly be alleged that they considered it their interest to invade them. But in fact it can be only amongst the most needy in the community that such an opinion can be entertained. The man of a small income must be aware how little his share would be if all the large fortunes in the kingdom were equally divided among the people. He must know that the little he would obtain by such a division could be no adequate compensation for the overturning of a principle which renders the produce of his industry secure. Whatever might be his gains after such a principle had been admitted, would be held by a very insecure tenure, and the chance of his making any future gains would be greatly diminished; for the quantity of employment in the country must depend, not only on the quantity of capital, but upon its advantageous distribution, and, above all, on the conviction of each capitalist that he will be allowed to enjoy unmolested the fruits of his capital, his skill, and his enterprise. To take from him this conviction is at once to annihilate half the productive industry of the country, and would be more fatal to the poor labourer than to the rich capitalist himself. This is so self-evident, that men very little advanced beyond the very lowest stations in the country cannot be ignorant of it; and it may be doubted whether any large number even of the lowest would, if they could, promote a division of property. It is the bugbear by which the corrupt always endeavour to rally those who have property to lose around them, and it is from this fear, or pretended fear, that so much jealousy is expressed of entrusting the least share of power to the people. But the objection, when urged against reform, is not an honest one, for, if it be allowed that those who have a sacred regard to the rights of property should have a voice in the choice of representatives, the principle is granted for which reformers contend.

Works of David Ricardo, ed. by J. R. McCulloch (2nd edn. 1888), pp. 554-5.

29. JEREMY BENTHAM: *Constitutional Code*
(1830)

(A)

To the devising of any well-grounded and rational course, for the surmounting of the obstacles opposed to good government, by the universal self-preference in the breasts of the functionaries of government—of the constituted guardians of the universal interest—the first step was the taking a true observation of the existence and shape of that same universally prevalent, particular, and sinister interest. This theory being accomplished, correspondent and accordant practice becomes a matter of course. Hence, into the compass of these two words, may be condensed the all-directing and leading rule—*minimize confidence*. Such, then, is the advice which the framer of this constitution has not been backward in giving to all who are disposed to accept it. Confine within the strictest limits of necessity, whatsoever confidence you may be tempted to repose either in them or their successors.

At the same time, here as in a watch, does this mainspring require another to antagonize with it. Of all constituents be it, at the same time the care, from no delegate to withhold any of that power, which may eventually be necessary to the due performance of the service looked for, at his hands. While confidence is minimized, let not power be withheld. For security against breach of trust, the sole apt remedy is, —on the part of trustees, not impotence, but constant responsibility, and as towards their creators—the authors of their political being—on every occasion, and at all times, the strictest and most absolute dependence.

(B)

No power of government ought to be employed in the endeavour to establish any system or article of belief on the subject of religion. . . .

But in truth, in no instance has a system in regard to religion been ever established, but for the purpose, as well as with the effect of its being made an instrument of intimidation, corruption, and delusion, for the support of depredation and oppression in the hands of governments. . . .

The affording such establishment to the religion of Jesus is inconsistent with his will, as evidenced by his own declarations as well as by his own practice. Nowhere is he stated to have directed that to the religion delivered by himself, any such establishment should be given. Nowhere, either in terms or in substance, has he said—give money to those who say they believe in what I have said, or give money to those who teach others to believe what I have said. Nowhere has he said—apply punishment to those who will not say they believe what I have said, or to those who say they believe that what I have said is false. . . .

The corruptive effect of opulence . . . was neither unperceived by him nor unproclaimed. No denunciations were more severe than those made by him against those who put their trust in riches. Wallowers in wealth and luxury, greater than any to which he could ever have been witness, are now to be seen,—men who, pretending to be preachers of *his* doctrine, and enjoying their wealth and luxury on that false pretence, never cease to say—take from our order any of the wealth it enjoys or may enjoy—set limits to our riches, and the religion of Jesus is at an end.

Bentham's Works, ed. Bowring (Edinburgh, 1843), vol. ix, (A), p. 62; (B), pp. 92-5.

30. JOHN STUART MILL: *Autobiography*

The other leading characteristics of the creed, which we held in common with my father, may be stated as follows:

In politics, an almost unbounded confidence in the efficacy of two things: representative government, and complete freedom of discussion. So complete was my father's reliance on the influence of reason over the minds of mankind, whenever it is allowed to reach them, that he felt as if all would be gained if the whole population were taught to read, if all sorts of opinions were allowed to be addressed to them by word and in writing, and if by means of the suffrage they could nominate a legislature to give effect to the opinions they adopted. He thought that when the legislature no longer represented a class interest, it would aim at the general interest, honestly and with adequate wisdom; since the people would be sufficiently under the guide of educated intelligence, to make in general a good choice of persons to represent them, and having done so, to leave to those whom they had chosen a liberal discretion. Accordingly aristocratic rule, the government of the Few in any of its shapes, being in his eyes the only thing which stood between mankind and an administration of their affairs by the best wisdom to be found among them, was the object of his sternest disapprobation, and a democratic suffrage the principal article of his political creed, not on the ground of liberty, Rights of Man, or any of the phrases, more or less significant, by which, up to that time, democracy had usually been defended, but as the most essential of 'securities for good government.' In this, too, he held fast only to what he deemed essentials; he was comparatively indifferent to monarchical or republican forms—far more so than Bentham, to whom a king, in the character of 'corrupter general', appeared necessarily very noxious. Next to aristocracy, an established church, or corporation of priests, as being by position the great depravers of religion, and interested in opposing the progress of the human mind, was the object of his greatest detestation.

J. S. Mill, *Autobiography* (World's Classics edn.), pp. 89-90.

PART III

THE AGE OF COBDEN AND BRIGHT

I. FREE TRADE AND THE REPEAL OF THE CORN LAWS

31. *Petition of the Manchester Chamber of Commerce to the House of Commons*, 1838

[This petition, drawn up by Richard Cobden, J. B. Smith and Henry Ashworth on behalf of the Manchester Anti-Corn Law Association, was adopted by the Manchester Chamber of Commerce on 20 December 1838.]

[After setting out the rapid growth of foreign competition to the Lancashire cotton trade and emphasising the extent to which English manufacturers were handicapped by the high price of bread, artificially maintained by the Corn Laws, the Petition concludes:]

. . . Your Petitioners cannot too earnestly make known that these evils are occasioned by our impolitic and urgent legislation, which, by preventing the British manufacturer from exchanging the produce of his labour for the corn of other countries, enables our foreign rivals to purchase their food at one half the price at which it is sold in this market; and your petitioners declare it to be their solemn conviction, that this is the commencement only of a state of things which, unless arrested by a timely repeal of all protective duties upon the importation of corn and of all foreign articles of subsistence, must eventually transfer our manufacturing industry into other and rival countries.

That, deeply impressed with such apprehensions, your petitioners cannot look with indifference upon, nor conceal from your honourable house the perilous condition of those surrounding multitudes, whose subsistence from day to day depends upon the prosperity of the cotton trade. Already the millions have raised the cry for food. Reason, compassion, and sound policy demand that the excited passions be allayed, otherwise evil consequences may ensue. The continuance of the loyal attachment of the people to the established institutions of the country can never be permanently secured on any other grounds than those of universal justice. Holding one of these eternal principles to be the unalienable right of every man, freely to exchange the results of his labour for the productions of other people, and maintaining the practice of protecting one part of the community at the expense of all other classes, to be unsound and unjustifiable, your petitioners earnestly implore your honourable house to repeal all laws relating to the importation of foreign corn and other foreign articles of subsistence, and to carry out to the fullest extent, both as affects agriculture and manufactures, the true and peaceful principles of free trade, by removing all existing obstacles to the unrestricted employment of industry and capital.

F. W. Hirst, *Free Trade and Other Fundamental Doctrines of the Manchester School* (1903), pp. 141-2.

32. RICHARD COBDEN: Speech in London, 8 February 1844

I am a manufacturer of clothing, and I do not know why, in this climate, and in the artificial state of society in which we live, the making of clothes should not be as honourable —because it is pretty near as useful—a pursuit as the manufacture of food. Well, did you ever hear any debates in the House to fix the price of my commodities in the market? Suppose we had a majority of cotton-printers (which happens to be my manufacture) in the House. . . . Let us suppose that you were reading the newspaper some fine morning, and saw an account of a majority of the House having been engaged the night before in fixing the price at which yard-wide prints should be sold: 'Yard-wide prints, of such a quality, 10d. a yard; of such a quality, 9d.; of such a quality, 8d.; of such a quality, 7d.', and so on. Why, you would rub your eyes with astonishment! . . .

Now, did it ever occur to you that there is no earthly difference between a body of men, manufacturers of corn, sitting down in the House, and passing a law enacting that wheat shall be so much, barley so much, beans so much, and oats so much?

Why, then, do you look at this monopoly of corn with such complacency? Simply because you and I and the rest of us have a superstitious reverence for the owners of those sluggish acres, and have a very small respect for ourselves and our own vocation. I say the Corn-law monopolists, who arrogate to themselves power in the House of Commons, are practising an injustice on every other species of capitalists. Take the iron trade, for example—a prodigious interest in this country. Iron of certain qualities has gone down in price, during the last five or six years, from £15 10s. to £5 10s. per ton. Men have seen their fortunes—ay, I have known them—dwindle away from £300,000 till now they could not sit down and write their wills for £100,000. Well, did any man ever hear in the House of Commons an attempt made to raise a cry about these grievances there, or to lodge a complaint against the Government or the country because they could not keep up the price of iron? Has any man come forward there proposing that by some law pig-iron should be so much, and bar-iron of such a price, and other kinds of iron in proportion? No; neither has this been the case with any other interest in the country. But how is it with corn? The very first night I was present in the House this session, I saw the Prime Minister get up, having a paper before him, and he was careful to tell us what the price of corn had been for the last fifty years, and what it was now. He is employed for little else but as a kind of corn-steward, to see how the prices may be kept up for his masters. . . .

Our opponents tell us that our object in bringing about the repeal of the Corn-laws is, by reducing the price of corn, to lower the rate of their wages. I can only answer upon this point for the manufacturing districts; but, as far as they are concerned, I state it most emphatically as a truth, that, for the last twenty years, whenever corn has been cheap wages have been high in Lancashire; and, on the other hand, when bread has been dear wages have been greatly reduced. . . .

Now, let me be fully understood as to what Free Traders really do want. We do not want cheap corn merely in order that we may have low money prices. What we desire is plenty of corn, and we are utterly careless what its price is, provided we obtain it at the natural price. All we ask is this, that corn shall follow the same law which the monopolists in food admit that labour must follow; that 'it shall find its natural level in the markets of the world.'. . .

To pay for that corn, more manufactures would be required from this country; this would lead to an increased demand for labour in the manufacturing districts, which would necessarily be attended with a rise of wages, in order that the goods might be made for the purpose of exchanging for the corn brought from abroad. . . . I observe there are narrow-minded men in the agricultural districts, telling us, 'Oh, if you allow Free Trade, and bring in a quarter of corn from abroad, it is quite clear that you will sell one quarter less in England.'. . . What! I would ask, if you set more people to work at better wages—if you can clear your streets of those spectres which are now haunting your thoroughfares begging their daily bread—if you can depopulate your work-houses and clear off the two millions of paupers which now exist in the land, and put them to work at productive industry —do you not think that they would consume some of the wheat as well as you; and may not they be, as we are now, consumers of wheaten bread by millions, instead of existing on their present miserable dietary? . . .

With free trade in corn, so far from throwing land out of use or injuring the cultivation of the poorer soils, free trade in corn is the very way to increase the production at home, and stimulate the cultivation of the poorer soils by compelling the application of more capital and labour to them. We do not contemplate deriving one quarter less corn from the soil of this country; we do not anticipate having one pound less of butter or cheese, or one head less of cattle or sheep: we expect to have a great increase in production and consumption at home; but all we contend for is this, that when we, the people here, have purchased all that can be raised at home, we shall be allowed to go 3,000 miles—to Poland, Russia or America—for more; and that there shall be no let or hindrance put in the way of our getting this additional quantity.

Speeches by Richard Cobden, M.P. (1870),
vol. i, pp. 118-33.

33. RICHARD COBDEN: Speech in London, 3 July 1844

In the first place, we want free trade in corn, because we think it just; we ask for the abolition of all restriction upon that article, exclusively, simply because we believe that, if we obtain that, we shall get rid of all other monopolies without any trouble. We do not seek free trade in corn primarily for the purpose of purchasing it at a cheaper money-rate; we require it at the natural price of the world's market, whether it becomes dearer with a free trade—as wool seems to be getting up now, after the abolition of the 1d. a pound —or whether it is cheaper, it matters not to us, provided the people of this country have it at its natural price, and every source of supply is freely opened, as nature and nature's God intended it to be;—then, and then only, shall we be satisfied. If they come to motives, we state that we do not believe that free trade in corn will injure the farmer; we are convinced that it will benefit the tenant-farmer as much as any trader or manufacturer in the community.

Neither do we believe it will injure the farm-labourer; we think it will enlarge the market for his labour, and give him an opportunity of finding employment, not only on the soil by the improvements which agriculturists must adopt, but that there will also be a general rise in wages from the increased demand for employment in the neighbouring towns, which will give young peasants an opportunity of choosing between the labour of the field and that of the towns. We do not expect that it will injure the land-owner, provided he looks merely to his pecuniary interest in the matter; we have no doubt it will interfere with his political despotism—that political union which now exists in the House of Commons, and to a certain extent also, though terribly shattered, in the counties of this country. We believe it might interfere with that; and that with free trade in corn men must look for political power rather by honest means —to the intelligence and love of their fellow-countrymen— than by the aid of this monopoly, which binds some men together by depressing and injuring their fellow-citizens.

We are satisfied that those landowners who choose to adopt the improvement of their estates, and surrender mere political power by granting long leases to the farmers— who are content to eschew some of their feudal privileges connected with vert and venison—I mean the feudal privileges of the chase—if they will increase the productiveness of their estates—if they choose to attend to their own business—then, I say, free trade in corn does not necessarily involve pecuniary injury to the landlords themselves. . . .

We believe that free trade will increase the demand for labour of every kind, not merely of the mechanical classes and those engaged in laborious bodily occupations, but for clerks, shopmen and warehousemen, giving employment to all those youths whom you are so desirous of setting out in the world. . . . Finally, we believe that Free Trade will not diminish, but, on the contrary, increase the Queen's revenue.

Ibid. pp. 187-208.

34. LORD JOHN RUSSELL: Letter to the Electors of the City of London, 22 November 1845

. . . I used to be of opinion that corn was an exception to the general rules of political economy; but observation and experience have convinced me that we ought to abstain from all interference with the supply of food. Neither a government nor a legislature can ever regulate the corn market with the beneficial effects which the entire freedom of sale and purchase are seen of themselves to produce. . . .

Let us then unite to put an end to a system which has been proved to be the blight of commerce, the bane of agriculture, the source of bitter divisions among classes, the cause of penury, fever, mortality and crime among the people.

. . . Let the Ministry propose such a revision of the taxes as in their opinion may render the public burdens more just and more equal; let them add any other provisions which caution and even scrupulous forbearance may suggest; but let the removal of restrictions on the admission of the main articles of food and clothing used by the mass of the people be required, in plain terms, as useful to all great interests, and indispensable to the progress of the nation.

I have the honour to be, Gentlemen, your obedient servant,

J. RUSSELL.

Edinburgh: November 22, 1845.

Spencer Walpole, *Life of Lord John Russell* (1889),
vol. i, pp. 407-9.

35. RICHARD COBDEN: Speech at Manchester, 15 January 1846

But I have been accused of looking too much to material interests. Nevertheless I can say that I have taken as large and great a view of the effects of this mighty principle as ever did any man who dreamt over it in his own study. I believe that the physical gain will be the smallest gain to humanity from the success of this principle. I look farther; I see in the Free Trade principle that which shall act on the moral world as the principle of gravitation in the universe, —drawing men together, thrusting aside the antagonism of race, and creed, and language, and uniting us in the bonds of eternal peace.

I believe that the effect will be to change the face of the world, so as to introduce a system of government entirely distinct from that which now prevails. I believe that the desire and the motive for large and mighty empires; for gigantic armies and great navies—for those materials which are used for the destruction of life and the desolation of the rewards of labour—will die away; I believe that such things will cease to be necessary, or to be used, when man becomes one family, and freely exchanges the fruits of his labour with his brother man. I believe that, if we could be allowed to reappear on this sublunary scene, we should see, at a far distant period, the governing system of this world revert to something like the municipal system; and I believe that the speculative philosopher of a thousand years hence will date the greatest revolution that ever happened in the world's history from the triumph of the principle which we have met here to advocate.

Speeches by Richard Cobden, M.P. (1870),
vol. i, pp. 362-3.

2. LAISSEZ-FAIRE

36. RICHARD COBDEN: *Russia*
(1836)

A few plain maxims may be serviceable to those who may in future have occasion to allude to the subject of commerce, in kings' speeches, or other state papers.

To make laws for the regulation of trade, is as wise as it would be to legislate about water finding a level, or matter exercising its centripetal force.

So far from large armaments being necessary to secure a regularity of supply and demand, the most obscure province on the west coast of America, and the smallest island in the South Pacific, are, in proportion to their wants, as duly visited by buyers and sellers as the metropolis of England itself.

The only naval force required in a time of peace for the protection of commerce, is just such a number of frigates and small vessels as shall form an efficient sea police.

If government desires to serve the interests of our commerce, it has but one way. War, conquest, and standing armaments cannot aid, but only oppress trade; diplomacy will never assist it—commercial treaties can only embarrass it. The only mode by which the Government can protect and extend our commerce, is by retrenchment, and a reduction of the duties and taxes upon the ingredients of our manufactures and the food of our artisans.

The Political Writings of Richard Cobden, ed. by
Sir Louis Mallet (1878), p. 135.

37. RICHARD COBDEN: Speech in the House of Commons, 27 February 1846

How can protection, think you, add to the wealth of a country? Can you by legislation add one farthing to the wealth of the country? You may, by legislation, in one evening, destroy the fruits and accumulations of a century of labour; but I defy you to show me how, by the legislation of this House, you can add one farthing to the wealth of the country. That springs from the industry and intelligence of the people of this country. You cannot guide that intelligence; you cannot do better than leave it to its own instincts. If you attempt by legislation to give any direction to trade or industry, it is a thousand to one that you are doing wrong; and if you happen to be right, it is a work of supererogation, for the parties for whom you legislate would go right without you, and better than with you.

Speeches by Richard Cobden, M.P. (1870),
vol. i, pp. 382-3.

38. THOMAS BABINGTON MACAULAY: Speech in the House of Commons, 22 May 1846

[Macaulay was speaking on the second reading of the Ten Hours Bill.]

This, they say, is one of those matters about which we ought not to legislate at all; one of those matters which settle themselves far better than any government can settle them. Now it is most important that this point should be fully cleared up. We certainly ought not to usurp functions which do not properly belong to us; but, on the other hand, we ought not to abdicate functions which do properly belong to us. I hardly know which is the greater pest to society, a paternal government, that is to say a prying, meddlesome government which intrudes itself into every part of human life, and which thinks that it can do everything for everybody better than anybody can do anything for himself; or a careless, lounging government, which suffers grievances, such as it could at once remove, to grow and multiply, and which to all complaint and remonstrance has only one answer: 'We must let things alone: we must let things take their course: we must let things find their level.' There is no more important problem in politics than to ascertain the just mean between these two most pernicious extremes, to draw correctly the line which divides those cases in which it is the duty of the state to interfere from those cases in which it is the duty of the state to abstain from interference. . . .

Our statesmen cannot now be accused of being busy-bodies. But I am afraid that there is, even in some of the ablest and most upright among them, a tendency to the opposite fault. I will give an instance of what I mean. Fifteen years ago it became evident that railroads would soon, in every part of the kingdom, supersede to a great extent the old highways. The tracing of the new routes which were to join all the chief cities, ports, and naval arsenals of the island was a matter of the highest national importance. But, unfortunately, those who should have acted for the nation, refused to interfere. Consequently, numerous questions which were really public, questions which concerned the public convenience, the public prosperity, the public security, were treated as private questions. That the whole society was interested in having a good system of internal communication seemed to be forgotten. The speculator who wanted a large dividend on his shares, the landowner who wanted a large price for his acres, obtained a full hearing. But nobody applied to be heard on behalf of the community. The effects of that great error we feel, and we shall not soon cease to feel. Unless I am greatly mistaken, we are in danger of committing tonight an error of the same kind. . . .

Trade, considered merely as trade, considered merely with reference to the pecuniary interest of the contracting parties, can hardly be too free. But there is a great deal of trade which cannot be considered merely as trade, and which affects higher than pecuniary interests. And to say that government never ought to regulate such trade is a monstrous proposition, a proposition at which Adam Smith would have stood aghast. . . .

For the science of political economy teaches us only that we ought not on commercial grounds to interfere with the liberty of commerce; and we, in the cases which I have put, interfere with the liberty of commerce on higher than commercial grounds. . . .

But your doctrine of free trade is an exaggeration, a caricature of the sound doctrine; and by exhibiting such a caricature you bring discredit on the sound doctrine. We should have nothing to do with the contracts between you and your tenants, if those contracts affected only pecuniary interests. But higher than pecuniary interests are at stake. It concerns the commonwealth that the great body of the people should not live in a way which makes life wretched and short, which enfeebles the body and pollutes the mind. . . .

If we consider man merely in a commercial point of view, if we consider him merely as a machine for the production of worsted and calico, let us not forget what a piece of mechanism he is, how fearfully and wonderfully made. We do not treat a fine horse or a sagacious dog exactly as we treat a spinning-jenny. Nor will any slaveholder, who has sense enough to know his own interest, treat his human chattels exactly as he treats his horses and his dogs. And would you treat the free labourer of England like a mere wheel or pulley? . . .

My honourable friend seems to me, in all his reasonings about the commercial prosperity of nations, to overlook entirely the chief cause on which that prosperity depends. What is it, Sir, that makes the great difference between country and country? Not the exuberance of soil; not the mildness of climate; not mines, nor havens, nor rivers. These things are indeed valuable when put to their proper use by human intelligence: but human intelligence can do much without them; and they without human intelligence can do nothing. They exist in the highest degree in regions of which the inhabitants are few, and squalid, and barbarous, and naked, and starving; while on sterile rocks, amidst unwholesome marshes, and under inclement skies, may be found immense populations, well fed, well lodged, well clad, well governed. Nature meant Egypt and Sicily to be

the gardens of the world. They once were so. Is it anything
in the earth or in the air that makes Scotland more prosperous than Egypt, that makes Holland more prosperous
than Sicily? No, it was the Scotchman that made Scotland;
it was the Dutchman that made Holland. . . . Man, man
is the great instrument that produces wealth. The natural
difference between Campania and Spitzbergen is trifling,
when compared with the difference between a country
inhabited by men full of bodily and mental vigour, and a
country inhabited by men sunk in bodily and mental
decrepitude.

Never will I believe that what makes a population
stronger, and healthier, and wiser, and better, can
ultimately make it poorer. You try to frighten us by telling
us that in some German factories the young work seventeen
hours in the twenty-four, that they work so hard that
among thousands there is not one who grows to such a
stature that he can be admitted into the army; and you
ask whether, if we pass this bill, we can posibly hold our
own against such competition as this? Sir, I laugh at the
thought of such competition. If ever we are forced to yield
the foremost place among commercial nations, we shall
yield it, not to a race of degenerate dwarfs, but to some
people pre-eminently vigorous in body and in mind.

Miscellaneous Writings and Speeches of Lord
Macaulay (1882), pp. 718-28.

39. JOSEPH HUME: Speech in the House
of Commons, 10 February 1847

[Hume was opposing the second reading of Fielden's Factories Bill.]

Some hon. gentlemen cast reflections upon the principles of political economy, not considering that it was by
those principles that the best interests of the community
were regulated. His hon. friend asked what these principles
were. . . . They were, that masters and men should be
allowed to make what arrangement they pleased between
themselves, both with regard to the length of hours and the

rate of wages; that Government should interfere as little as possible, except in every instance to remove prohibitions and protections. The only condition on which this right was acceded to was, that no man should carry it on to the injury of others. . . .

For three hundred years laws had been passed, interfering with the labourer and the employer. . . . But the evils arising from this practice had become so severe, and at the same time so obvious, that, by common consent, a great proportion of the laws so enacted, were repealed two or three and twenty years ago; and he could not help thinking that hon. gentlemen who supported the present measure, were proceeding on a course likely to add to the evils which he was sure they were anxious to avoid. They thought they knew better than the labourers themselves what were their interests. . . . Now he objected to that doctrine altogether. He held that the common sense of the working classes was capable of enabling them to take care of themselves. . . .

Every interference which prevented men, whatever might be their talents, from employing their capital, and exercising their ingenuity under protection of the laws, in any manner they thought proper, was injurious and bad. . . . After having relieved trade and emancipated commerce, were they to be so insane as again to place themselves under shackles and trammels? . . . Parliament had no right to interfere with either labour or capital; and for his part he was prepared to sweep away every restriction that now remained, and to let one general and uniform principle of perfect liberty pervade our legislation. Having stated these general principles, he asked hon. gentlemen to give him an answer to these following points: Were they desirous that England should maintain her manufacturing superiority? If so, were they disposed to give fair play to capital and industry in this country? Were they aware of what was going on in Belgium and Germany? Was there any restriction in the United States? . . . He had read a report drawn up by a committee of the legislature of Massachusetts upon a petition praying for a restriction in the hours of labour. It was a most sensible report:—

'We cannot interfere,' said the committee. 'We admit the evil; we wish we could lessen the hours of labour for all classes; we wish that every man could maintain himself and his family by eight or nine hours of labour per day. But we find it cannot be done. Our manufacturers have competition to meet in neutral markets, and we must leave them to their own exertions.'

The committee further stated, that the best means by which labour and capital could be employed, was to leave them free. If this principle were true in America, did it not hold good here?

Parliamentary Debates, House of Commons,
3rd Series, lxxxix, pp. 1074-80.

40. JOHN STUART MILL: *Principles of Political Economy*
(1848)

(A)

The restraints of Communism would be freedom in comparison with the present condition of the majority of the human race. The generality of labourers in this and most other countries have as little choice of occupation or freedom of locomotion, are practically as dependent on fixed rules and on the will of others, as they could be on any system short of actual slavery; to say nothing of the entire domestic subjection of one half the species, to which it is the signal honour of Owenism and most other forms of Socialism that they assign equal rights, in all respects, with those of the hitherto dominant sex. But it is not by comparison with the present bad state of society that the claims of Communism can be estimated; nor is it sufficient that it should promise greater personal and mental freedom than is now enjoyed by those who have not enough of either to deserve the name. The question is, whether there would be any asylum left for individuality of character; whether public opinion would not be a tyrannical yoke; whether the absolute dependence of each on all, and surveillance of each by all, would not grind all down into a tame uniformity of thoughts, feelings, and actions. This is already one of the glaring evils of the existing state of society, notwithstanding a much greater diversity of education and pursuits, and a much less absolute dependence of the individual on the mass, than would exist in the Communistic régime. No society in which eccentricity is a matter of reproach can be in a wholesome state. It is yet to be ascertained whether the Communistic scheme would be consistent with that multiform development of human nature, those manifold unlikenesses, that diversity of tastes and talents, and variety of intellectual points of view, which not only form a great part of the interest of human life, but by bringing intellects into stimulating collision, and by presenting to each innumerable notions that he would not have conceived of himself, are the mainspring of mental and moral progression.

(B)

Government may interdict all persons from doing certain things; or from doing them without its authorization; or may prescribe to them certain things to be done, or a certain manner of doing things which it is left optional with them to do or to abstain from. This is the *authoritative* interference of government. There is another kind of intervention which is not authoritative: when a government, instead of issuing a command and enforcing it by penalties, adopts the course so seldom resorted to by governments, and of which such important use might be made, that of giving advice, and promulgating information; or when, leaving individuals free to use their own means of pursuing any object of general interest, the government, not meddling with them, but not trusting the object solely to their care, establishes, side by side with their arrangements, an agency of its own for a like purpose. Thus, it is one thing to maintain a Church Establishment, and another to refuse toleration to other religions, or to persons professing no religion. It is one thing to provide schools or colleges, and another to require that no person shall act as an instructor of youth without a government licence. There might be a national bank, or a government manufactory, without any monopoly against private banks and manufactories. There might be a post-office, without penalties against the conveyance of letters by other means. There may be a corps of government engineers for civil purposes, while the profession of a civil engineer is free to be adopted by every one. There may be public hospitals, without any restriction upon private medical or surgical practice.

It is evident, even at first sight, that the authoritative form of government intervention has a much more limited sphere of legitimate action than the other. It requires a much stronger necessity to justify it in any case; while there are large departments of human life from which it must be unreservedly and imperiously excluded. Whatever theory we adopt respecting the foundation of the social union, and under whatever political institutions we live, there is a circle around every individual human being which no government, be it that of one, of a few, or of the many, ought to be permitted to overstep: there is a part of the life of every person who has come to years of discretion, within which the individuality of that person ought to reign uncontrolled either by any other individual or by the public collectively. That there is, or ought to be, some space in human existence thus entrenched around, and sacred from authoritative intrusion, no one who professes the smallest regard to human freedom or dignity will call in question. . . . I apprehend that it ought to include all that part which concerns only the life, whether inward or outward, of the individual, and does not affect the interests of others, or affects them only through the moral influence of example. . . .

Even in those portions of conduct which do affect the interest of others, the onus of making out a case always lies on the defenders of legal prohibitions. . . . To be prevented from doing what one is inclined to, or from acting according to one's own judgment of what is desirable, is not only always irksome, but always tends, *pro tanto*, to starve the development of some portion of the bodily or mental faculties, either sensitive or active; and unless the conscience of the individual goes freely with the legal restraint, it partakes, either in a great or in a small degree, of the degradation of slavery. Scarcely any degree of utility, short of absolute necessity, will justify a prohibitory regulation, unless it can also be made to recommend itself to the general conscience...

A second general objection to government agency is that every increase of the functions devolving on the government is an increase of its power, both in the form of authority, and still more, in the indirect form of influence. The importance of this consideration, in respect to political freedom, has in general been quite sufficiently recognised, at least in England; but many, in latter times, have been prone to think that limitation of the powers of the government is only essential when the government itself is badly constituted; when it does not represent the people, but is the organ of a class, or coalition of classes: and that a government of sufficiently popular constitution might be trusted with any amount of power over the nation, since its power would be only that of the nation over itself. This might be true, if the nation, in such cases, did not practically mean a mere majority of the nation, and if minorities were only capable of oppressing, but not of being oppressed. Experience, however, proves that the depositaries of power who are mere delegates of the people, that is of a majority, are quite as ready (when they think they can count on popular support) as any organs of oligarchy, to assume arbitrary power, and encroach unduly on the liberty of private life. The public collectively is abundantly ready to impose, not only its generally narrow views of its interests, but its abstract opinions, and even its tastes, as laws binding upon individuals. And the present civilization tends so strongly to make the power of persons acting in masses the only substantial power in society, that there never was more necessity for surrounding individual independence of thought, speech, and conduct, with the most powerful defences, in order to maintain that originality of mind and individuality of character, which are the only source of any real progress, and of most of the qualities which make the human race much superior to any herd of animals. Hence it is no less important in a democratic than in any other government, that all tendency on the part of public authorities to stretch their interference, and assume a power of any sort which can easily be dispensed with, should be regarded with unremitting jealousy. . . .

Though a better organisation of governments would greatly diminish the force of the objection to the mere multiplication of their duties, it would still remain true that in all the more advanced communities the great majority of things are worse done by the intervention of government, than the individuals most interested in the matter would do them, or cause them to be done, if left to themselves. The grounds of this truth are expressed with tolerable exactness in the popular dictum, that people understand their own business and their own interests better, and care for them more, than the government does, or can be expected to do. This maxim holds true throughout the greatest part of the business of life, and wherever it is true we ought to condemn every kind of government intervention that conflicts with it. The inferiority of government agency, for example, in any of the common operations of industry or commerce, is proved by the fact, that it is hardly ever able to maintain itself in equal competition with individual agency, where the individuals possess the requisite degree of industrial enterprise, and can command the necessary assemblage of means. All the facilities which a government enjoys of access to information; all the means which it possesses of remunerating, therefore of commanding, the best available talent in the market—are not an equivalent for the one great disadvantage of an inferior interest in the result.

The preceding are the principal reasons of a general character, in favour of restricting to the narrowest compass the intervention of a public authority in the business of the community: and few will dispute the more than sufficiency of these reasons, to throw, in every instance, the burthen of making out a strong case, not on those who resist, but on those who recommend, government interference. *Laisser-faire*, in short, should be the general practice: every departure from it, unless required by some great good, is a certain evil.

John Stuart Mill, *The Principles of Political Economy*
(1848), (A), p. 210; (B), pp. 942-7.

3. EDUCATION

41. THOMAS BABINGTON MACAULAY: Speech in the House of Commons, 18 April 1847

[Both Macaulay and Bright (No. 42) were speaking in the debate on the Government's scheme for education.]

I believe, Sir, that it is the right and the duty of the state to provide means of education for the common people. This proposition seems to me to be implied in every definition that has ever yet been given of the functions of a government. . . .

This new theory of politics has at least the merit of originality. It may be fairly stated thus. All men have hitherto been utterly in the wrong as to the nature and objects of civil government. The great truth, hidden from every preceding generation, and at length revealed, in the year 1846, to some highly respectable ministers and elders of dissenting congregations, is this. Government is simply a great hangman. Government ought to do nothing except by harsh and degrading means. The one business of government is to handcuff, and lock up, and scourge, and shoot, and stab, and strangle. It is odious tyranny in a government to attempt to prevent crime by informing the understanding and elevating the moral feeling of a people. A statesman may see hamlets turned, in the course of one generation, into great seaport towns and manufacturing towns. He may know that on the character of the vast population which is collected in those wonderful towns, depends the prosperity, the peace, the very existence of society. But he must not think of forming that character. He is an enemy of public liberty if he attempts to prevent those hundreds of thousands of his countrymen from becoming mere Yahoos. He may, indeed, build barrack after barrack to overawe them. If they break out into insurrection, he may send cavalry to sabre them: he may mow them down with grape shot: he may hang them, draw them, quarter them, anything but teach them. He may see, and may shudder as he sees, throughout large rural districts, millions of infants growing up from infancy to manhood as ignorant, as mere slaves of sensual appetite, as the beasts that perish. No matter. He is a traitor to the cause of civil and religious freedom if he does not look on with folded arms, while absurd hopes and evil passions ripen in that rank soil. He must wait for the day of his harvest. He must wait till the Jacquerie comes, till farm houses are burning, till threshing machines are broken in pieces; and then begins his business, which is simply to send one poor ignorant savage to the county gaol, and another to the Antipodes, and a third to the gallows.

Such, Sir, is the new theory of government which was first propounded, in the year 1846, by some men of high note among the Nonconformists of England. It is difficult to understand how men of excellent abilities and excellent intentions—and there are, I readily admit, such men among those who hold this theory—can have fallen into so absurd and pernicious an error. One explanation only occurs to me. This is, I am inclined to believe, an instance of the operation of the great law of reaction. We have just come victorious out of a long and fierce contest for the liberty of trade. While that contest was undecided, much was said and written about the advantages of free competition, and about the danger of suffering the State to regulate matters which should be left to individuals. There has consequently arisen in the minds of persons who are led by words, and who are little in the habit of making distinctions, a disposition to apply to political questions and moral questions principles which are sound only when applied to commercial questions. These people, not content with having forced the government to surrender a province wrongfully usurped, now wish to wrest from the government a domain held by a right which was never before questioned, and which cannot be questioned with the smallest show of reason. 'If', they say, 'free competition is a good thing in trade, it must surely be a good thing in education. The supply of other commodities, of sugar, for example, is left to adjust itself to the demand; and the consequence is, that we are better supplied with sugar than if the government undertook to supply us. Why then should we doubt that the supply of instruction will,

without the intervention of the government, be found equal
to the demand?'

Never was there a more false analogy. Whether a man
is well supplied with sugar is a matter which concerns himself alone. But whether he is well supplied with instruction
is a matter which concerns his neighbours and the State. If
he cannot afford to pay for sugar, he must go without sugar.
But it is by no means fit that, because he cannot afford to
pay for education, he should go without education.

Miscellaneous Writings and Speeches of Lord
Macaulay (1882), pp. 734-48.

42. JOHN BRIGHT: Speech in the House of Commons, 20 April 1847

The right hon. Gentleman appeared to me to prove too
much. He tried to prove that it was the duty of the Government to educate the people; but if it be the duty of Government to educate them, it must be the duty of the Government
to enforce education. I do not know where the line can be
drawn. If it be its solemn duty to afford opportunity for
education, and to see that all the people are educated, it
appears to me we must come inevitably to the conclusion,
that Government has the power, and that it is also its right
and its duty, to enforce education on all the people subject
to its rule.

The noble Lord at the head of the Government objected
to the Dissenters that they had supported the Committee of
Privy Council in 1839, whilst they oppose it in 1847; that
they were then in favour of this interference, and are now
against it. I admit that many, or at least, that some of the
Dissenters were in favour of it eight years ago. But we have
had some experience from 1839 to 1847. At that time the
Dissenters regarded the institution of the Committee of
Privy Council as a step leading away from that power which
the Church of England wished to usurp, of educating the
whole people; and the Dissenters hoped we were on the
road at last to overcome the pretensions which the Church
of England had so long asserted, that she was called upon

and bound to undertake the business of education, and that she ought to be entrusted with the education of the people. But from 1839 to this year we have found no step taken by the Government which has not had a tendency to aggrandize the Established Church. . . . In 1847, the noble Lord comes forward with another scheme. It has the same defect; its object, tendency, and result will be to give increased and enormous power to the clergy of the Established Church. It is a scheme of which the Dissenters cannot avail themselves, in accordance with the principles by which they are Dissenters; and, therefore, they are bound now to step forward and to protest against this as against the former schemes. And I wonder not they have come to the conclusion that it is dangerous to them as members of Dissenting bodies, and dangerous also to the civil liberty of the people, that the State should interfere with education, since the Government, it appears, is not able to interfere without giving increased power to the clergy of an already dominant Church.

If there be one principle more certain than another, I suppose it is this, that what a people is able to do for itself, that the Government should not attempt to do for it. For nothing tends so much to strengthen a people—to make them great and good—as the constant exercise of all their faculties for public objects, and the carrying on of all public works and objects by voluntary contributions among themselves. . . .

It is not because the Church of England receives money from this grant that Nonconformists object to the grant; but it is because Nonconformists themselves, in accordance with the principles by which they are so, cannot receive public money for the teaching of religion in their schools; and, therefore, they object to the State giving money as an advantage to the Church schools—an advantage by which they must profit, and which will certainly be most damaging to the Dissenting schools. . . .

The right hon. Gentleman tells us that they are abandoning all the principles which the Nonconformists of past times ever taught; he tells us what republican statesmen and leaders in the United States have said, what has been done or held by Washington, Jefferson, and the commonwealth of Massachusetts. But is there any comparison between the United States and the United Kingdom? Is there any Established Church in the United States? . . . Give us, if you please, the state of things which exists in the United States, and particularly in that State of Massachusetts. Free us from the trammels of your Church—set religion apart from the interference of the State—if you will make public provision for education, let it not depend upon the doctrines of a particular creed—and then you will find the various sects in this country will be as harmonious on the question of education as are the people in the United States of America. . . .

Just recollect, when the whole of the Nonconformists are charged with clamour, what they mean by being Non-conformists. They object, as I understand, at least I object, to the principle by which the Government seizes public funds in order to give salaries and support to the teachers of all sects of religion, or of one sect of religion, for I think the one plan nearly as unjust as the other. Either the Nonconformists hold this opinion, or they are a great imposture. They object to any portion of the public money going to teachers of religion belonging either to the Established Church or to Dissenting bodies; they object to the receiving it for themselves. . . .

I will now conclude; and if I have been betrayed into some warmth of expression, let it be remembered that I am a member of the Nonconformist body. My forefathers languished in prison by the acts of that Church which you now ask me to aggrandise. Within two years places of worship of the sect to which I belong have been despoiled of their furniture to pay the salary of a minister of the Established Church; and when I look back and see how that Church has been uniformly hostile to the progress of public liberty, it is impossible for me to withhold my protest against the outrage committed by the Government on the Nonconformist body for the sake of increasing the power of a political institution, which I believe is destined to fall before the growing Christianity and the extending freedom of the people.

Speeches by John Bright, M.P., ed. by J. H. T. Rogers (1868), vol. ii, pp. 497-512.

4. RELIGIOUS LIBERTY

43. THOMAS BABINGTON MACAULAY: Speech in the House of Commons, 17 April 1833

[Macaulay was speaking in the debate on the civil disabilities of the Jews.]

When the question was about Catholic emancipation, the cry was, 'See how restless, how versatile, how encroaching, how insinuating, is the spirit of the Church of Rome. See how her priests compass earth and sea to make one proselyte, how indefatigably they toil, how attentively they study the weak and strong parts of every character, how skilfully they employ literature, arts, sciences, as engines for the propagation of their faith. You find them in every region and under every disguise, collating manuscripts in the Bodleian, fixing telescopes in the observatory of Pekin, teaching the use of the plough and the spinning-wheel to the savages of Paraguay. Will you give power to the members of a church so busy, so aggressive, so insatiable?' Well, now the question is about people who never try to seduce any stranger to join them, and who do not wish anybody to be of their faith who is not also of their blood. And now you exclaim, 'Will you give power to the members of a sect which remains sullenly apart from other sects, which does not invite, nay, which hardly even admits neophytes?' The truth is, that bigotry will never want a pretence. Whatever the sect be which it is proposed to tolerate, the peculiarities of that sect will, for the time, be pronounced by intolerant men to be the most odious and dangerous that can be conceived. . . .

But what if it were true that the Jews are unsocial? What if it were true that they do not regard England as their country? Would not the treatment which they have undergone explain and excuse their antipathy to the society in which they live? Has not similar antipathy often been felt by persecuted Christians to the society which persecuted them? While the bloody code of Elizabeth was enforced against the English Roman Catholics, what was the

patriotism of Roman Catholics? Oliver Cromwell said that
in his time they were Espaniolised. At a later period it
might have been said that they were Gallicised. It was the
same with the Calvinists. What more deadly enemies had
France in the days of Louis the Fourteenth than the persecuted Huguenots? . . . Why not try what effect would be
produced on the Jews by that tolerant policy which has
made the English Roman Catholic a good Englishman, and
the French Calvinist a good Frenchman? . . .

The honourable member for Oldham tells us that the
Jews are naturally a mean race, a sordid race, a money-
getting race; that they are averse to all honourable callings;
that they neither sow nor reap; that they have neither flocks
nor herds; that usury is the only pursuit for which they are
fit; that they are destitute of all elevated and amiable
sentiments. Such, Sir, has in every age been the reasoning
of bigots. They never fail to plead in justification of persecution the vices which persecution has engendered. England
has been to the Jews less than half a country; and we revile
them because they do not feel for England more than a half
patriotism. We treat them as slaves, and wonder that they
do not regard us as brethren. We drive them to mean
occupations, and then reproach them for not embracing
honourable professions. We long forbade them to possess
land; and we complain that they chiefly occupy themselves
in trade. We shut them out from all the paths of ambition;
and then we despise them for taking refuge in avarice.
During many ages we have, in all our dealings with them,
abused our immense superiority of force; and then we are
disgusted because they have recourse to that cunning which
is the natural and universal defence of the weak against the
violence of the strong. But were they always a mere money-
changing, money-getting, money-hoarding race? Nobody
knows better than my honourable friend the member for
the University of Oxford that there is nothing in their
national character which unfits them for the highest duties
of citizens. He knows that, in the infancy of civilisation,
when our island was as savage as New Guinea, when letters
and arts were still unknown to Athens, when scarcely a
thatched hut stood on what was afterwards the site of Rome,

this contemned people had their fenced cities and cedar palaces, their splendid Temple, their fleets of merchant ships, their schools of sacred learning, their great statesmen and soldiers, their natural philosophers, their historians and their poets. What nation ever contended more manfully against overwhelming odds for its independence and religion? What nation ever, in its last agonies, gave such signal proofs of what may be accomplished by a brave despair? And if, in the course of many centuries, the oppressed descendants of warriors and sages have degenerated from the qualities of their fathers, if, while excluded from the blessings of law, and bowed down under the yoke of slavery, they have contracted some of the vices of outlaws and of slaves, shall we consider this as matter of reproach to them? Shall we not rather consider it as matter of shame and remorse to ourselves? Let us do justice to them. Let us open to them the door of the House of Commons. Let us open to them every career in which ability and energy can be displayed. Till we have done this, let us not presume to say that there is no genius among the countrymen of Isaiah, no heroism among the descendants of the Maccabees.

Miscellaneous Writings and Speeches of Lord Macaulay (1882), pp. 544-50.

44. JOHN BRIGHT: Speech in the House of Commons, 12 May 1851

[Bright was speaking in the debate on the Ecclesiastical Titles Bill which prohibited the assumption of ecclesiastical titles already taken by clergy of the Church of England. In 1850 Pius IX had decided to re-establish a regular Roman Catholic diocesan hierarchy in England.]

I beg to ask the noble Lord, then, as a question of politics, who is injured by the Bill? The noble Lord does not touch the Pope. I believe the Pope acted very foolishly, and that Cardinal Wiseman also acted foolishly; but both will go unscathed. The true sufferers will be the wearer of the Crown, and the millions of subjects professing the Roman Catholic religion. Look at the speeches, the writings, and the denunciations of the last six months. Is it possible that all these could have occurred in the United Kingdom without producing a permanent evil as regards the harmony and the well-being and strength of the nation? Then take Ireland alone. There has been a great gulf heretofore existing between England and Ireland, a gulf created by past legislation. The noble Lord has helped to widen and deepen that gulf, and there is now a more marked separation between the countries than has existed at any period in the last twenty years. We have by our legislation taught 8,000,000 of our fellow-subjects that their priests are hated by the British Legislature, and that they themselves are treated with disrespect, and their loyalty denied by this House and the leading Minister of the country. That is an evil of great magnitude, and one which we are bound to take into consideration. . . .

In 1829 a measure was passed—long delayed—which professed to give Roman Catholics all the liberty we ourselves enjoy. I will stand upon that Act. It is far better to have faith in the population of this country, to bind them to the Legislature and the Crown by a generous and confiding treatment, than to proceed in such a course as the House is now invited to enter on. . . .

The noble Lord has drawn up an indictment against 8,000,000 of his countrymen; he has increased the power of the Pope over the Roman Catholics, for he has drawn closer the bonds between them and their Church and the head of their Church. The noble Lord has quoted Queen Elizabeth and the great man of the Commonwealth, as though it were necessary now to adopt the principles which prevailed almost universally two hundred years ago. Does the noble Lord forget that we are the true ancients, that we stand on the shoulders of our forefathers, and can see farther? We have seen the working of these principles, and their result, and have concluded to abandon them.

I have not touched on any matter purely religious; this House is not the place for religious questions. But reflecting on the deep mysteries of religion, on my own doubts and frailties, on the shortness of the present time, and on the awful and unknown future—I ask what am I that I should judge another in religious things, and condemn him to exclusion and persecution? I fear not for the country on

questions like this. England, with a united population—
though the noble Lord has done much to disunite them—
cares nothing for foreign potentates, be their combinations
what they may. England with her free press, her advancing
civilization, her daily and hourly progress in the arts, sciences,
industry, and morals, will withstand any priestly attempt to
subjugate the mind, and successfully resist any menaces,
whether coming from Lambeth or from Rome. I am one
of a sect which has invariably held the principles I now
advocate, which has in past years suffered greatly from those
principles which the noble Lord now wishes to introduce into
our Legislature. I cannot do otherwise than raise my voice
against such an attempt, and ask the noble Lord to proceed
no further.

Speeches by John Bright, M.P., ed. by J. H. T.
Rogers (1868), vol. ii, pp. 471-85.

45. JOHN BRIGHT: Speech in the House of Commons, 15 April 1853

[Bright was speaking in the debate on the admission of Jews to Parliament.]

Now I have endeavoured, in the course of these discussions,
to trace whence this notion or feeling of unchristianising
springs, and I think I can trace it backwards through the
changes of the law, by which successive parties and sects,
and sections of the people of this country, have, during the
last 160 years, been admitted to full participation in the
rights of citizenship. The very same feeling, though it was
called something else, was in operation when you excluded
the Roman Catholics from Parliament. The very same feeling
under a somewhat different title was in operation when the
Unitarians were subjected to oppressive statutes; and it was
the very same spirit, however much you may attempt to
disguise it, under which, previous to the repeal of the Test
and Corporation Acts, the Dissenters of this country were
excluded from municipal and other offices. It always seems
to me to come from that appetite for supremacy which
springs from the fact that we have had in this country a

powerful and dominant Church, connected chiefly with a powerful ruling class, and that step by step the people of this country, one section after another, have wrested from that Church, and from that class, the rights of citizenship which we have claimed, and which we now enjoy.

Now what can be more marvellous than that any sane man should propose that doctrinal differences in religion should be made the test of citizenship and political rights? Doctrinal differences in religion, in all human probability, will last for many generations to come, and may possibly last so long as man shall inhabit this globe; but if you permit these differences to be the test of citizenship, what is it but to admit into your system this fatal conclusion, that social and political differences in all nations can never be eradicated, but must be eternal?

Ibid. vol. ii, p. 488.

5. FOREIGN POLICY

46. RICHARD COBDEN: Speech in the House of Commons, 12 June 1849

[Cobden's motion ran: 'That an humble address be presented to Her Majesty, praying that she will be graciously pleased to direct her Principal Secretary of State for Foreign Affairs to enter into communications with Foreign Powers, inviting them to concur in Treaties, binding the respective parties, in the event of any future misunderstanding, which cannot be arranged by amicable negotiation, to refer the matter in dispute to the decision of arbitrators.']

It is not necessary that anyone in this House, or out of it, who accedes to this motion, should be of opinion that we are not justified, under any circumstances, in resorting to war, even in self-defence. It is only necessary that you should be agreed that war is a great calamity, which it is desirable we should avoid if possible. . . .

I assume that every one in this House would only sanction war, in case it was imperatively demanded on our part, in defence of our honour, or our just interests. . . .

My object is to see if we cannot devise some better method than war for attaining those ends; and my plan is, simply and solely, that we should resort to that mode of settling disputes in communities, which individuals resort to in private life. I only want you to go one step farther, to carry out in another instance the principle which you recognise in other cases—that the intercourse between communities is nothing more than the intercourse of individuals in the aggregate. I want to know why there may not be an agreement between this country and France, or between this country and America, by which the nations should respectively bind themselves, in case of any misunderstanding arising which could not be settled by mutual representation or diplomacy, to refer the dispute to the decision of arbitrators. . . . I do not confine myself to the plan of referring disputes to neutral Powers. I see the difficulty of two independent states, like England and France, doing so, as one might prefer a republic for the arbitrator, and the other a monarchy. I should prefer to see these disputes referred to individuals, whether designated commissioners, or plenipotentiaries, or arbitrators, appointed from one country to meet men appointed from another country to inquire into the matter and decide upon it; or, if they cannot do so, to have the power of calling in an umpire, as is done in all arbitrations. I propose that these individuals should have absolute power to dispose of the question submitted to them.

We are now spending every year on our armaments more than we spent annually, on the seven years' war, in the middle of the last century. . . . I wish to know where this system is to end. I have sat on the army, navy, and ordnance committees, and I see no limit to the increase of our armaments under the existing system. Unless you can adopt some such plan as I propose, unless you can approach foreign countries in a conciliatory spirit, and offer to them some kind of assurance that you do not wish to attack them, and receive the assurance that you are not going to be assailed by them, I see no necessary or logical end to the increase of our establishments. . . .

Will any one, for a moment, tell me that the disputes about the boundary between Maine and New Brunswick, and the misunderstanding respecting Oregon, might not have been settled by arbitration? . . . Supposing the case to have been left to the decision of such an umpire as Baron Humboldt, for example; would he not have decided far more correctly than any war would be likely to do? I know that the Oregon question caused the liveliest apprehensions to those who were engaged on both sides, in this dispute, in 1846. . . . The great difficulty was lest party spirit and popular excitement should arise on either side of the water, to hinder and perplex the efforts of those who were interested in its settlement. It is to remove that difficulty in future— to prevent the interposition of bad passions and popular prejudices in these disputes—that I desire to have provision made, beforehand, for the settlement of any quarrel that may arise by arbitration. . . .

Now, I would ask, in the face of these facts, where is the argument you can use against the reasonable proposition which I now put forward? I may be told that, even if you make treaties of .this kind, you cannot enforce the award. I admit it. . . .

I do not, myself, advocate an appeal to arms; but that which follows the violation of a treaty, under the present system, may follow the violation of a treaty of arbitration, if adopted. What I say, however, is, if you make a treaty with another country, binding it to refer any dispute to arbitration, and if that country violates that treaty, when the dispute arises, then you will place it in a worse position before the world—you will place 'it in so infamous a position, that I doubt if any country would enter into war on such bad grounds as that country must occupy. . . .

I shall be quite satisfied, as a beginning, if I see the noble Lord, or any one filling his place, trying to negotiate an arbitration treaty with the United States, or with France. But I should like to bind ourselves to the same principle with the weakest and smallest States. I should be as willing to see it done with Tuscany, Belgium, or Holland, as with France or America, because I am anxious to prove to the world that we are prepared to submit our misunderstandings, in all cases, to a pure and more just arbitrament than that of brute force. Whilst I do not agree with those who are in favour of a Congress of nations, I do think that if the larger and more civilised Powers were to enter into treaties of this kind, their decisions would become precedents and you would in this way, in the course of time, establish a kind of common law amongst nations, which would save the time and trouble of arbitration in each individual case.

I do not anticipate any sudden or great change in the character of mankind, nor do I expect a complete extinction of those passions which form part of our nature. But I do not think there is anything very irrational in expecting that nations may see that the present system of settling disputes is barbarous, demoralising, and unjust; that it wars against the best interests of society, and that it ought to give place to a mode more consonant with the dictates of reason and humanity.

Speeches by Richard Cobden, M.P. (1870),
vol. ii, pp. 159-67.

47. VISCOUNT PALMERSTON: Speech at Tiverton, 31 July 1847

. . . We took part with the people of Spain—with those who wanted constitutional liberty, equal laws, a Parliament, justice, no Inquisition—against those who were for having no Parliament, no justice, but much Inquisition. We succeeded; and by means of very trifling assistance, which could not possibly have determined events, if the Spanish people had not been on that side, we enabled them to work out their liberties with smaller sacrifices than they must otherwise have submitted to, and with less suffering than they must otherwise have encountered. . . . There was a struggle in Portugal very similar to that which I have mentioned as taking place in Spain. . . . Did we set up Dom Miguel? No; we put him down. We threw our influence into the scale of liberty, freedom, and constitutional rights; and, by our assistance, that cause conquered, and the Portuguese nation became possessed of a Parliament, and of all those rights which are essential for securing the liberties of a nation.

H. W. V. Temperley and L. M. Penson,
Foundations of British Foreign Policy
(Cambridge, 1938), pp. 106-7.

48. RICHARD COBDEN: Speech in the House of Commons, 28 June 1850

[Cobden was speaking in the debate on Don Pacifico.]

I never in public advocated interference with the Government of foreign countries, even in cases where my feelings were most strongly interested in anything relating to their domestic affairs or concerns. When I see that principle violated by others, as in the case of the Russian invasion of Hungary, and when I see a portion of the press of this civilised nation hounding on that semi-barbarous empire, then, believing that this is almost the only country where there is a free platform, and where it cannot be corrupted, as a portion of the press may have been, I shall denounce it, as I denounced the Government of Russia, and, as I stated at the same time, I was ready to denounce our own Government also. But it is a matter of very small importance what my individual opinion may be, when you come to the question, whether the Government of this country shall become the propagandist of their opinions in foreign countries. I maintain this Government has no right to communicate except through the Government of other countries; and that, whether it be a republic, a despotism, or a monarchy, I hold it has no right to interfere with any other form of Government. Mark the effect of your own principle, if you take the opposite ground. If you recognise the principle of intervention in your Government, you must tolerate it in other nations also. With what face could you get up and denounce the Emperor of Russia for invading Hungary, after the doctrine advocated by the hon. and learned Member (Mr. Cockburn) to-night had been adopted by this country? I say, if you want to benefit nations who are struggling for their freedom, establish as one of the maxims of international law the principle of non-intervention. If you want to give a guarantee for peace, and as I believe, the surest guarantee for progress and freedom, lay down this principle, and act on it, that no foreign State has a right by force to interfere with the domestic concerns of another State, even to confer a benefit on it, without its own consent.

Do you want to benefit the Hungarians and Italians? I think I know more of them than most people in this country. I sympathised with them during their manly struggle for freedom, and I have admired and respected them not less in their hour of adversity. I will tell you the sentiments of the leading men of the Hungarians. . . .

These men say,—'We don't ask you to help us, or to come to our assistance. Establish such a principle as shall provide we shall not be interfered with by others.' And what do the Italians say? They don't want the English to interfere with them, or to help them. 'Leave us to ourselves,' they say. 'Establish the principle that we shall not be interfered with by foreigners.'

I will answer the hon. and learned Gentleman's cheer. He seems to ask, How will you keep out Austria from Italy, and Russia from Hungary? I will give him an illustration of what I mean. Does he remember when Kossuth took refuge in Turkey, and that Austria and the Emperor of Russia demanded him back? I beg him to understand that this illustrious refugee was not saved by any intervention of the Foreign Secretary. Has it not been admitted that the Emperor of Russia gave up his claim before the courier arrived from England? What was it, then, that liberated them? It was the universal outbreak of public opinion and public indignation in Western Europe. And why had public opinion this power? Because this demand for the extradition of political offenders was a violation of the law of nations, which declares that persons who have committed political offences on one state shall find a sanctuary in another, and ought not to be delivered up. If our Government were always to act upon this principle of non-intervention, we should see the law of nations declaring itself as clearly against the invasion of a foreign country as it has spoken out against the extradition of political refugees. Let us begin, and set the example to other nations of this non-intervention. . . .

I believe the progress of freedom depends more upon the maintenance of peace, the spread of commerce, and the diffusion of education, than upon the labours of Cabinets or Foreign-offices. And if you can prevent those perturbations which have recently taken place abroad in consequence of your foreign policy, and if you will leave other nations in greater tranquillity, those ideas of freedom will continue to progress, and you need not trouble yourselves about them.

Speeches by Richard Cobden, M.P. (1870),
vol. ii, pp. 225-7.

49. JOHN BRIGHT: Letter to Absalom Watkin on the Crimean War, 29 October 1854

At this moment England is engaged in a murderous warfare with Russia, although the Russian Government accepted her own terms of peace, and has been willing to accept them in the sense of England's own interpretation of them ever since they were offered; and at the same time England is allied with Turkey, whose Government rejected the award of England, and who entered into the war in opposition to the advice of England. Surely, when the Vienna note was accepted by Russia, the Turks should have been prevented from going to war, or should have been allowed to go to war at their own risk.

I have said nothing here that all these troubles have sprung out of the demands made by France upon the Turkish Government, and urged in language more insulting than any which has been shown to have been used by Prince Menchikoff. I have said nothing of the diplomatic war which has been raging for many years past in Constantinople, and in which England has been behind no other Power in attempting to subject the Porte to foreign influences. I have said nothing of the abundant evidence there is that we are not only at war with Russia, but with all the Christian population of the Turkish Empire, and that we are building up our Eastern policy on a false foundation—namely, on the perpetual maintenance of the most immoral and filthy of all despotisms over one of the fairest portions of the earth which it has desolated, and over a population it has degraded but has not been able to destroy. I have said nothing of the wretched delusion that we are fighting for civilization in supporting the Turk against the Russian and against the subject Christian population of Turkey. I have said nothing about our pretended sacrifices for freedom in this war, in which our great and now dominant ally is a monarch who, last in Europe, struck down a free constitution, and dispersed by military violence a national Representative Assembly.

My doctrine would have been non-intervention in this case. The danger of the Russian power was a phantom; the necessity of permanently upholding the Mahometan rule in Europe is an absurdity. Our love for civilization, when we subject the Greeks and Christians to the Turks, is a sham; and our sacrifices for freedom, when working out the behests of the Emperor of the French and coaxing Austria to help us, is a pitiful imposture. The evils of non-intervention were remote and vague, and could neither be weighed nor described in any accurate terms. The good we can judge something of already, by estimating the cost of a contrary policy. And what is that cost? War in the north and south of Europe, threatening to involve every country of Europe. Many, perhaps fifty millions sterling, in the course of expenditure by this country alone, to be raised from the taxes of a people whose extrication from ignorance and poverty can only be hoped for from the continuance of peace. The disturbance of trade throughout the world, the derangement of monetary affairs, and difficulties and ruin to thousands of families. Another year of high prices of food, notwithstanding a full harvest in England, chiefly because war interferes with imports, and we have declared our principal foreign food-growers to be our enemies. The loss of human life to an enormous extent. Many thousands of our own countrymen have already perished of pestilence and in the field; and hundreds, perhaps thousands, of English families will be plunged into sorrow, as a part of the penalty to be paid for the folly of the nation and its rulers.

When the time comes for the 'inquisition for blood', who shall answer for these things? You have read the tidings from the Crimea; you have, perhaps, shuddered at the slaughter; you remember the terrific picture—I speak not of the battle, and the charge, and the tumultuous excitement of the conflict, but of the field after the battle—Russians, in their frenzy or their terror, shooting Englishmen who would have offered them water to quench their agony of thirst; Englishmen, in crowds, rifling the pockets of the men they had slain or wounded, taking their few shillings or roubles, and discovering among the plunder of the stiffening corpses images of the 'Virgin and the Child.' You have read this, and your imagination has followed the fearful details. This is war,—every crime which human nature can commit or imagine, every horror it can perpetrate or suffer; and this it is which our Christian Government recklessly plunges into, and which so many of our countrymen at this moment think it patriotic to applaud! You must excuse me if I cannot go with you. I will have no part in this terrible crime. My hands shall be unstained with the blood which is being shed. The necessity of maintaining themselves in office may influence an administration; delusions may mislead a people; *Vattel* may afford you a law and a defence; but no respect for men who form a Government, no regard I have for 'going with the stream', and no fear of being deemed wanting in patriotism, shall influence me in favour of a policy which, in my conscience, I believe to be as criminal before God as it is destructive of the true interest of my country.

> *Speeches by John Bright, M.P.*, ed. by J. H. T. Rogers (1868), vol. i, pp. 529-35.

50. WILLIAM EWART GLADSTONE: Speech in the House of Commons, 3 March 1857

[This speech was subsequently reprinted as a pamphlet, *War in China*.]

My right honourable friend the member for Carlisle was forbidden to appeal to the principles of Christianity. . . . As it seems to give offence, I will make no appeal to those principles; but I will appeal to that which is older than Christianity, because it was in the world before it—to that which is broader than Christianity, because it extends in the world beyond it—and to that which underlies Christianity, for Christianity itself appeals to it—I appeal to that justice which binds man to man. . . . We have spoken of the treaty obligations of China towards ourselves; but let not our treaty obligations to China be forgotten.

[Mr. Gladstone, referring to Article 12 of the Treaty ceding Hong Kong to Great Britain, continued:]

By that article you have contracted, under the most solemn obligations, to put down smuggling to the very best of your power. Is there anything peculiar in your smuggling on the coast of China to give special stringency to this obligation? It comprises the worst, the most pernicious, the most demoralizing and destructive of all the contraband trades that are carried on upon the surface of the globe. . . .

Your greatest and most valuable trade with China is this trade with opium. It is a smuggling trade. You promised to put it down. You received Hong-Kong for the purpose of careening and refitting your vessels, and instead of that you have drawn together those 60,000 Chinese within it, and from them you find the materials for manning, sustaining and organizing a fleet of coasters whose business is to enlarge, who have enlarged and who are enlarging, that smuggling traffic that you are bound by treaty to put down. So stands the case so far as the treaty is concerned. And now, having taken Hong-Kong for purposes that you have not fulfilled, having applied it to different purposes, having failed entirely, or rather not having endeavoured to put down this smuggling trade, having organised this coasting trade for purposes which included an enlargement of that smuggling trade, you accumulate all these acts of injustice by trumping up a claim built upon the most pitiable technicalities to cover this coasting fleet with the British flag; and when we are told that such proceedings ought not to be endured, then you reproach us with indifference to the honour of the ensign of our country. . . .

My right honourable friend the Secretary of State for the Colonies said there is no war in China. I agree with him. No, Sir, there is not war in China, but what is there? There is hostility. There is bloodshed. There is a trampling down of the weak by the strong. There is the terrible and abominable retaliation of the weak upon the strong. You are now occupied in this House by revolting and harrowing details about a Chinese baker who poisoned bread—about proclamations for the capture of British heads,—about the waylaying of a postal steamer, and the murder of those on board. And these things you think strengthen your case. Why, they deepen your guilt. . . . You go to China and make war upon those who stand before you as women or as children. They try to resist you; they call together their troops; they load their guns; they kill one or wound perhaps two in action, while you perhaps slay thousands. They are unable to meet you in the field. You have no equality of ground on which to meet them. You can earn no glory in such warfare, and it is those who put the British flag to such uses who stain it. . . .

But we are told to beware of an adverse vote of the House of Commons. We are told to consider the effect of such a vote upon the Chinese. We are told to consider the ruinous consequences to our trade. We are asked if we wish to extend the ruinous conflagration which has broken out, and to injure those interests of humanity which it is our duty to assert. . . . But of all the cases in which warlike operations were ever begun, I do not know of any in which the political problem to be solved was so simple. The Chinese are not making war upon us. If, when the vote of this Parliament goes to China they should be making war on us, that would be a very different matter. The defence of the lives and properties of the subjects of the Queen would be, under all circumstances, an imperative obligation. But there is nothing so improbable as that they should make war on us. They have never shown any skill or daring in the nature of aggressive operations. We are making war upon them. . . .

I find an appeal has been made to this House which appears to me to be a false and illegitimate appeal. It is an appeal to fear, which is seldom a rightful and noble senti-ment, and it is to that fear which is the basest and worst kind of fear—the fear of being thought afraid. The Govern-ment are afraid of the mischievous impression that will be produced upon the Chinese if the acts of our officials are disavowed. . . . Presently we shall be told by the noble lord (Palmerston) of the wise caution that we ought to display, of the solemn predicament in which we are placed, of the political mischief which may ensue. Shadowy pictures will be drawn of the dangers, the confusion, the weakness, and the paralysis of British power in the East. . . .

The confessions and avowals of the supporters of the Government have been, it appears to me, perfectly fatal either to the continuance of that power, or else to the character and fame of England. They talk of the consequences, they admit in full the injustice; and then they say that we must go on with that injustice. There is a general admission, either express or tacit, that the conduct of the British authorities cannot be defended on its merits. Few have justified the proceedings that have taken place. Many of those who intend to support the Government have openly condemned them. . . . I will ask what the effect will be throughout the world, if it goes forth that in the debates held in the two Houses of Parliament the majority, nay almost the whole of the speakers condemned the proceedings, and that even among those who sustained the Government with their vote there was a large number who condemned and scarcely any that ventured to uphold them. Why, Sir, the opinion will be that England is a power which, while it is higher and more daring in its pretensions to Christianity than any other power on the face of the globe, yet in a case when her own interests have been concerned, and when she has been acting in the remote and distant East, when fairly put to it and asked whether she would do right or wrong, she was ready to adopt for fear of political inconvenience the principle—'I will make the law of wrong the law of my Eastern policy, and will lay the foundation of that Empire which is my proudest boast in nothing more nor less than gross injustice.' Sir, this is not my opinion. . . . I will not believe that England will lay the foundation of its Eastern Empire in sin and in shame like this. I believe, on the contrary, that if you have the courage to assert your prerogatives as the British House of Commons, you will pursue a course which is more consistent with sound policy as well as with the eternal principles of justice. . . .

It does not rest with subordinate functionaries abroad—it does not rest with the Executive Government—it does not rest with the House of Lords, finally, and in the last resort, to say what shall be the policy of England and to what purpose her power shall be directed. Sir, that function lies within these walls. . . . England is not yet committed. With everyone of us it rests to take his part in showing that this House, which is the first, the most ancient, and the noblest temple of freedom in the world, is also the temple of that everlasting justice without which freedom itself would be only a name or only a curse to mankind.

War in China, A Speech by W. E. Gladstone (1857).

51. JOHN BRIGHT: Speech at Birmingham, 29 October 1858

I believe that I understate the sum when I say that, in pursuit of this Will-o'-the-wisp, (the liberties of Europe and the balance of power,) there has been extracted from the industry of the people of this small island no less an amount than 2,000,000,000 l. sterling. I cannot imagine how much 2,000,000,000 l. is, and therefore I shall not attempt to make you comprehend it. I presume it is something like those vast and incomprehensible astronomical distances with which we have been lately made familiar, we feel that we do not know one bit more about them than we did before. When I try to think of that sum of 2,000,000,000 l., there is a sort of vision passes before my mind's eye. I see your peasant labourer delve and plough, sow and reap, sweat beneath the summer's sun, or grow prematurely old before the Winter's blast. I see your noble mechanic, with his manly countenance and his matchless skill, toiling at his bench or his forge. I see one of the workers in our factories in the north, a woman—a girl, it may be— gentle and good, as many of them are, as your sisters and daughters are—I see her intent upon the spindle, whose revolutions are so rapid that the eye fails altogether to detect them, or watching the alternating flight of the unresting shuttle. I turn again to another portion of your population, which, 'plunged in mines, forgets a sun was made,' and I see the man who brings up from the secret chambers of the earth the elements of the riches and greatness of his country. When I see all this, I have before me a mass of produce and of wealth which I am no more able to comprehend than I am that 2,000,000,000 l. of which I have spoken, but I behold in its full proportions the hideous error of your Government, whose fatal policy consumes in some cases a half, never less than a third, of all the results of that industry which God intended should fertilize and bless every home in England, but the fruits of which are squandered in every part of the surface of the globe, without producing the smallest good to the people of England.

How, indeed, can I, any more than any of you, be un-English and anti-national? Was I not born upon the same soil? Do I not come of the same English stock? Are not my family committed irrevocably to the fortunes of this country? Is not whatever property I may have depending as much as yours is depending upon the good government of our common fatherland? Then how shall any man dare to say to any one of his countrymen, because he happens to hold a different opinion on questions of great public policy, that therefore he is un-English, and is to be condemned as anti-national?

We have been at war since that time, I believe, with, for, and against every considerable nation in Europe. . . . We have been all round Europe, and across it over and over again, and after a policy so distinguished, so pre-eminent, so long-continued, and so costly, I think we have a fair right—I have, at least—to ask those who are in favour of it to show us its visible result. Europe is not at this moment, so far as I know, speaking of it broadly, and making allowance for certain improvements in its general civilisation, more free politically than it was before. The balance of power is like perpetual motion, or any of those impossible things which some men are always racking their brains and spending their time and money to accomplish. . . .

The more you examine this matter the more you will come to the conclusion which I have arrived at, that this foreign policy, this regard for 'the liberties of Europe,' this care at one time for 'the Protestant interests,' this excessive love for the 'balance of power,' is neither more nor less than a gigantic system of out-door relief for the aristocracy of Great Britain. . . .

Perhaps there are in this room, I am sure there are in the country, many persons who hold a superstitious traditionary belief that, somehow or other, our vast trade is to be attributed to what we have done in this way, that it is thus that we have opened markets and advanced commerce, that English greatness depends upon the extent of English conquests and English military renown. But I am inclined to think that, with the exception of Australia, there is not a single dependency of the Crown which, if we come to reckon what it has cost in war and protection, would not be found to be a positive loss to the people of this country. . . . Wherever you turn, you will find that the opening of markets, developing of new countries, introducing cotton cloth with cannon balls, are vain, foolish, and wretched excuses for wars.

What are we to say of a nation which lives under a perpetual delusion that it is about to be attacked—a nation which is the most combined on the face of the earth, with little less than 30,000,000 of people all united under a Government which, though we intend to reform it, we do not the less respect it, and which has mechanical power and wealth to which no other country offers any parallel? There is no causeway to Britain; the free waves of the sea flow day and night for ever round her shores, and yet there are people going about with whom the hallucination is so strong that they do not merely discover it quietly to their friends, but they write it down in double-leaded columns, in leading articles,—nay, some of them actually get up on platforms and proclaim it to hundreds and thousands of their fellow-countrymen. I should like to ask you whether these delusions are to last for ever, whether this policy is to be the perpetual policy of England, whether these results are to go on gathering and gathering until there come, as come there must inevitably, some dreadful catastrophe on our country.

I should like to-night, if I could, to inaugurate one of the best and holiest revolutions that ever took place in this country. We have had a dozen revolutions since some of us were children. . . .

It is not from statesmen that these things come. It is not from them that have proceeded these great revolutions of opinion on the questions of Reform, Protection, Colonial Government and Criminal Law—it was from public meetings such as this, from the intelligence and conscience of the great body of the people who have no interest in wrong, and who never go from the right but by temporary error and under momentary passion.

It is for you to decide whether our greatness shall be only temporary or whether it shall be enduring. When I am told that the greatness of our country is shown by the 100,000,000 l. of revenue produced, may I not also ask how it is that we have 1,100,000 paupers in this kingdom, and why it is that 7,000,000 l. should be taken from the industry chiefly of the labouring classes to support a small nation, as it were, of paupers? . . .

While these things continue, I say that we have no reason to be self-satisfied and contented with our position; but that we who are in Parliament and are more directly responsible for affairs, and you who are also responsible, though in a lower degree, are bound by the sacred duty which we owe our country to examine why it is that with all this trade, all this industry, and all this personal freedom, there is still so much that is unsound at the base of our social fabric?

I believe there is no permanent greatness to a nation except it be based upon morality. I do not care for military greatness or military renown. I care for the condition of the people among whom I live. There is no man in England who is less likely to speak irreverently of the Crown and Monarchy of England than I am; but crowns, coronets, mitres, military display, the pomp of war, wide colonies, and a huge empire, are, in my view, all trifles light as air, and not worth considering, unless with them you can have a fair share of comfort, contentment, and happiness among the great body of the people. Palaces, baronial castles, great halls, stately mansions, do not make a nation. The nation in every country dwells in the cottage; and unless the light of your Constitution can shine there, unless the beauty of your legislation and the excellence of your statesmanship are impressed there on the feelings and condition of the people, rely upon it you have yet to learn the duties of government.

I have not, as you have observed, pleaded that this country should remain without adequate and scientific means of defence. I acknowledge it to be the duty of your statesmen, acting upon the known opinions and principles of ninety-nine out of every hundred persons in the country, at all times, with all possible moderation, but with all possible efficiency, to take steps which shall preserve order within and on the confines of your kingdom. But I shall repudiate and denounce the expenditure of every shilling, the engagement of every man, the employment of every ship, which has no object but intermeddling in the affairs of other countries, and endeavouring to extend the boundaries of an Empire which is already large enough to satisfy the greatest ambition, and I fear is much too large for the highest statesmanship to which any man has yet attained.

The most ancient of profane historians has told us that the Scythians of his time were a very warlike people, and that they elevated an old cimeter upon a platform as a symbol of Mars, for to Mars alone, I believe, they built altars and offered sacrifices. To this cimeter they offered sacrifices of horses and cattle, the main wealth of the country, and more costly sacrifices than to all the rest of their gods. I often ask myself whether we are at all advanced in one respect beyond those Scythians. What are our contributions to charity, to education, to morality, to religion, to justice and to civil government, when compared with the wealth we expend in sacrifices to the old cimeter?

May I ask you, then, to believe, as I do most devoutly believe, that the moral law was not written for men alone in their individual character, but that it was written as well for nations, and for nations great as this of which we are citizens. If nations reject and deride that moral law, there is a penalty which will inevitably follow. It may not come at once, it may not come in our lifetime; but, rely upon it, the great Italian is not a poet only, but a prophet, when he says,—

> 'The sword of heaven is not in haste to smite,
>   Nor yet doth linger.'

We have experience, we have beacons, we have landmarks enough. We know what the past has cost us, we know how much and how far we have wandered, but we are not left without a guide. It is true we have not, as an ancient people had, Urim and Thummim—those oraculous gems on Aaron's breast—from which to take counsel, but we have the unchangeable and eternal principles of the moral law to guide us, and only so far as we walk by that guidance can we be permanently a great nation, or our people a happy people.

Speeches by John Bright, M.P., ed. by J. H. T. Rogers (1868), vol. ii, pp. 373-99.

52. JOHN BRIGHT: Speech at Glasgow, 21 December 1858

I am not about for a moment to discuss the question, whether our foreign policy has been, or is now, good, bad, or indifferent, because that does not very much affect the question to which I wish to call your attention. In our home affairs we have a very open system of government. If the Home Office is about to do anything, somebody hears of it, and somebody approves of it, or somebody objects to it. In all matters connected with our personal freedom, with the administration of justice, in all things which may be called internal, we have the freest opportunity of obtaining information, expressing our opinion, and enforcing our views on the Government.

But when you come to our foreign policy, you are no longer Englishmen; you are no longer free; you are recommended not to inquire. If you do, you are told you cannot understand it; you are snubbed, you are hustled aside. We are told that the matter is too deep for common understandings like ours—that there is great mystery about it. We have what is called diplomacy. We have a great many lords engaged in what they call diplomacy. We have a lord in Paris, we have another in Madrid, another in Berlin, another (at least we had until very lately) in Vienna, and another lord in Constantinople; and we have another at Washington; in fact, almost all over the world; particularly where the society is most pleasant, and the climate most agreeable, there is almost certain to be an English nobleman to represent the English Foreign Office, but you never know what he is doing. You have three or four columns every other day in most of the leading London papers—not a little of which is copied into the provincial journals—all about our foreign affairs, and yet, notwithstanding this, you are not a bit better acquainted with the matter when you read it, if you do read it at all, than you were before. Yet you have the great fact, that you have paid 28,000,000 l. a-year for more than forty years, and, since the year 1815, more than 1,000,000,000 l. out of the industry of the population. And out of all this comes the supposed necessity of armaments twice as large as were necessary twenty-five years ago; and yet you have no control over, and know nothing of the matter.

Lately, our Minister for Foreign Affairs was candid enough to tell you that Government drifted into war, and you know what is meant when a ship drifts. And other Foreign Ministers have drifted us into a great many wars; and I expect, if some change be not made with regard to this question, that they will either find it convenient, or that they cannot avoid it, from some cause or other, to allow us to drift into a war at some future period. I will not talk of what war is—we have had a specimen of it. Be it necessary or be it unnecessary—be the quarrel just or be it unjust—be it for the rights of the nation or to gratify the stupidity of a monarch or the intrigues of a minister —war, nevertheless, is one of the greatest calamities that can afflict any kingdom of the human race; and you, the people, are ignorant of the steps by which you are drawn into war.

It is a curious thing to observe the evils which nations live under, and the submissive spirit with which they yield to them. I have often compared, in my own mind, the people of England with the people of ancient Egypt, and the

Foreign Office of this country with the temples of the Egyptians. We are told by those who pass up and down the Nile, that on its banks are grand temples with stately statues and massive and lofty columns—statues each one of which would have appeared almost to have exhausted a quarry in its production. You have, further, vast chambers, and gloomy passages; and some innermost recess, some holy of holies, in which, when you arrive at it, you find some loathsome reptile which a nation reverenced and revered, and bowed itself down to worship. In our Foreign Office we have no massive columns; we have no statues; but we have a mystery as profound; and in the innermost recesses of it we find some miserable intrigue, in defence of which your fleets are traversing every ocean, your armies are perishing in every clime, and the precious blood of our country's children is squandered as though it had no price. I hope that an improved representation will change all this; that the great portion of our expenditure which is incurred in carrying out the secret and irresponsible doings of our Foreign Office will be placed directly under the free control of a Parliament elected by the great body of the people of the United Kingdom.

Ibid. pp. 73-8.

6. INDIA AND IRELAND

53. THOMAS BABINGTON MACAULAY: Speech in the House of Commons, 10 July 1833

We are told that the time can never come when the natives of India can be admitted to high civil and military office. We are told that this is the condition on which we hold our power. We are told that we are bound to confer on our subjects every benefit—which they are capable of enjoying?—no;—which it is in our power to confer on them? —no;—but which we can confer on them without hazard to the perpetuity of our own domination. Against that proposition I solemnly protest as inconsistent alike with sound policy and sound morality. . . .

I feel that, for the good of India itself, the admission of natives to high office must be effected by slow degrees. But that, when the fulness of time is come, when the interest of India requires the change, we ought to refuse to make that change lest we should endanger our own power, this is a doctrine of which I cannot think without indignation. Governments, like men, may buy existence too dear. . . .

What is power worth if it is founded on vice, on ignorance, and on misery; if we can hold it only by violating the most sacred duties which as governors we owe to the governed, and which, as a people blessed with far more than an ordinary measure of political liberty and of intellectual light, we owe to a race debased by three thousand years of despotism and priestcraft? We are free, we are civilised, to little purpose, if we grudge to any portion of the human race an equal measure of freedom and civilisation.

Are we to keep the people of India ignorant in order that we may keep them submissive? Or do we think that we can give them knowledge without awakening ambition? Or do we mean to awaken ambition and to provide it with no legitimate vent? Who will answer any of these questions in the affirmative? Yet one of them must be answered in the affirmative, by every person who maintains that we ought permanently to exclude the natives from high office. . . .

It may be that the public mind of India may expand under our system till it has outgrown that system; that by good government we may educate our subjects into a capacity for better government; that, having become instructed in European knowledge, they may, in some future age, demand European institutions. Whether such a day will ever come I know not. But never will I attempt to avert or to retard it. Whenever it comes, it will be the proudest day in English history. To have found a great people sunk in the lowest depths of slavery and superstition, to have so ruled them as to have made them desirous and capable of all the privileges of citizens, would indeed be a title to glory all our own. The sceptre may pass away from us. Unforeseen accidents may derange our most profound schemes of policy. Victory may be inconstant to our arms.

But there are triumphs which are followed by no reverse. There is an empire exempt from all natural causes of decay. Those triumphs are the pacific triumphs of reason over barbarism; that empire is the imperishable empire of our arts and our morals, our literature and our laws.

Miscellaneous Writings and Speeches of Lord
Macaulay (1882), pp. 551-72.

54. JOHN BRIGHT: Speech in the House of Commons, 24 June 1858

You may govern India, if you like, for the good of England, but the good of England must come through the channels of the good of India. There are but two modes of gaining anything by our connection with India. The one is by plundering the people of India, and the other by trading with them. I prefer to do it by trading with them. But in order that England may become rich by trading with India, India itself must become rich, and India can only become rich through the honest administration of justice and through entire security of life and property.

I admit that this is a great work; I admit, also, that the further I go into the consideration of this question, the more I feel that it is too large for me to grapple with, and that every step we take in it should be taken as if we were men walking in the dark. We have, however, certain great principles to guide us, and by their light we may make steps in advance, if not fast, at any rate sure. But we start from an unfortunate position. We start from a platform of conquest by force of arms extending over a hundred years. . . . The people of India have only seen England in its worst form in that country. They have seen it in its military power, its exclusive Civil Service, and in the supremacy of a handful of foreigners. When Natives of India come to this country, they are delighted with England and with Englishmen. They find themselves treated with a kindness, a consideration, a respect, to which they were wholly strangers in their own country; and they cannot understand how it is that men who are so just, so attentive to them here, sometimes, indeed too often, appear to them in a different character in India.

You must change all this if you mean to keep India. I do not now make any comment upon the mode in which this country has been put into possession of India. I accept that possession as a fact. There we are; we do not know how to leave it, and therefore let us see if we know how to govern it. It is a problem such as, perhaps, no other nation has had to solve. Let us see whether there is enough of intelligence and virtue in England to solve the difficulty. In the first place, then, I say, let us abandon all that system of calumny against the Natives of India which has lately prevailed. . . . The less we say about atrocities the better. Great political tumults are, I fear, never brought about or subdued without grievous acts on both sides deeply to be regretted. At least, we are in the position of invaders and conquerors—they are in the position of the invaded and the conquered. . . .

I would, immediately after this Bill passes, issue a Proclamation in India which should reach every subject of the British Crown in that country. . . . I would have a general amnesty, which should be put forth as the first great act done directly by the Queen of England in the exercise of Sovereign power over the territories of India. In this Proclamation I would promise to the Natives of India a security for their property as complete as we have here at home. . . .

I would tell them also in the Proclamation, that while the people of England hold that their own, the Christian religion, is true and the best for mankind, yet that it is consistent with that religion that they who profess it should hold inviolable the rights of conscience and the rights of religion in others. I would show, that whatever violent, over-zealous, and fanatical men may have said in this country, the Parliament of England, the Ministers of the Queen, and the Queen herself, are resolved that upon this point no kind of wrong should be done to the millions who profess the religions held to be true in India. I would do another thing. I would establish a Court of Appeal, the Judges of which should be Judges of the highest character in India, for the settlement of those many disputes which have arisen between the Government of India and its subjects, some Native and some

European. . . . Then I would carry out the proposition which the noble Lord has made tonight, that a commission should be issued to inquire into the question of finance. I would have other commissions, one for each Presidency, and I would tell the people of India that there should be a searching inquiry into their grievances, and that it was the interest and the will of the Queen of England that those grievances should be redressed.

Now, perhaps I may be told that I am proposing strange things, quite out of the ordinary routine of government. I admit it. We are in a position that necessitates something out of the ordinary routine. There are positions and times in the history of every country, as in the lives of individuals, when courage and action are absolute salvation. . . . The people of India do not like us, but they scarcely know where to turn if we left them. They are sheep literally without a shepherd. They are people whom you have subdued, and who have the highest and strongest claims upon you—claims which you cannot forget—claims which, if you do not act upon, you may rely upon it that, if there be a judgment for nations—as I believe there is—as for individuals, our children in no distant generation must pay the penalty which we have purchased by neglecting our duty to the populations of India.

Speeches by John Bright, M.P., ed. by J. H. T. Rogers (1868), vol. i, pp. 35-62.

55. JOHN BRIGHT: Speech in the House of Commons, 1 August 1859

I did hope when the noble Lord spoke to-night that he would have told us something which I am sure he must have known; that there is no such thing as a real Government in India at all; that there is no responsibility either to a public opinion there, or to a public opinion at home; and that therefore we cannot expect a better policy or happier results. Let hon. gentlemen imagine a Government like that in India, over which the payers of the taxes have not the slightest control; for the great body of the people in India have, as we all know, no control in any way over the Government.

Neither is there any independent English opinion that has any control over the Government, the only opinions being those of the Government itself, or those of the Military and Civil Services, and chiefly of the latter. They are not the payers of taxes; they are the spenders and enjoyers of the taxes. The Civil Service, being privileged, is arrogant, and I had almost said tyrannous, as any one may see who reads the Indian papers, which mainly represent the opinion of that Service and the Military Service, which, as everywhere else where it is not checked by the resolution of the taxpayers and civilians, is clamorous and insatiable for greater expenditure.

The Governor-General of India goes out knowing little or nothing of India. I know exactly what he does when he is appointed. He shuts himself up to study the first volumes of Mr. Mill's *History of India*, and he reads through this laborious work without nearly so much effect in making him a good Governor-General as a man might ignorantly suppose. He goes to India, a country of twenty nations, speaking twenty languages. He knows none of those nations, and he has not a glimmer of the grammar and pronunciation or meaning of those languages. . . . He knows nothing of the country or the people, and they are really unknown to the Government of India. . . . Observe the position, then, in which the Governor-General is placed. He is surrounded by an official circle, he breathes an official air, and everything is dim or dark beyond it. You lay duties upon him which are utterly beyond the mental or bodily powers of any man who ever existed, and which he cannot therefore adequately perform.

What you want is to decentralize your Government. I hold it to be manifestly impossible to govern 150,000,000 of persons, composing twenty different nations, speaking as many different languages, by a man who knows nothing of India, assisted by half-a-dozen councillors belonging to a privileged order, many of whom have had very little experience in India, except within narrow limits, and whose experience never involved the consideration and settlement of great questions of statesmanship. If you could have an independent Government in India for every 20,000,000 of its people, I do not hesitate to say, though we are so many thousand miles away, that there are Englishmen who, settling down among those 20,000,000 of people, would be able to conduct the government of that particular province on conditions wholly different and immeasurably better than anything in the way of administration which we have ever seen in India.

I am not the inventor of local government for India; but the more I have considered the subject—the more I have discussed it with the Members of this House and with gentlemen connected with India—the more I am convinced that you will not make a single step towards the improvement of India unless you change your whole system of government —unless you give to each Presidency a government with more independent powers than are now possessed by it. What would be thought if the whole of Europe was under one governor, who knew only the language of the Feejee Islands, and that his subordinates were like himself, only more intelligent than the inhabitants of the Feejee Islands are supposed to be? You set a Governor over 150,000,000 of human beings, in a climate where the European cannot do the work he has to do so well as here, where neither the moral nor physical strength of the individual is equal to what it is at home,—and you do not always furnish the most powerful men for the office;—you seem to think that the atmosphere will be always calm and the sea always smooth. And so the government of India goes on; there are promises without number of beneficial changes, but we never hear that India is much better or worse than before. Now, that is not the way to do justice to a great empire like India.

Look at your responsibilities. India is ruled by Englishmen, but remember that in that unfortunate country you have destroyed every form of government but your own; that you have cast the thrones of the Natives to the ground. . . . All over those vast regions there are countless millions, helpless and defenceless, deprived of their natural leaders and their ancient chiefs, looking with only some small ray of hope to that omnipresent and irresistible Power by which they have been subjected. I appeal to you on behalf of that people. . . . I hope that you will not show to the world that, although your fathers conquered the country, you have not the ability to govern it. You had better disencumber yourselves of the fatal gift of empire than that the present generation should be punished for the sins of the past. . . . I hope that no future historian will have to say that the arms of England in India were irresistible, and that an ancient empire fell before their victorious progress,—yet that finally India was avenged, because the power of her conqueror was broken by the intolerable burdens and evils which she cast upon her victim, and that this wrong was accomplished by a waste of human life and a waste of wealth which England, with all her power, was unable to bear.

Ibid. pp. 85-112.

56. RICHARD COBDEN: Speech at Rochdale, 24 November 1863

Well, now is it not deplorable that we English, directly we get east the Cape of Good Hope, lose our morality and our Christianity—that we resort to all the meanness and chicanery, and treachery with which we accuse those Oriental people of practising upon us? But we forget what De Tocqueville says in speaking of similar proceedings of ours in India. He says: 'You ought not, as Englishmen and Christians, to lower yourselves to the level of that people. Remember, your sole title to be there at all is because you are supposed to be superior to them.' Do you suppose these things can be done by us Englishmen with impunity—do you think there is no retributive justice that will mete out vengeance to us as a people if we continue to do this; and if there is no compunction on the part of this community?

. . . Professor Goldwin Smith, treating of this very subject, says: 'There is no example, I believe, in history, from that of imperial Rome down to that of imperial France, of a nation which has trampled out the rights of others, but that ultimately forfeited its own.' Do you think those maxims, which we tolerated in the treatment of three, four, or five millions of people in the East—do you think that they will not turn back to curse us in our own daily lives, and in our own political organization? You have India; you have acquired India by conquest, and by means which no Englishman can look back upon with satisfaction. You hold India; your white faces are predominating and ruling in that country; and has it ever occurred to you at what cost you rule? We have lately had a report of the sanitary state of the army in India; why, if you take into account the losses we sustain in that country by fever, by debauchery, by ennui, and by climate; if you take into account the extra number of deaths and invalids in the army and civil service, in consequence of the climate, you are holding India at a cost —if I may be permitted to use the term—of a couple of battles of Waterloo every year. Is there not a tremendous responsibility accompanied with this, that you are to tolerate your lawless adventurers to penetrate not only into China, but in Japan, in your name? The history of all the proceedings in China at this time is as dishonourable to us as a nation as were the proceedings in Spain in the times of Cortes and Pizarro. When they fought, they did not commit greater atrocities than Englishmen have done in China. They have them mixing up themselves in this civil war and rebellion for the sake of loot, for the sake of plunder, entering towns, and undertaking to head these Chinese— aiding the Chinese Government—in storming these defenceless towns. They are so far off; their proceedings are done at so great a distance, that you don't feel them or see them, or know your responsibility; but they will find you out, and find out your children.

Speeches by Richard Cobden, M.P. (1870),
vol. ii, pp. 113-14.

57. JOHN BRIGHT: Speech in the House of Commons, 25 August 1848

The condition of Ireland requires two kinds of remedies— one political, the other social; and it is hard to tell where the one ends and the other begins. I will speak first of the political remedies. At present, there prevails throughout three-fourths of the Irish people a total unbelief in the honesty and integrity of the Government of this country. There may or may not be good grounds for all this ill feeling; but that it exists, no man acquainted with Ireland will deny. The first step to be taken is to remove this feeling; and, to do this, some great measure or measures should be offered to the people of Ireland, which will act as a complete demonstration to them that bygones are to be bygones, with regard to the administration of Irish affairs, and that henceforth new, generous, and equal principles of government are to be adopted.

Ireland has long been a country of jars and turmoil, and its jars have arisen chiefly from religious dissensions. In respect of matters of religion she has been governed in a manner totally unknown in England and Scotland. If Ireland has been rightly governed—if it has been wise and just to maintain the Protestant Church established there, you ought, in order to carry out your system, to establish Prelacy in Scotland, and Catholicism in England; though, if you were to attempt to do either the one or the other, it would not be a sham but a real insurrection that you would provoke. There must be equality between the great religious sects in Ireland—between Catholic and Protestant. It is impossible that this equality can be much longer denied.

I do not mean that you should withdraw from the Protestant Church every sixpence now in its possession; what I mean is, that you should separate it from the State, and appropriate all the funds of which it might justly be deprived to some grand national object, such as the support and extension of the system of education now established in Ireland; an appropriation of money which would, I am sure, produce in the minds of the people of Ireland an entire change of feeling with regard to the legislation of Parliament in relation to their country.

With regard to the Parliamentary representation of Ireland, I assert most distinctly that the representation which exists at this moment is a fraud; and I believe it would be far better if there were no representation at all, because the people would not then be deluded by the idea that they had a representative Government to protect their interests. The number of taxes which the people have to pay, in order to secure either the municipal or Parliamentary franchise, is so great that it is utterly impossible for the constituencies to be maintained and for public opinion—the honest, real opinion of intelligent classes in Ireland—to obtain any common or decent degree of representation in the Imperial Legislature. I feel quite confident that in the next Session of Parliament, the questions of religious equality in Ireland and of Irish representation must receive a much more serious attention than they have obtained in any past Session.

I come now to those social questions which must also receive the attention of Parliament; for if they do not, the political remedies will, after all, be of very little permanent use. I advocate these political changes on the ground, not that they will feed the hungry or employ the idle, but that they will be as oil thrown upon the waters, and will induce the people no longer to feel themselves treated as a conquered race. It is agreed on all sides that the social remedies which are immediately possible to us, are those having reference to the mode in which the land of Ireland is owned. . . .

The true solution of this matter is to get the lands out of the hands of men who are the nominal, and not the real, possessors. But Parliament maintains laws which act most injuriously in this particular. The law and practice of entails tends to keep the soil in large properties, and in the hands of those who cannot perform their duty to it. . . . A code of laws exists, under which it is impossible for the land and the people to be brought together.

The law and practice of primogeniture is another evil of the same character. It is a law unnatural and unjust at all times; but in the present condition of Ireland it cannot much longer be endured. . . . I would establish, for a limited period at least, a special court in Ireland to adjudicate on all questions connected with the titles and transfers of landed property. This court should finally decide questions of title; it should prepare and enforce a simple and short form of conveyance, as short almost as that by which railway stock is transferred; and, without regard to the public revenue, I would abolish every farthing of expense which is now incurred in the duties on stamps, for the purpose of facilitating the distribution of land in Ireland, and of allowing the capital and industry of the people to work out its salvation. All this is possible; and, more than this, it is all necessary. . . .

Let the House, if it can, regard Ireland as an English country. Let us think of eight millions of people, and of the millions of them doomed to this intolerable suffering. Let us think of the half-million who, within two years past, have perished miserably in the workhouses, and on the highways, and in their hovels—more, far more than ever fell by the sword in any war this country ever waged; let us think of the crop of nameless horrors which is even now growing up in Ireland, and whose disastrous fruit may be gathered in years and generations to come. Let us examine what are the laws and the principles under which alone God and nature have permitted that nations should become industrious and provident. . . .

It may be thought I am opposed to much that exists in the present order of things; but whether it tended to advance democracy, or to uphold aristocracy, or any other system, I would wish to fling to the winds any prejudice I have entertained, and any principle that may be questioned, if I can thereby do one single thing to hasten by a single day the time when Ireland shall be equal to England in that comfort and that independence which an industrious people may enjoy, if the Government under which they live is equal and just.

Speeches by John Bright, M.P., ed. by J. H. T. Rogers (1868), vol. i, pp. 313-21.

58. JOHN BRIGHT: Speech in the House of Commons,
2 April 1849

On looking over the reports of the Poor-law Inspectors, I find them teeming with statements of the wretchedness which prevails in the distressed districts of Ireland. The general character of the reports is, that starvation is, literally speaking, gradually driving the population into their graves. . . .

The prisons are crowded, the chapels deserted, society is disorganized and ruined; labour is useless, for capital is not to be had for its employment. The reports of the Inspectors say that this catastrophe has only been hastened, and not originated, by the failure of the potato crop during the last four years, and that all men possessed of any intelligence must have foreseen what would ultimately happen.

This being the case, in what manner are the Irish people to subsist in future? There is the land, and there is labour enough to bring it into cultivation. But such is the state in which the land is placed, that capital cannot be employed upon it. You have tied up the raw material in such a manner —you have created such a monopoly of land by your laws and your mode of dealing with it, as to render it alike a curse to the people and to the owners of it. . . .

I want Parliament to remove every obstacle in the way of the free sale of land. I believe that in this policy lies the only security you have for the restoration of the distressed districts of Ireland.

I probably shall be told that I propose schemes which are a great interference with the rights of property. My opinion is that nothing can be a greater interference and infringement of the rights of property than the laws which regulate property now. . . . You speak of interference with property; but I ask what becomes of the property of the poor man, which consists of his labour? Take those 4,000,000 persons who live in the distressed districts. Their property in labour is almost totally destroyed. There they are—men whom God made and permitted to come into this world, endowed with faculties like ourselves, but who are unable to maintain themselves, and must either starve or live upon others. The interference with their property has been enormous— so great as absolutely to destroy it. . . .

I shall be told that I an injuring aristocratical and territorial influence. What is that in Ireland worth to you now? What is Ireland worth to you at all? Is she not the very symbol and token of your disgrace and humiliation to the whole world? Is she not an incessant trouble to your Legislature, and the source of increased expense to your people, already over-taxed? Is not your legislation all at fault in what it has hitherto done for the country? The people of Ulster say that we shall weaken the Union. It has been one of the misfortunes of the legislation of this House that there has been no honest attempt to make a union with the whole people of Ireland up to this time. We have had a union with Ulster, but there has been no union with the whole people of Ireland, and there never can be a union between the Government and the people whilst such a state of things exists as has for many years past prevailed in the south and west of Ireland.

Ibid. pp. 323-47.

PART IV

THE AGE OF GLADSTONE

I. THE PHILOSOPHY OF LIBERTY

59. JOHN STUART MILL: *On Liberty*
(1859)

(A)

This, then, is the appropriate region of human liberty. It comprises, first, the inward domain of consciousness; demanding liberty of conscience in the most comprehensive sense; liberty of thought and feeling; absolute freedom of opinion and sentiment on all subjects, practical or speculative, scientific, moral, or theological. The liberty of expressing and publishing opinions may seem to fall under a different principle, since it belongs to that part of the conduct of an individual which concerns other people; but, being almost of as much importance as the liberty of thought itself, and resting in great part on the same reasons, is practically inseparable from it. Secondly, the principle requires liberty of tastes and pursuits; of framing the plan of our life to suit our own character; of doing as we like, subject to such consequences as may follow: without impediment from our fellow-creatures, so long as what we do does not harm them, even though they should think our conduct foolish, perverse, or wrong. Thirdly, from this liberty of each individual, follows the liberty, within the same limits, of combination among individuals; freedom to unite, for any purpose not involving harm to others: the persons combining being supposed to be of full age, and not forced or deceived.

No society in which these liberties are not, on the whole, respected is free, whatever may be its form of government; and none is completely free in which they do not exist absolute and unqualified. The only freedom which deserves the name, is that of pursuing our own good in our own way, so long as we do not attempt to deprive others of theirs, or impede their efforts to obtain it. . . . Mankind are greater gainers by suffering each other to live as seems good to themselves, than by compelling each to live as seems good to the rest.

Let us suppose that the government is entirely at one with the people, and never thinks of exerting any power of coercion unless in agreement with what it conceives to be their voice. But I deny the right of the people to exercise such coercion, either by themselves or by their government. The power itself is illegitimate. The best government has no more title to it than the worst. It is as noxious, or more noxious, when exerted in accordance with public opinion, than when in opposition to it. If all mankind minus one were of one opinion, and only one person were of the contrary opinion, mankind would be no more justified in silencing that one person, than he, if he had the power, would be justified in silencing mankind. . . .

But, indeed, the dictum that truth always triumphs over persecution is one of those pleasant falsehoods which men repeat after one another till they pass into commonplaces, but which all experience refutes. History teems with instances of truth put down by persecution. If not suppressed for ever, it may be thrown back for centuries. . . . It is a piece of idle sentimentality that truth, merely as truth, has any inherent power denied to error of prevailing against the dungeon and the stake. Men are not more zealous for truth than they often are for error, and a sufficient application of legal or even of social penalties will generally succeed in stopping the propagation of either. . . .

There have been, and may again be, great individual thinkers in a general atmosphere of mental slavery. But there never has been, nor ever will be, in that atmosphere an intellectually active people. Where any people has made a temporary approach to such a character, it has been because the dread of heterodox speculation was for a time suspended. Where there is a tacit convention that principles are not to be disputed; where the discussion of the greatest questions which can occupy humanity is considered to be closed, we cannot hope to find that generally high scale of mental activity which has made some periods of history so remarkable. Never when controversy avoided the subjects which are large and important enough to kindle enthusiasm, was the mind of a people stirred up from its foundations, and the impulse given which raised even persons of the most ordinary intellect to something of the dignity of thinking beings. Of such we have had an example in the condition of Europe during the times immediately following the Reformation; another, though limited to the Continent and to a more cultivated class, in the speculative movement of the latter half of the eighteenth century; and a third, of still briefer duration, in the intellectual fermentation of Germany during the Goethian and Fichtean period. These periods differed widely in the particular opinions which they developed; but were alike in this, that during all three the yoke of authority was broken. In each, an old mental despotism had been thrown off, and no new one had yet taken its place. The impulse given at these three periods has made Europe what it now is. . . .

In our times, from the highest class of society down to the lowest, every one lives as under the eye of a hostile and dreaded censorship. . . . They ask themselves, what is suitable to my position? what is usually done by persons of my station and pecuniary circumstances? or (worse still) what is usually done by persons of a station and circumstance superior to mine? . . . It does not occur to them to have any inclination, except for what is customary. Thus the mind itself is bowed to the yoke: even in what people do for pleasure, conformity is the first thing thought of; they live in crowds; they exercise choice only among things commonly done; peculiarity of taste, eccentricity of conduct, are shunned equally with crimes; until by dint of not following their own nature they have no nature to follow: their human capacities are withered and starved: they become incapable of any strong wishes or native pleasures, and are generally without either opinions or feelings of home growth, or properly their own. . . .

It will not be denied by anybody, that originality is

a valuable element in human affairs. There is always need of persons not only to discover new truths, and point out when what were once truths are true no longer, but also to commence new practices, and set the example of more enlightened conduct, and better taste and sense in human life. It is true that this benefit is not capable of being rendered by everybody alike: there are but few persons, in comparison with the whole of mankind, whose experiments, if adopted by others, would be likely to be any improvement on established practice. But these few are the salt of the earth; without them, human life would become a stagnant pool. Not only is it they who introduce good things which did not before exist; it is they who keep the life in those which already exist. . . . There is only too great a tendency in the best beliefs and practices to degenerate into the mechanical; and unless there were a succession of persons whose ever-recurring originality prevents the grounds of those beliefs and practices from becoming merely traditional, such dead matter would not resist the smallest shock from anything really alive, and there would be no reason why civilization should not die out, as in the Byzantine Empire. Persons of genius, it is true, are, and are always likely to be, a small minority; but in order to have them, it is necessary to preserve the soil in which they grow. Genius can only breathe freely in an *atmosphere* of freedom. . . .

No government by a democracy or a numerous aristocracy, either in its political acts or in the opinions, qualities, and tone of mind which it fosters, ever did or could rise above mediocrity, except in so far as the sovereign Many have let themselves be guided (which in their best times they have always done) by the counsels and influence of a more highly gifted and instructed One or Few. The initiation of all wise or noble things comes and must come from the individuals; generally at first from some one individual. The honour and glory of the average man is that he is capable of following that initiative; that he can respond internally to wise and noble things, and be led to them with his eyes open. I am not countenancing the sort of 'hero-worship' which applauds the strong man of genius for forcibly seizing on the government of the world and making it do his bidding in spite of itself. All he can claim is, freedom to point out the way. . . .

The despotism of custom is everywhere the standing hindrance to human advancement, being in unceasing antagonism to that disposition to aim at something better than customary, which is called, according to circumstances, the spirit of liberty, or that of progress or improvement. The spirit of improvement is not always a spirit of liberty, for it may aim at forcing improvements on an unwilling people; and the spirit of liberty, in so far as it resists such attempts, may ally itself locally and temporarily with the opponents of improvement; but the only unfailing and permanent source of improvement is liberty, since by it there are as many possible independent centres of improvement as there are individuals. The progressive principle, however, in either shape, whether as the love of liberty or of improvement, is antagonistic to the sway of Custom, involving at least emancipation from that yoke; and the contest between the two constitutes the chief interest of the history of mankind. The greater part of the world has, properly speaking, no history, because the despotism of Custom is complete. . . .

It is not progress that we object to; on the contrary, we flatter ourselves that we are the most progressive people who ever lived. It is individuality that we war against: we should think we had done wonders if we had made ourselves all alike; forgetting that the unlikeness of one person to another is generally the first thing which draws the attention of either to the imperfection of his own type, and the superiority of another, or the possibility, by combining the advantages of both, of producing something better than either. We have a warning example in China.

What is it that has hitherto preserved Europe from this lot? What has made the European family of nations an improving, instead of a stationary portion of mankind? Not any superior excellence in them, which, when it exists, exists as the effect, not as the cause; but their remarkable diversity of character and culture. Individuals, classes, nations, have been extremely unlike one another: they have struck out a great variety of paths, each leading to something valuable; and although at every period those who travelled in different paths have been intolerant of one another, and each would have thought it an excellent thing if all the rest could have been compelled to travel his road, their attempts to thwart each other's development have rarely had any permanent success, and each has in the time endured to receive the good which the others have offered. Europe is, in my judgment, wholly indebted to this plurality of paths for its progressive and many-sided development.

(B)

The third and most cogent reason for restricting the interference of government is the great evil of adding unnecessarily to its power. . . .

If the roads, the railways, the banks, the insurance offices, the great joint-stock companies, the universities, and the public charities, were all of them branches of the government; if, in addition, the municipal corporations and local boards, with all that now devolves on them, became departments of the central administration, if the employees of all these different enterprises were appointed and paid by the government, and looked to the government for every rise in life; not all the freedom of the press and popular constitution of the legislature would make this or any other country free otherwise than in name. And the evil would be greater, the more efficiently and scientifically the administrative machinery was constructed. . . .

All the enlarged culture and practised intelligence in the country, except the purely speculative, would be concentrated in a numerous bureaucracy, to whom alone the rest of the community would look for all things: the multitude for direction and dictation in all they had to do, the able and aspiring for personal advancement. To be admitted into the ranks of this bureaucracy, and when admitted, to rise therein, would be the sole objects of ambition. Under this *régime*, not only is the outside public ill-qualified, for want of practical experience, to criticise or check the mode of operation of the bureaucracy, but even if the accidents of despotic or the natural working of popular institutions occasionally raise to the summit a ruler of reforming inclinations, no reform can be effected which is contrary to the interest of the bureaucracy. Such is the melancholy condition of the Russian empire, as shown in the accounts of those who have had sufficient opportunity of observation. The Czar himself is powerless against the bureaucratic body; he can send any one of them to Siberia, but he cannot govern without them, or against their will. On every decree of his they have a tacit veto by merely refraining from carrying it into effect. In countries of more advanced civilisation and of a more insurrectionary spirit . . . when the evil exceeds their amount of patience, they rise against the government, and make what is called a revolution; whereupon somebody else, with or without legitimate authority from the nation, vaults into the seat, issues his orders to the bureaucracy, and everything goes on much as it did before, the bureaucracy being unchanged, and nobody else being capable of taking their place.

A very different spectacle is exhibited among a people accustomed to transact their own business. . . . Let them be left without a government, every body of Americans is able to improvise one, and to carry on that or any other public business with a sufficient amount of intelligence, order, and decision. This is what every free people ought to be: and a people capable of this is certain to be free; it will never let itself be enslaved by any man or body of men because these are able to seize and pull the reins of the central administration. No bureaucracy can hope to make such a people as this do or undergo anything that they do not like. But where everything is done through the bureaucracy, nothing to which the bureaucracy is really adverse can be done at all. . . . The governors are as much the slaves of their organisation and discipline as the governed are of the governors. A Chinese mandarin is as much the tool and creature of a despotism as the humbled cultivator. . . .

To determine the point at which evils, so formidable to human freedom and advancement, begin, or rather at which they begin to predominate over the benefits attending the collective application of the force of society, under its recognised chiefs, for the removal of the obstacles which stand in the way of its well-being; to secure as much of the advantages of centralised power and intelligence as can be had without turning into governmental channels too great a proportion of the general activity—is one of the most difficult and complicated questions in the art of government. It is, in a great measure, a question of detail, in which many and various considerations must be kept in view, and no absolute rule can be laid down. But I believe that the practical principle in which safety resides, the ideal to be kept in view, the standard by which to test all arrangements intended for overcoming the difficulty, may be conveyed in these words: the greatest dissemination of power consistent with efficiency; but the greatest possible centralisation of information, and diffusion of it from the centre. Thus, in municipal administration, there would be, as in the New England States, a very minute division among separate officers, chosen by the localities, of all business which is not better left to the persons directly interested; but besides this, there would be, in each department of local affairs, a central superintendence, forming a branch of the general government. The organ of this superintendence would concentrate, as in a focus, the variety of information and experience derived from the conduct of that branch of public business in all the localities, from everything analogous which is done in foreign countries, and from the general principles of political science. This central organ should have a right to know all that is done, and its special duty should be that of making the knowledge acquired in one place available for others. Emancipated from the petty prejudices and narrow views of a locality by its elevated position and comprehensive sphere of observation, its advice would naturally carry much authority; but its actual power, as a permanent institution, should, I conceive, be limited to compelling the local officers to obey the laws laid down for their guidance. In all things not provided for by general rules, those officers should be left to their own judgment, under responsibility to their constituents. For the violation of rules, they should be responsible to law, and the rules themselves should be laid down by the legislature, the central administrative authority only watching over their execution. . . .

A Government cannot have too much of the kind of activity which does not impede, but aids and stimulates, individual exertion and development. The mischief begins when, instead of calling forth the activity and powers of individuals and bodies, it substitutes its own activity for theirs; when, instead of informing, advising, and, upon occasion, denouncing, it makes them work in fetters, or bids them stand aside and does their work instead of them. The worth of a State, in the long run, is the worth of the individuals composing it; and a State which postpones the interests of *their* mental expansion and elevation to a little more of adminstrative skill, or of that semblance of it which practice gives, in the details of business; a State which dwarfs its men, in order that they may be more docile instruments in its hands even for beneficial purposes—will find that with small men no great thing can really be accomplished; and that the perfection of machinery to which it has sacrificed everything will in the end avail it nothing, for want of the vital power which, in order that the machine might work more smoothly, it has preferred to banish.

> J. S. Mill, *On Liberty* and *Representative Government*, ed. R. B. McCallum (1948), (A), pp. 11-64; (B), pp. 99-104.

60. JOHN STUART MILL: *Considerations on Representative Government* (1861)

It has long been a common saying, that if a good despot could be ensured, despotic monarchy would be the best form of government. I look upon this as a radical and most pernicious misconception of what good government is. . . .

It is not much to be wondered at if impatient or disappointed reformers, groaning under the impediments opposed to the most salutary public improvements by the ignorance, the indifference, the intractableness, the perverse obstinacy of a people, and the corrupt combinations of selfish private interests armed with the powerful weapons afforded by free institutions, should at times sigh for a strong hand to bear down all these obstacles, and compel a recalcitrant people to be better governed. But (setting aside the fact, that for one despot who now and then reforms an abuse, there are ninety-nine who do nothing but create them) those who look in any such direction for the realization of their hopes leave out of the idea of good government its principal element, the improvement of the people themselves. One of the benefits of freedom is that under it the ruler cannot pass by the people's minds, and amend their affairs for them without amending them. If it were possible for the people to be well governed in spite of themselves, their good government would last no longer than the freedom of a people usually lasts who have been liberated by foreign arms without their own co-operation. It is true, a despot may educate the people; and to do so really, would be the best apology for his despotism. But any education which aims at making human beings other than machines, in the long run makes them claim to have the control of their own actions. . . .

It is an adherent condition of human affairs that no intention, however sincere, of protecting the interests of others can make it safe or salutary to tie up their own hands. Still more obviously true is it, that by their own hands only can any positive and durable improvement of their circumstances in life be worked out. Throughout the joint influence of these two principles, all free communities have both been more exempt from social injustice and crime, and have attained more brilliant prosperity, than any others, or than they themselves after they lost their freedom. Contrast the free states of the world, while their freedom lasted, with the contemporary subjects of monarchical or oligarchical despotism: the Greek cities with the Persian satrapies; the Italian republics and the free towns of Flanders and Germany, with the feudal monarchies of Europe; Switzerland, Holland, and England, with Austria or ante-revolutionary France. Their superior prosperity was too obvious ever to have been gainsaid: while their superiority in good government and social relations is proved by the prosperity, and is manifest besides in every page of history. If we compare, not one age with another, but the different

governments which co-existed in the same age, no amount
of disorder which exaggeration itself can pretend to have
existed amidst the publicity of the free states can be compared
for a moment with the contemptuous trampling upon the
mass of the people which pervaded the whole life of the
monarchical countries, or the disgusting individual tyranny
which was of more than daily occurrence under the systems
of their frightful courts of justice.

Ibid. pp. 136-43.

61. LORD ACTON: Review of Goldwin Smith's *Irish History* (1862)

There were, therefore, two opinions in the revolutionary party. Those who overthrew the monarchy,
established the republic, and commenced the war, were
content with having secured political and legal equality,
and wished to leave the nation in the enjoyment of those
advantages which fortune distributes unequally. But the
consistent partisans of equality required that nothing should
be allowed to raise one man above another. The Girondists
wished to preserve liberty, education, and property; but
the Jacobins, who held that an absolute equality should be
maintained by the despotism of the government over the
people, interpreted more justly the democratic principles
which were common to both parties.

Three weeks after the fall of the Gironde, the Constitution
of 1793, by which a purely ideal democracy was instituted,
was presented to the French people. . . . Robespierre
explains the system in his report on the principles of political
morality, presented to the Convention at the moment of
his greatest power:—

'If the principle of a popular government in time of
peace is virtue, its principle during revolution is virtue
and terror combined; virtue, without which terror is
pernicious; terror, without which virtue is powerless.
Terror is nothing but rapid, severe, inflexible justice;

therefore a product of virtue. It is not so much a principle in itself, as a consequence of the universal principle of democracy in its application to the urgent necessities of the country.'

This is perfectly true. Envy, revenge, fear, were motives by which individuals were induced or enabled to take part in the administration of such a system; but its introduction was not the work of passion, but the inevitable result of a doctrine. The democratic Constitution required to be upheld by violence, not only against foreign arms, but against the state of society and the nature of things. . . .

The same theory of an original state of nature, from which the principle of equality was deduced, also taught men where they might find the standard of equality. . . . Those who were least tainted by the temptations of civilised society remained in the natural state. This was the definition of the new notion of the People, which became the measure of virtue and of equality. The democratic theory required that the whole nation should be reduced to the level of the lower orders in all those things in which society creates disparity, in order to be raised to the level of that republican virtue which resides among those who have retained a primitive simplicity by escaping the influence of civilisation.

The form of government and the condition of society must always correspond. Social equality is therefore a postulate of pure democracy. It was necessary that it should exist if the Constitution was to stand, and if the great ideal of popular enthusiasm was ever to be realised. The Revolution had begun by altering the social condition of the country; the correction of society by the State had already commenced. It did not, therefore, seem impossible to continue it until the nation should be completely remodelled in conformity with the new principles. . . . The difference between the actual society and the ideal equality was so great that it could be removed only by violence. The great mass of those who perished were . . . condemned, not for particular acts, but for their position, or for acts which denoted, not so much a hostile design, as an incompatible habit. . . . Hence the proscription was wholesale. Criminals were judged and executed in categories; and the merits of individual cases were, therefore, of little account. . . . The question was not, what crimes has the prisoner committed? but, does he belong to one of those classes whose existence the Republic cannot tolerate? . . . Most of the Terrorists were swayed by fear for themselves, or by the frenzy which is produced by familiarity with slaughter. But this is of small account. The significance of that sanguinary drama lies in the fact, that a political abstraction was powerful enough to make men think themselves right in destroying masses of their countrymen in the attempt to impose it on their country. . . . No man who admits their theory has a right to complain of their acts. The one proceeded from the other with the inflexible logic of history. The Reign of Terror was nothing else than the reign of those who conceive that liberty and equality can coexist.

> Lord Acton, *The History of Freedom and Other Essays*,
> ed. by J. N. Figgis and R. V. Laurence (1907),
> pp. 262-7.

62. LORD ACTON: *The History of Freedom in Antiquity* (1877)

[An address delivered to the Bridgnorth Institute, 26 February 1877.]

Liberty, next to religion, has been the motive of good deeds and the common pretext of crime, from the sowing of the seed at Athens, two thousand four hundred and sixty years ago, until the ripened harvest was gathered by men of our race. It is the delicate fruit of a mature civilisation; and scarcely a century has passed since nations, that knew the meaning of the term, resolved to be free. In every age its progress has been beset by its natural enemies, by ignorance and superstition, by lust of conquest and by love of ease, by the strong man's craving for power, and the poor man's craving for food. During long intervals it has been utterly arrested, when nations were being rescued from barbarism and from the grasp of strangers, and when the perpetual struggle for existence, depriving men of all interest and understanding in politics, has made them eager to sell their birthright for a pottage, and ignorant of the treasure they resigned. At all times sincere friends of freedom have been rare, and its triumphs have been due to minorities, that have prevailed by associating themselves with auxiliaries whose object often differed from their own. . . .

Liberty is not a means to a higher political end. It is itself the highest political end. It is not for the sake of a good public administration that it is required, but for security in the pursuit of the highest objects of civil society and of private life. Increase of freedom in the State may sometimes promote mediocrity, and give vitality to prejudice; it may even retard useful legislation, diminish the capacity for war, and restrict the boundaries of Empire. It might be plausibly argued that, if many things would be worse in England or Ireland under an intelligent despotism, some things would be managed better; that the Roman Government was more enlightened under Augustus and Antoninus than under the Senate, in the days of Marius or of Pompey. A generous spirit prefers that his country should be poor, and weak, and of no account, but free, rather than powerful, prosperous, and enslaved. It is better to be the citizen of a humble commonwealth in the Alps, without a prospect of influence beyond the narrow frontier, than a subject of the superb autocracy that overshadows half of Asia and of Europe. But it may be urged, on the other side, that liberty is not the sum or the substitute of all the things men ought to live for; that to be real it must be circumscribed, and that the limits of circumscription vary; that advancing civilisation invests the State with increased rights and duties, and imposes increased burdens and constraint on the subject; that a highly instructed and intelligent community may perceive the benefit of compulsory obligations which, at a lower stage, would be thought unbearable; that liberal progress is not vague or indefinite, but aims at a point where the public is subject to no restrictions but those of which it feels the advantage; that a free country may be less capable of doing much for the advancement of religion, the prevention of vice, or the relief of suffering, than one that does not shrink from confronting great emergencies by some sacrifice of individual rights, and some concentration of power; and that the supreme political object ought to be sometimes postponed to still higher moral objects. My argument involves no collision with these qualifying reflections.

> Lord Acton, *The History of Freedom in Antiquity*, address delivered at the Bridgnorth Institute, 26 February 1877, pp. 1-23.

63. LORD ACTON: Review of Sir Erskine May's *Democracy in Europe* (1878)

Since the Revolution of July and the Presidency of Jackson gave the impulse which has made democracy preponderate, the ablest political writers, Tocqueville, Calhoun, Mill, and Laboulaye, have drawn, in the name of freedom, a formidable indictment against it. They have shown democracy without respect for the past or care for the future, regardless of public faith and of national honour, extravagant and inconstant, jealous of talent and of knowledge, indifferent to justice but servile towards opinion, incapable of organisation, impatient of authority, averse from obedience, hostile to religion and to established law. . . . But it is not to these symptoms that we must impute the permanent danger and the irrepressible conflict. . . . The manifest, the avowed difficulty is that democracy, no less than monarchy or aristocracy, sacrifices everything to maintain itself, and strives, with an energy and a plausibility that kings and nobles cannot attain, to override representation, to annul all the forces of resistance and deviation, and to secure, by Plebiscite, Referendum, or Caucus, free play for the will of the majority. The true democratic principle, that none shall have power over the people, is taken to mean that none shall be able to restrain or to elude its power. The true democratic principle, that the people shall not be made to do what it does not like, is taken to mean that it shall never be required to tolerate what it does not like. The true democratic principle, that every man's free will shall be as unfettered as possible, is taken to mean that the free will of the collective

people shall be fettered in nothing. . . . Democracy claims
to be not only supreme, without authority above, but
absolute, without independence below; to be its own master,
not a trustee. The old sovereigns of the world are exchanged
for a new one, who may be flattered and deceived, but whom
it is impossible to corrupt or to resist, and to whom must
be rendered the things that are Caesar's and also the things
that are God's. The enemy to be overcome is no longer the
absolutism of the State, but the liberty of the subject. . . .

For the old notions of civil liberty and of social order
did not benefit the masses of the people. Wealth increased,
without relieving their wants. The progress of knowledge left
them in abject ignorance. Religion flourished, but failed to
reach them. Society, whose laws were made by the upper
class alone, announced that the best thing for the poor is not
to be born, and the next best, to die in childhood, and suffered
them to live in misery and crime and pain. As surely as the
long reign of the rich has been employed in promoting the
accumulation of wealth, the advent of the poor to power
will be followed by schemes for diffusing it. Seeing how
little was done by the wisdom of former times for education
and public health, for insurance, association, and savings,
for the protection of labour against the law of self-interest,
and how much has been accomplished in this generation,
there is reason in the fixed belief that a great change was
needed, and that democracy has not striven in vain. Liberty,
for the mass, is not happiness; and institutions are not an
end but a means. The thing they seek is a force sufficient to
sweep away scruples and the obstacle of rival interests, and,
in some degree, to better their condition. They mean that
the strong hand that heretofore has formed great States,
protected religions, and defended the independence of
nations, shall help them by preserving life, and endowing
it for them with some, at least, of the things men live for.
That is the notorious danger of modern democracy. That
is also its purpose and its strength. And against this threatening power the weapons that struck down other despots do
not avail. The greatest happiness principle positively con-
firms it. The principle of equality, besides being as easily
applied to property as to power, opposes the existence of

persons or groups of persons exempt from the common law, and independent of the common will; and the principle, that authority is a matter of contract, may hold good against kings, but not against the sovereign people, because a contract implies two parties.

The Quarterly Review, January 1878.

64. LORD ACTON: Letter to Bishop Creighton
(1887)

[Occasioned by Bishop Creighton's review of the *History of the Papacy* in the *English Historical Review*.]

I cannot accept your canon that we are to judge Pope and King unlike other men, with a favourable presumption that they did no wrong. If there is any presumption it is the other way, against the holders of power, increasing as the power increases. Historic responsibility has to make up for the want of legal responsibility. Power tends to corrupt, and absolute power corrupts absolutely. Great men are almost always bad men, even when they exercise influence and not authority, still more when you superadd the tendency or the certainty of corruption by authority. There is no worse heresy than that the office sanctifies the holder of it. That is the point at which the negations of Liberalism meet and keep high festival, and the end learns to justify the means. You would hang a man of no position like Ravaillac; but if what one hears is true, then Elizabeth asked the gaoler to murder Mary, and William III ordered his Scots minister to extirpate a clan. Here are the greatest names coupled with greatest crimes; you would spare those criminals, for some mysterious reason. I would hang them higher than Haman, for reasons of quite obvious justice. . . .

The inflexible integrity of the moral code is, to me, the secret of the authority, the dignity, the utility of History.

If we may debase the currency for the sake of genius, or success, or rank or reputation, we may debase it for the sake of a man's influence, of his religion, of his party, of the good cause which prospers by his credit and suffers by his disgrace. Then History ceases to be a science, an arbiter of controversy, a guide of the Wanderer, the upholder of that moral standard which the powers of earth and religion itself tend constantly to depress. It serves where it ought to reign; and it serves the worst cause better than the purest. . . . My dogma is not the special wickedness of my own spiritual superiors, but the general wickedness of men in authority—of Luther and Zwingli, and Calvin and Cranmer and Knox, of Mary Stuart and Henry VIII, of Philip II and Elizabeth, of Cromwell and Louis XIV, James and Charles and William, Bossuet and Ken.

Lord Acton, *Historical Essays and Studies*, ed. by J. N. Figgis and R. V. Laurence (1907), pp. 503-5.

65. LORD ACTON: Letter to Mary Gladstone, 24 April 1881

As to Democracy, it is true that masses of new electors are utterly ignorant, that they are easily deceived by appeals to prejudice and passion, and are consequently unstable, and that the difficulty of explaining economic questions to them, and of linking their interests with those of the State, may become a danger to the public credit, if not to the security of private property. A true Liberal, as distinguished from a Democrat, keeps this peril always before him.

The answer is, that you cannot make an omelette without breaking eggs—that politics are not made up of artifices only, but of truths, and that truths have to be told.

We are forced, in equity, to share the government with the working class. . . . If there is a free contract, in open market, between capital and labour, it cannot be right that one of the two contracting parties should have the making of the laws, the management of the conditions, the keeping of the peace, the administration of justice, the distribution of taxes, the control of expenditure, in its own hands exclusively. It is unjust that all these securities, all these advantages, should be on the same side. . . . Before this argument, the ancient dogma, that power attends on property, broke down. Justice required that property should—not abdicate, but—share its political supremacy.

Without this partition, free contract was as illusory as a fair duel in which one man supplies seconds, arms, and ammunition.

That is the flesh and blood argument. That is why Reform, full of questions and expediency and policy in detail is, in the gross, not a question of expediency or of policy at all; and why some of us regard our opponents as men who should imagine sophisms to avoid keeping promises, paying debts, or speaking truths.

They will admit much of my theory, but then they will say, like practical men, that the ignorant classes cannot understand affairs of state, and are sure to go wrong. But the odd thing is that the most prosperous nations in the world are both governed by the masses—France and America. So there must be a flaw in the argument somewhere. The fact is that education, intelligence, wealth are a security against certain faults of conduct, not against errors of policy. There is no error so monstrous that it fails to find defenders among the ablest men. Imagine a congress of eminent celebrities, such as More, Bacon, Grotius, Pascal, Cromwell, Bossuet, Montesquieu, Jefferson, Napoleon, Pitt, etc. The result would be an Encyclopaedia of Error. They would assert Slavery, Socialism, Persecution, Divine Right, military despotism, the reign of force, the supremacy of the executive over legislation and justice, purchase in the magistracy, the abolition of credit, the limitation of laws to nineteen years, etc. If you were to read Walter Scott's pamphlets, Southey's Colloquies, Ellenborough's Diary, Wellington's Despatches —distrust of the select few, of the chosen leaders of the community, would displace the dread of the masses. The danger is not that a particular class is unfit to govern. Every class is unfit to govern. The law of liberty tends to abolish the reign of race over race, of faith over faith, of class over class. It is not the realisation of a political ideal: it is the discharge of a moral obligation. . . .

To many people the idea is repugnant that there is a moral question at the bottom of politics. They think that it is only by great effort and the employment of every resource that property and religion can be maintained. If you embarrass their defence with unnecessary rules and scruples, you risk defeat, and set up a rather arbitrary and unsanctioned standard above the interest of their class or of their church. Such men are not at their ease with the Prime Minister, especially if he is against them, and even when they are on his side. I am thinking of Argyll in Lytton's first debate; of Kimberley always; of soldiers and diplomatists generally. . . .

Nor do I admit the other accusation, of rousing class animosities. The upper class used to enjoy undivided sway, and used it for their own advantage, protecting their interests against those below them, by laws which were selfish and often inhuman. Almost all that has been done for the good of the people has been done since the rich lost the monopoly of power, since the rights of property were discovered to be not quite unlimited. Think not only of the Corn Laws, but of the fact that the State did nothing for primary education fifty years ago. The beneficent legislation of the last half-century has been due to the infusion of new elements in the electoral body. Success depended on preventing the upper class from recovering their lost ground, by keeping alive in the masses the sense of their responsibility, of their danger, of the condition from which they had been rescued, of the objects still before them, and the ancient enemy behind. Liberal policy has largely consisted in so promoting this feeling of self-reliance and self-help, that political antagonism should not degenerate into social envy, that the forces which rule society should be separate from the forces which rule the state. . . .

Lord Acton, *Letters to Mary Gladstone* (1904), pp. 91-6.

66. JOHN MORLEY: *On Compromise*
(1874)

The history of civilisation is the history of the displacement of old conceptions by new ones more conformable to the facts. It is the record of the removal of old institutions and ways of living, in favour of others of greater convenience and ampler capacity, at once multiplying and satisfying human requirements.

Now compromise, in view of the foregoing theory of social advance, may be of two kinds, and of these two kinds one is legitimate and the other not. . . . It may mean the deliberate suppression or mutilation of an idea, in order to make it congruous with the traditional idea or the current prejudice on the given subject, whatever that may be. Or else it may mean a rational acquiescence in the fact that the bulk of your contemporaries are not yet prepared either to embrace the new idea, or to change their ways of living in conformity to it. The first prolongs the duration of the empire of prejudice, and retards the arrival of improvement. The second does his best to abbreviate the one, and to hasten and make definite the other, yet he does not insist on hurrying changes which, to be effective, would require the active support of numbers of persons not yet ripe for them. It is legitimate compromise to say:—'I do not expect you to execute this improvement, or to surrender that prejudice, in my time. But at any rate it shall not be my fault if the improvement remains unknown or rejected. There shall be one man at least who has surrendered the prejudice, and who does not hide that fact.' It is illegitimate compromise to say:—'I cannot persuade you to accept my truth; therefore I will pretend to accept your falsehood.'. . .

'It is a very great mistake', said Burke, . . . 'to imagine that mankind follow up practically any speculative principle either of government or of freedom, as far as it will go in argument and logical illation. All government, indeed every human benefit and enjoyment, every virtue, and every prudent act, is founded on compromise and barter. We balance inconveniences; we give and take—we remit some rights that we may enjoy others. . . . Man acts from motives relative to his interests; and not on metaphysical speculations.'[1] In France such words ought to be printed in capitals on the front of every newspaper, and written up in letters of burnished gold over each faction of the Assembly, and on the door of every bureau in the Administration. In England they need a commentary which shall bring out the very simple truth, that compromise and barter do not mean the undisputed triumph of one set of principles.

[1] Speech on Conciliation with America.

Nor, on the other hand, do they mean the mutilation of both sets of principles, with a view to producing a tertium quid that shall involve the disadvantages of each, without securing the advantages of either. What Burke means is that we ought never to press our ideas up to their remotest logical issues, without reference to the conditions in which we are applying them. In politics we have an art. Success in politics, as in every other art, obviously before all else implies both knowledge of the material with which we have to deal, and also such concession as is necessary to the qualities of the material. Above all, in politics we have an art in which development depends upon small modifications. That is the true side of the conservative theory.... That fatal French saying about small reforms being the worst enemies of great reforms, is in the sense in which it is commonly used, a formula of social ruin.

On the other hand, let us not forget that there is a sense in which this very saying is profoundly true. A small and temporary improvement may really be the worst enemy of a great and permanent improvement, unless the first is made on the lines and in the direction of the second. And so it may, if it be successfully palmed off upon a society as actually being the second. In such a case as this, and our legislation presents instances of the kind, the small reform, if it be not made with reference to some large progressive principle and with a view to further extension of its scope, makes it all the more difficult to return to the right line and direction when improvement is again demanded. . . .

In a different way the second possible evil of a small reform may be equally mischievous—where the small reform is represented as settling the question. The mischief here is not that it takes us out of the progressive course, as in the case we have just been considering, but that it sets men's minds in a posture of contentment, which is not justified by the amount of what has been done, and which makes it all the harder to arouse them to new effort when the inevitable time arrives. . . .

In either of these senses, the small reform may become the enemy of the great one. But a right conception of political method, based on a rightly interpreted experience of the conditions on which societies unite progress with order, leads the wise conservative to accept the small change, lest a worse thing befall him, and the wise innovator to seize the chance of a small improvement, while incessantly working in the direction of great ones. The important thing is that throughout the process neither of them should lose sight of his ultimate ideal; nor fail to look at the detail from the point of view of the whole.

If the process seems intolerably slow, we may correct our impatience by looking back upon the past. People seldom realise the enormous period of time which each change in men's ideas requires for its full accomplishment. We speak of these changes with a peremptory kind of definiteness, as if they had covered no more than the space of a few years. Thus we talk of the time of the Reformation, as we might talk of the Reform Bill or the Repeal of the Corn Duties. Yet the Reformation is the name for a movement of the mind of northern Europe, which went on for three centuries. . . . We lose the reality of history, we fail to recognize one of the most striking aspects of human affairs, and above all we miss that most invaluable practical lesson, the lesson of patience, unless we remember that the great changes of history took up long periods of time which, when measured by the little life of a man, are almost colossal, like the vast changes of geology. . . .

This much, concerning moderation in political practice. No such considerations present themselves in the matters which concern the shaping of our own lives, or the publication of our social opinions. In this region we are not imposing changes upon others, either by law or otherwise. We therefore owe nothing to the prejudices or habits of others. If any one sets serious value upon the point of difference between his own ideal and that which is current, if he thinks that his 'experiment in living' has promise of real worth, and that if more persons could be induced to imitate it, some portion of mankind would be thus put in possession of a better kind of happiness, then it is selling a birthright for a mess of pottage to abandon hopes so rich and generous, merely in order to avoid the passing and casual penalties of social disapproval. . . . We lose not only the possible advantage of the given change. Besides that, we lose also the certain advantage of maintaining or increasing the amount of conscientiousness in the world. And everybody can perceive the loss incurred in a society where diminution of the latter sort takes place. The advance of the community depends not merely on the improvement and elevation of its moral maxims, but also on the quickening of moral sensibility. . . .

The great importance of leaving this priceless element in a community as free, as keen, and as active as possible, is overlooked by the thinkers who uphold coercion against liberty, as a saving social principle. Every act of coercion directed against an opinion or a way of living is in so far calculated to lessen the quantity of conscience in the society where such acts are practised. Of course, where ways of living interfere with the lawful rights of others, . . . it is necessary to force the dissidents, however strong may be their conscientious sentiment. The evil of attenuating that sentiment is smaller than the evil of allowing one set of persons to realise their own notions of happiness, at the expense of all the rest of the world. But where these notions can be realised without unlawful interference of that kind, then the forcible hindrance of such realisation is a direct weakening of the force and amount of conscience on which the community may count. . . . All that we have been saying may appear to cut both ways. If the innovator should decline to practise silence or reserve, why should the possessor of power be less uncompromising, and why should he not impose silence by force? If the heretic ought to be uncompromising in expressing his opinions, and in acting upon them, in the fulness of his conviction that they are right, why should not the orthodox be equally uncompromising in his resolution to stamp out the heretical notions and unusual ways of living, in the fulness of his conviction that they are thoroughly wrong? To this question the answer is that the hollow kinds of compromise are as bad in the orthodox as in the heretical. Truth has as much to gain from sincerity and thoroughness in one as in the other. But the issue between the partisans of the two opposed schools turns upon the sense which we design to give to the process of stamping out. Those who cling to the tenets of liberty limit the action of the majority, as of the minority, strictly to persuasion. Those who dislike liberty, insist that earnestness of conviction justifies either a majority or a minority in using not persuasion only, but force. . . .

You have not converted a man, because you have silenced him. Opinion and force belong to different elements. To think that you are able by social disapproval or other coercive means to crush a man's opinion, is as one who should fire a blunderbuss to put out a star. The acquiescence in current notions which is secured by law or by petulant social disapproval, is as worthless and as essentially hypocritical, as the conversion of an Irish pauper to protestantism by means of soup-tickets, or that of a savage to Christianity by the gift of a string of beads. . . .

The absence of a strait-waistcoat is a negation; but it is a useful condition for the activity of sane men. No doubt there must be a definite limit to this absence of external interference with conduct, and that limit will be fixed at various points by different thinkers. We are now only urging that it cannot be wisely fixed for the more complex societies by any one who has not grasped this fundamental preconception, that liberty, or the absence of coercion, or the leaving people to think, speak, and act as they please, is in itself a good thing. It is the object of a favourable presumption. The burden of proving it inexpedient always lies, and wholly lies, on those who wish to abridge it by coercion, whether direct or indirect.

One reason why this truth is so reluctantly admitted, is men's irrational want of faith in the self-protective quality of a highly developed and healthy community. The timid compromiser on the one hand, and the advocate of coercive restriction on the other, are equally the victims of a superfluous apprehension. The one fears to use his liberty for the same reason that makes the other fearful of permitting liberty. This common reason is the want of a sensible confidence that, in a free western community, which has reached our stage of development, religious, moral, and social novelties—provided they are tainted by no element of compulsion or interference with the just rights of others—may be trusted to find their own level. . . .

Stable societies are amply furnished with force enough to

resist all effort in a destructive direction. There is seldom much fear, and in our own country there is hardly any fear at all, of hasty reformers making too much way against the spontaneous conservatism which belongs to a healthy and well-organised community. If dissolvent ideas do make their way, it is because the society was already ripe for dissolution. New ideas, however ardently preached, will dissolve no society which was not already in a condition of profound disorganisation.

The recognition of the self-protecting quality of society is something more than a point of speculative importance. It has a direct practical influence. For it would add to the courage and intrepidity of the men who are most attached to the reigning order of things. If such men could only divest themselves of a futile and nervous apprehension, that things as they are have no root in their essential fitness and harmony, and that order consequently is ever hanging on a trembling and doubtful balance, they would not only gain by the self-respect which would be added to them and the rest of the community, but all discussion would become more robust and real. If they had a larger faith in the stability for which they profess so great an anxiety, they would be more free alike in understanding and temper to deal generously, honestly, and effectively with those whom they count imprudent innovators.

John Morley, On Compromise (1874), pp. 206-64.

2. PARLIAMENTARY REFORM

67. RICHARD COBDEN: Speech at Rochdale, 18 August 1859

I would ask the middle class who have now got the franchise, whether they may not incur some difficulties and dangers themselves if they keep out of the electoral pale the vast majority of the community who have now no interest in the suffrage? The working class, and those who are not entitled now to vote, I believe amount to five millions of persons. Well, I say to those who have the vote, 'Take into partnership with you a portion of those who are now excluded from the right of voting, and do it, if you have no other motive, from the selfish motive of being secure in the possession of the power you have.' For your electoral system is standing now upon so narrow a foundation that it is hardly safe to reckon upon its standing at all in case of some certain contingencies arising, which we can imagine may some day arise. Why, what have we seen abroad? I remember quite well when Louis Philippe, the last king of France, was strongly urged by the reformers in France to double the electoral body in that country. They then had only about 250,000 voters. He was urged to double the number of votes. He refused; he continued to govern the country through this small minority of voters; and one evening when we were sitting in the House of Commons, the telegraph flashed the news from Paris that the Government of Louis Philippe had been overthrown, and a Republic proclaimed in its place. And I remember quite well when the buzz of the conversation ran round the House as this piece of news was passed from Member to Member, I remember saying to the late Mr. Joseph Hume, who sat beside me, 'Go across to Sir Robert Peel, and tell him the news.' Sir Robert Peel was sitting then just on the front seat on the other side of the House, having been repudiated by his large party, which he had lost by having previously repealed the Corn-laws. I remember Mr. Hume going and sitting by the side of Sir R. Peel, and whispering the news to him, and his immediate answer was this: 'This comes of trying to govern the country through a narrow representation in Parliament, without regarding the wishes of those outside. It is what this party behind me wanted me to do in the matter of the Corn-laws, and I would not do it.' . . .

Recollect that it is our boast that the people here do rule, and that they have ruled for centuries; and I say that, taking into account our great pretensions in regard to the freedom of the subject in this country, and comparing our present state, when we have but a million of voters, I declare that our state is less defensible than the case of Louis Philippe was in the time of which I speak, because, compared with our pretensions, our system of representation is no doubt an enormous sham; and there is no security in shams at any time, because they are very liable to be upset by any sudden reality such as that which occurred in the streets of Paris at the time of which I speak.

Well, but still we have the bugbear, that the working class of this country are not to be trusted with the franchise; the saying is that the people would injure themselves if you gave them the franchise; that they cannot take care of themselves. Now, in answer to that, I will put another question which has often occurred to me in my travels in distant countries: 'If the people are not fit to take care of themselves, who are to be trusted to take care of them?' That is the question which I have asked myself in many countries. I have asked it of myself where they are governed as they are in Russia, I have asked it where they are governed as they are in Austria, where they are ruled as they now are in France—I have asked myself this question: Where will you find a resting-place—how will you ever establish a system by which the people can be governed unless you come to this, that they must be left to govern themselves?

Speeches by Richard Cobden, M.P. (1870),
vol. ii, pp. 548-9.

68. JOHN BRIGHT: Speech at Rochdale, 3 February 1863

Now, the people of Europe owe much more than they are often aware of to the Constitution of the United States of America, and to the existence of that great Republic. The United States have been in point of fact an ark of refuge to the people of Europe, when fleeing from the storms and the revolutions of the old continent. They have been, as far as the artisans and labouring population of this country are concerned, a life-boat to them; and they have saved hundreds of thousands of men and of families from disastrous ship-wreck. The existence of that free country and that free government has had a prodigious influence upon freedom in Europe and in England. If you could have before you a chart of the condition of Europe when the United States became a nation, and another chart of the condition of Europe now, you would see the difference, the enormous stride which has been made in Europe; and you may rely upon it that not a little of it has been occasioned by the influence of the great example of that country, free in its political institutions beyond all other countries, and yet maintaining its course in peace, preserving order, and conferring upon all its people a degree of prosperity which in these old countries is as yet unknown.

I should like now to speak specially to the working men who are here, who have no capital but their skill and their industry and their bodily strength. In fifteen years from 1845 to 1860—and this is a fact which I stated in this room more than a year ago, when speaking on the question of America, but it is a fact which every working man ought to have in his mind always when he is considering what America is—in fifteen years there have emigrated to the United States from Great Britain and Ireland not less than two million four hundred thousand persons. Millions are easily spoken, not easily counted, with great difficulty comprehended; but the twenty-four hundred thousand persons that I have described means a population equal to not less than sixty towns, every one of them of the size and population of Rochdale. And every one of these men who have emigrated, as he crossed the Atlantic—if he went by steam, in a fortnight, and if he went by sail, in a month or five weeks—found himself in a country where to his senses a vast revolution had taken place, comprehending all that men anticipate from any kind of revolution that shall advance political and social equality in their own land—a revolution which commenced in the War of Independence, which has been going on, and which has been confirmed by all that has transpired in subsequent years.

He does not find that he belongs to what are called the 'lower classes'; he is not shut out from any of the rights of citizenship; he is admitted to the full enjoyment of all political privileges, as far as they are extended to any portion of the population; and he has there advantages which the people of this country have not yet gained, because we are but gradually making our way out of the darkness and the errors and the tyrannies of past ages. But in America he finds the land not cursed with feudalism; it is free to every man to buy and sell, and possess and transmit. He finds in the town in which he lives that the noblest buildings are the school-houses to which his children are freely admitted. And among those twenty millions—for I am now confining my observations to the Free States—the son of every man has easy admission to School, has fair opportunity for improvement; and, if God has gifted him with power of head and of heart, there is nothing of usefulness, nothing of greatness, nothing of success of that country to which he may not fairly aspire.

Speeches by John Bright, M.P., ed. by J. H. T. Rogers (1868), vol. i, pp. 230-1.

69. RICHARD COBDEN: Speech at Rochdale, 24 November 1863

It has been a fashion of late to talk of an extension of the franchise as something not to be tolerated, because it is assumed that the manners of the people were not fitted to take a part in the Government; and they point to America and France, and other places, and they draw comparisons between this country and other countries. Now, I hope I shall not be considered revolutionary—because at my age I don't want any revolutions—they won't serve me, I am sure, or anybody that belongs to me. England may perhaps compare very favourably with most other countries, if you draw the line in society tolerably high—if you compare the condition of the rich and the upper classes of this country, or a considerable portion of the middle classes, with the same classes abroad. . . .

I have been a great traveller—I have travelled in most civilised countries, and I assert that the masses of the people of this country do not compare so favourably with the masses of other countries as I could wish. I find in other countries a greater number of people with property than there are in England. I don't know, perhaps, any country in the world where the masses of the people are so illiterate as in England. It is no use your talking of your army and navy, your exports and your imports; it is no use telling me you have a small portion of your people exceedingly well off. I want to make the test in a comparison of the majority of the people against the majority in any other country. I say that with regard to some things in foreign countries we don't compare so favourably. The English peasantry has no parallel on the face of the earth. You have no other peasantry like that of England—you have no other country in which it is entirely divorced from the land. There is no other country of the world where you will not find men turning up the furrow in their own freehold. You won't find that in England.

I don't want any revolution or agrarian outrages by which we should change all this. But this I find to be quite consistent with human nature, that wherever I go the condition of the people is very generally found to be pretty good in comparison to the power they have to take care of themselves. And if you have a class entirely divorced from political power, and there is another country where they possess it, the latter will be treated with more consideration, they will have greater advantages, they will be better educated, and have a better chance of having property than in a country where they are deprived of the advantage of political power. But we must remember this: we have been thirty years—it is more than thirty years since our Reform Bill was passed; and during that time great changes have taken place in other countries. Nearly all your colonies since that time have received representative institutions. They are much freer in Australia and New Zealand, and much freer in their representative system than we are in England; and thirty years ago they were entirely under the domination of our Colonial Office. Well, go on the Continent, you find there wide extension of political franchises all over the country. Italy, and Austria even, is stirring its dry bones; you have all Germany now more or less invested with popular sovereignty; and I say, that, with all our boasted maxims of superiority as a self-governing people, we don't maintain our relative rank in the world, for we are all obliged to acknowledge that we dare not entrust a considerable part of the population of this country with political power, for fear they should make a revolutionary and dangerous use of it.

If you exclude to the present extent the masses of the people from the franchise, you are always running the risk of that which a very sagacious old Conservative statesman once said in the House of Commons. He said, 'I am afraid we shall have an ugly rush some day.' Well, I want to avoid that 'ugly rush.' I would rather do the work tranquilly, and do it gradually.

Speeches by Richard Cobden, M.P. (1870),
vol. ii, pp. 116-17.

70. JOHN BRIGHT: Speech at Birmingham, 18 January 1865

The Tories, and those Whigs who are like Tories, have an uncomfortable feeling which approaches almost to a shiver. What is this apparition which alarms them? . . . I will tell you what it is. They are afraid of the five or six millions of Englishmen, grown-up men who are allowed to marry, to keep house, to rear children, who are expected to earn their living, who pay taxes, who must obey the law, who must be citizens in all honourable conduct—they are afraid of the five or six millions who by the present system of representation are shut out, and insultingly shut out, from the commonest right of citizenship.

You know the boast we have of what takes place when negro-slaves land in England; you know what one of our best poets has said, that if their lungs but breathe our air, that moment they are free; they touch our country, and their shackles fall. But how is it with an Englishman? An Englishman, if he goes to the Cape, can vote; if he goes further, to Australia, to the nascent empires of the New World, he can vote; if he goes to the Canadian Confederation, he can vote; and if he goes to those grandest colonies of England not now dependent upon the English Crown, there . . . he can give his free and independent vote. It is only in his own country, on his own soil, where he was born, the very soil which he has enriched with his labour and with the sweat of his brow, that he is denied this right which in every other community of Englishmen in the world would be freely accorded to him.

This state of things I hold to be dangerous, and one that cannot last. It may happen, as it happened thirty years ago, that the eyes of the five millions all through the United Kingdom may be fixed with an intense glare upon the doors of Parliament; it was so in the years 1831–32. There are men in this room who felt then, and know now, that it required but an accident—but one spark to the train, and this country would have been in the throes of revolution; and these gentlemen who are so alarmed now lest a man who lives in a £10 house in a county, and a £6 house in a borough, should have a vote, would have repented in sack-cloth and ashes that they had ever said one word or given one vote against Lord Grey's Reform Bill. I say that accidents always are happening, not to individuals only, but to nations. It was the accident of the French Revolution of 1830 that preceded that great movement in this country. You may have accidents again, but I do not hold that to be states-manship which allows the security, the tranquillity, the loyalty of a people to be disturbed by any accident which they are able to control. If the five millions should once unitedly fix their eyes with an intense look upon the door of that House where my hon. Friend and I expect so soon to enter, I would ask who shall say them nay? . . . I say there is no power in this country, as opinion now stands, and as combination is now possible, there is no power in this country that can say 'Nay' for one single week to the five millions if they are intent upon making their way within the doors of Parliament.

But perhaps our friends who oppose us will say, 'We do not fear about elections and order. What we fear is this—the legislative results of this wide extension of the franchise.' I am ready to test it in any country by the results of legisla-tion. I say, whether you go to South Africa, or to Australia, or to the British North American provinces, or to the States of the American Union, you will find—excluding always those States where slavery injures the state of society—you will find that life and property are as secure, you will find that education is much more extended amongst the people, that there is quite as wide a provision for their religious interests, that the laws are as merciful and just, that taxes are imposed and levied with as great equality, and that the millions of your countrymen who are now established in those countries are at least as well off in all the circumstances of life as are the people of this country whom they have left behind them. I confess that I never yet heard of a man who returned to this country from any of those countries under the impression that he would be more secure here than he would be there.

But this, I suspect, is what they fear. I have sought a good deal into this question, and it seems to me as if they had a notion that in this country we have some institutions which have come down to us from the middle ages—from what some people call the dark ages—and that these institutions may not permanently harmonize with the intelligence and the necessities of the nineteenth century in which we live. The 'institutions' are truly safe enough if the Government be in the hands of the institution; and if the Peerage and the Established Church are to rule in England, then I presume that the Peerage and the Established Church, in their present condition, will be permanently safe; and if the great patronage of our vast expenditure is to be dispensed perpetually amongst the ruling class, the ruling class as a matter of course will take extreme care of the patronage. There is something very sacred in that patronage. There are many families in this country with long lines of ancestry, who, if patronage were curtailed, would feel very much as some of us feel in Lancashire when the American war has stopped our supplies of cotton. They look upon patronage as a holy thing, not to be touched by profane hands. I have no doubt they have in their minds the saying of a great friend of mine, though he is an imaginary character—I mean Hosea Bigelow, the author of the *Bigelow Papers*. He says—

'It is something like a fulfilling the prophecies,
    When all the first families have all the best offices.'

I would insist on this; since the power of the Crown was limited two hundred years ago, and since the power of the nobles was limited thirty years ago, good government has gained greatly in this country, and the people are in all circumstances better, and I am quite sure that the respect shown to the Crown is more general by far than it was at an earlier period. But our Constitution involves necessarily the representation of the people, and in calling for this representation we stand upon a foundation from which no argument and no sophistry can ever remove us. The House of Commons is in reality the only guarantee we have for freedom. If you looked at any other country, and saw nothing but a monarch, he might be a good king and might do his best, but you would see that there is no guarantee for freedom—you know not who will be his successor. If you saw a country with no Crown, but with a handful of nobles, administering the government of the country, you would say there is no guarantee there for freedom, because a number of individuals acting together have not the responsibility, or the feeling of responsibility, that one man has, and they do things which one man would not dare to do. If there be a man here who feels himself and his prejudices rise up against the statements I am making, he, at least, will admit that the real and only permanent foundation for political freedom in any country is in the establishment and maintenance of a system of political representation—in your Houses of Parliament.

These gentlemen do not comprehend our Constitution at all. They do not know, apparently, that it is only because there is something which the people still believe to be in some degree a representative body, and which stands between them and monarchical and aristocratic despotism—that it is only the existence of that House which makes the institution they are so fond of safe and permanent at all—and they are afraid that the five millions somehow or other will get into it. Now, I beg to tell them that the five millions will get into it, though they may not get into it all at once; and perhaps few men desire that they should, for I am opposed myself to great and violent changes, which create needless shocks, and which are accepted, if they are accepted, with great alarm.

But I will undertake to say that some portion, a considerable and effective portion, of those five millions will before many years are passed be freely allowed to vote for Members of the House of Commons. It is not the democracy which these gentlemen are always afraid of that is the peril of this country. It was not democracy in 1832 that was the peril. It was the desperate antagonism of the class that then had power to the just claims and rights of the people. And at this moment, when they dine and when I speak, I tell them that Conservatism—they give it that name, but it is worthy of a very different name—that Conservatism, be it Tory or be it Whig, is the true national peril which we have to face. They may dam the stream, they may keep back the waters, but the volume is ever increasing, and it descends with accelerated force, and the time will come when, in all probability, and to a certainty, if wisdom does not take the place of folly, the waters will burst their banks, and these men, who fancy they are stemming this imaginary apparition of democracy, will be swept away by the resolute will of a united and determined people.

Speeches by John Bright, M.P., ed. by J. H. T.
Rogers (1868), vol. ii, pp. 104-29.

71. W. E. GLADSTONE: Speech at Chester, 31 May 1865

And what do I understand by the Liberal principle? I understand, in the main, it is a principle of trust in the people only qualified by prudence. By the principle which is opposed to the Liberal principle, I understand mistrust of the people, only qualified by fear. . . .

Now we are in this singular predicament. I believe that a smaller portion of working men enjoy the franchise now than enjoyed it thirty years ago, after the Reform Bill was passed. But if the electors of the working class have diminished, what has happened to the working class itself? Has the working class diminished? No, it has increased. Has the condition of the working class deteriorated? No, it is amended. Is the education of the people worse? No, it is infinitely extended and improved. Is the loyalty of the working class more doubtful? No, . . . Yet one word more: has the character of the working class been specially tested in that interval? Yes, it was tried in the fire of affliction—in that fire of affliction which wasted Lancashire, when, in a day, the subsistence and employment of a people were swept away, and yet public order was secure, the laws were revered, respect was paid to every more fortunate class, want was endured with silence, patience, and heroic fortitude. I must say that proofs of competency such as those ought to have some influence on the spirit of privileged classes, and to induce them, not as a matter of conflict and controversy, not from a regard for abstract theory, but upon grounds the most strictly practical, and with a view of strengthening the laws and institutions of the country, to make some sensible, ay, some liberal, though some safe extension of the franchise.

W. E. Gladstone, *Speeches and Addresses delivered at the Election of 1865*, pp. 47-9.

72. W. E. GLADSTONE: Speech at Manchester, 18 July 1865

[This is the speech in which Gladstone said: 'At last my friends I am come amongst you. And I am come among you unmuzzled.']

Promises have been recorded in the face of the English people, which promises either ought not to have been made, or else ought to have been redeemed; and if such promises remain over long in suspense, if after being profusely tendered in times when it was politically convenient, they are cast aside when it appears to be safe to make short work with them, the inevitable consequence is, I will not indeed say discontent and disaffection in the mass of the community, but certainly loss of credit, loss of dignity, loss of confidence in the powers and institutions of the country. . . . In 1832 was passed a Reform Bill. Since that time what has happened? The fitness of the labouring class for the franchise has increased; the proportion which the labouring class enfranchised bears to the rest of the community I greatly fear has diminished. . . . Gentlemen, I have ever been, and I still

am, opposed to every sudden and to every violent change.
. . . But this I say, that the true and just balance of the
powers of the constitution would be, not destroyed, but
improved, by a fair, and liberal, and sensible, though not a
sweeping, nor an overwhelming, admission of our brethen
of the labouring community to the privilege of the suffrage.
And I must say I could heartily wish that it might still be
possible to keep this question out of the vortex of party
politics. . . . As far as I am concerned, I have ever desired
to have it treated calmly, impartially, upon social grounds,
upon a rational view of the characters of our fellow countrymen, upon a calm estimate of the experience we have had
of them; an estimate which shall not omit to take into view,
as it deserves, their conduct during the difficulties of the
last few years. I should earnestly desire to see an extension
of the franchise, not wrung, not extorted, as it was in 1832,
at the cost almost, at the hazard certainly, of something
like revolution, but given freely, generously, spontaneously;
given in that way which excites confidence and gratitude,
instead of engendering something, perhaps even much, of
resentment, or even disaffection.

Ibid. pp. 13-15.

73. W. E. GLADSTONE: Speech in the House of Commons, 27 April 1866

I am justified, then, in stating that the working classes
are not adequately represented in this House. They are
not, it is admitted, represented in any proportion to their
numbers . . . They are not represented, as I have previously
shown, in accordance with their share of the income of the
country. Especially after the events of the last few years, I
may boldly proceed to say they are not represented in
proportion to their intelligence, their virtue, or their loyalty.
Finally, they are less represented now than they were
thirty-six years ago, when they were less competent to
exercise the franchise. . . . If these are not good reasons
for extending the suffrage at the present, I know not what
reason can be good. But if hon. Members think they can

hold their ground in a policy of resistance and refusal for the present, I have to ask them, how do they regard the future? My right hon. friend the Member for Calne has prophesied to us, in the most emphatic terms, the ruin of the British Constitution. His prophecies were beautiful so far as his masterly use of the English language is concerned. But many prophecies quite as good may be found in the pages of Mr. Burke and Mr. Canning, and other almost equally distinguished men. What has been the fate of these prophecies? What use do they now serve? They form admirable material of declamations for schoolboys, and capital exercises to be translated into Greek.

My hon. friend says we know nothing about the labouring classes. Is not one single word a sufficient reply? That word is Lancashire; Lancashire, associated with the sufferings of the last four years, so painful and bitter in themselves to contemplate, but so nobly and gloriously borne? The qualities then exhibited were the qualities not of select men here and there among a depraved multitude, but of the mass of a working community. The sufferings were sufferings of the mass. The heroism was heroism of the mass. For my own part, I cannot believe that the men who exhibited those qualities were only a sample of the people of England, and that the rest would have wholly failed in exhibiting the same great qualities had occasion arisen. I cannot see what argument could be found for some wise and temperate experiment of the extension of civil rights among such people, if the experience of the past few years does not sufficiently afford it.

And now, Sir, let us for a moment consider the enormous and silent changes which have been going forward among the labouring population. May I use the words to hon. and right hon. gentlemen once used by way of exhortation by Sir Robert Peel to his opponents, 'elevate your vision'? Let us try and raise our views above the fears, the suspicions, the jealousies, the reproaches, and the recriminations of this place and this occasion. Let us look onward to the time of our children and of our children's children. Let us know what preparation it behoves us should be made for that coming time. Is there or is there not, I ask, a steady movement of the labouring classes, and is or is not that movement a movement onwards and upwards? I do not say that it falls beneath the eye, for, like all great processes, it is unobservable in detail, but as solid and undeniable as it is resistless in its essential character. It is like those movements of the crust of the earth which science tells us are even now going on in certain portions of the globe. The sailor courses over them in his vessel, and the traveller by land treads them without being conscious of these changes; but from day to day, from hour to hour, the heaving forces are at work, and after a season we discern from actual experience that things are not as they were. Has my right hon. friend, in whom mistrust rises to its utmost height, ever really considered the astonishing phenomena connected with some portion of the conduct of the labouring classes, especially in the Lancashire distress? Has he considered what an amount of self-denial was exhibited by these men in respect to the American war? They knew that the source of their distress lay in the war, yet they never uttered or entertained the wish that any effort should be made to put an end to it, as they held it to be a war for justice and for freedom. Could any man have believed that a conviction so still, so calm, so firm, so energetic, could have planted itself in the minds of a population without becoming a known patent fact throughout the whole country? But we knew nothing of it. And yet when the day of trial came we saw that noble sympathy on their part with the people of the North; that determination that, be their sufferings what they might, no word should proceed from them that would hurt a cause which they so firmly believed to be just. On one side there was a magnificent moral spectacle; on the other side was there not also a great lesson to us all, to teach us that in those little tutored, but yet reflective minds, by a process of quiet instillation, opinions and sentiments gradually form themselves of which we for a long time remain unaware, but which, when at last they make their appearance, are found to be deep-rooted, mature and ineradicable?

Gladstone's Speeches ed. by A. Tilney Bassett (1916), pp. 374-6.

74. JOHN BRIGHT: Speech at Glasgow, 16 October 1866

With the Parliament which we have now and have had, facts and arguments go for very little. Take that question to which I have referred, of limiting the supply of bread to the people. The Corn-law was on the Statute-book for thirty-one years—sixteen years before the Reform Bill, and fifteen years after the passing of that Bill—but from the first hour of its enactment until the hour of its destruction the facts and the arguments against it were equally clear and equally conclusive. They would not be convinced though one arose from the dead, and that which convinced them at last was the occurrence of a great famine in Ireland, which destroyed or drove from the country hundreds of thousands of the citizens of the empire. I maintain with the most perfect conviction that the House of Commons, representing as it now does counties and boroughs such as I have described, does not represent the intelligence and the justice of the nation, but the prejudices, the privileges, and the selfishness of a class.

Your Address refers to pauperism—the gulf of pauperism. In the United Kingdom at this moment there are more than 1,200,000 paupers. . . . Now look, I beg of you, to this mass of misery. It is so great a mass that benevolence cannot reach it. . . .

Benevolence can touch scarcely the fringe of this vast disorder. There is another virtue we could add, and that virtue and that quality is justice. It is not benevolence but justice that can deal with giant evils. It was not benevolence that gave the people bread twenty years ago, but it was justice embodied in the abolition of a cruel and guilty law. But justice is impossible from a class. It is most certain and easy from a nation; and I believe we can only reach the depths of ignorance and misery and crime in this country by an appeal to the justice, the intelligence, and the virtues of the entire people.

I am of opinion that the rich people of a country, invested with power, and speaking generally for rich people alone, cannot sufficiently care for the multitude and the poor. They are personally kind enough, but they do not care for the people in the bulk. . . . They imagine that it is a providential arrangement that a small section of the people should be rich and powerful, and that the great mass of the people should be hardworking and poor. It is a long distance from castles, and mansions, and great houses, and abounding luxuries, to the condition of the great mass of the people who have no property, and too many of whom are always on the verge of poverty. We know very well all of us how much we are influenced by the immediate circumstances by which we are surrounded. The rich find everything just as they like. The country needs no Reform. There is no other country in the world so pleasant for rich people as this country. But I deny altogether that the rich alone are qualified to legislate for the poor, any more than the poor alone would be qualified to legislate for the rich. My honest belief is, that if we could be all called upon to legislate for all, that all would be more justly treated, and would be more happy than we are now. We should have then an average; we should have the influence of wealth and of high culture, and of those qualities that come from leisure, and the influence of those more robust qualities that come from industry and from labour.

Suppose now, without arguing for this or that particular measure of Reform, that we could add another million to the existing constituencies, what would be the result? We should modify the constituencies. Instead of the people coming to the hustings at the nomination and holding up their hands for this candidate or that, and having for the most part no power in the election, the inhabitants of the town would have a much greater power than they have now. The constituency would be less open to management than it is at present; majorities on one side or the other would be larger and less open to corruption; and we should have Members whose opinions and whose conduct would be modified by this infusion of new and fresh blood into the constituencies which send them to Parliament. We should do this further—we should bring the rich and the great more into contact with the people, and into a better acquaintance with human wants and with the necessities and feelings of their countrymen. . . . And if there was more knowledge of the people, there would assuredly be more sympathy with them; and I believe the legislation of the House, being more in accordance with the public sentiment, would be wiser and better in every respect.

Speeches by John Bright, M.P., ed. by J. H. T. Rogers (1868), vol. ii, pp. 203-11.

75. JOHN BRIGHT: Speech to the Members of various Trades' Unions and Trade Societies in St. James's Hall, London, 4 December 1866

It is about eight years since, in a speech which I delivered on the question of Parliamentary Reform, that I took the opportunity of giving what I thought was somewhat wholesome counsel to the unenfranchised working-men of this country. I told them that the monopolists of political power in this country would not willingly surrender that power or any portion of it; and further, that no class which was excluded could rely upon the generosity of any other class for that justice which it could demand, and that, therefore, although large numbers of the middle class were then, and are now, in favour of the enfranchisement of a large number of the working class, yet that they would not make that great effort which is necessary to wring political power from those who now hold it, and to extend it to those who are now and were then excluded from it. I said that if the working-men wished for political power they had only to ask for it in a manner to show the universality of their desire, and the union and the power which they were able to bear upon it; and I recollect particularly making a suggestion that involved me in a good deal of unfriendly criticism, namely, that I thought the time had come, or would soon come, when it would be the duty of the working class to make use of that great organisation of theirs which extends over the whole country—the organisation of trades' and friendly societies— for the purpose of bringing to bear upon the Government the entire power of their just demand. I said, further, that I

believed one year only of the united action of the working
class through this existing organisation would wholly change
the aspect of the question of Reform.

But these critics of ours say that this measure—the
combination of trades' unions for political purposes—is one
that excites their fears, and is of a very formidable nature.
It was precisely because it would be of a formidable nature
that I first recommended it. . . .

But if these associations and the combinations of these
societies are formidable, who have made them formidable?
These societies took no part in political movements until
they were challenged to it by the speeches, the resolutions,
the divisions, and the acts of a great party in the Parliament
of the kingdom. Did they fail to have fact and argument in
favour of the change proposed last session? No; but fact and
argument had no effect upon whatever there is of reasoning
power in the ranks of the Tory party. Did they think that
the working-men of this country—who built this great city
—who have covered the country with great cities—who
have cultivated every acre of its cultivated area—who have
made this country a name of power through all time and
throughout the whole world—did they for one moment
imagine that you would lie down and submit, without
raising your voice against them, to the scandalous and unjust
imputations that were heaped upon you? Did they think
that you would be silent for ever, and patient for ever, under
a perpetual exclusion from the benefits of the constitution of
your country? If they are dissatisfied with this movement,
what would they have? Would they wish that, as men did
fifty or sixty years ago, instead of making open demonstration of your opinions, you should conspire with the view of
changing the political constitution of your country? . . .

But surely one of two modes must be taken. If there be a
deep and widespread sentiment, that injustice is no longer
tolerable, than, judging from all past history of all people,
one of two modes will be taken, either that mode so sad and
so odious of secret conspiracy, or that mode so grand and so
noble which you have adopted. . . .

Now, I have said before—I repeat it again—that there is
no security whatsoever for liberty under any government

unless there be an essential power in a fair representation of the nation. An illustrious man, the founder of the great province, and now the great State of Pennsylvania— William Penn—in the preface to his Constitution for that province—a Constitution of the widest and most generous freedom—uses these words:—'Any government is free to the people under it, whatever be the frame, where the laws rule, and the people are a party to the laws; and more than this is tyranny, oligarchy, or confusion.' Now, let us ask ourselves, can it be fairly said, can it be said without the most direct falsehood, that the people of this country, through the House of Commons, are really a party to the laws that are made? It is not at all disputed that only sixteen out of every hundred men are now on the electoral rolls, and are able, all other circumstances favouring, to give their vote at a general election; and it is not disputed that half the House of Commons—that an absolute majority of that House —is elected by a number of electors not exceeding altogether three men out of every hundred in the United Kingdom. . . .

These opponents of ours, many of them in Parliament openly, and many of them secretly in the press, have charged us with being the promoters of a dangerous excitement. They say we are the source of the danger which threatens. . . . If I speak to the people of their rights, and indicate to them the way to secure them—if I speak of their danger to the monopolists of power—am I not a wise counsellor, both to the people and to their rulers? Suppose I stood at the foot of Vesuvius or Etna, and seeing a hamlet or a homestead planted on its slope, I said to the dwellers in that hamlet or in the homestead, You see that vapour which ascends from the summit of the mountain. That vapour may become a dense, black smoke that will obscure the sky. You see that trickling of lava from the crevices or fissures in the side of the mountain. That trickling of lava may become a river of fire. You hear that muttering in the bowels of the mountain. That muttering may become a bellowing thunder, the voice of a violent convulsion that may shake half a continent. You know that at your feet is the grave of great cities for which there is no resurrection, as history tells us that dynasties and aristocracies have passed away and their name has been known no more for ever. If I say this to the dwellers upon the slope of the mountain, and if there comes hereafter a catastrophe which makes the world to shudder, am I responsible for that catastrophe? I did not build the mountain, or fill it with explosive materials. I merely warned the men that were in danger.

So, now, it is not I who am stimulating men to the violent pursuit of their acknowledged constitutional rights. We are merely about our lawful business—and you are the citizens of a country that calls itself free, yet you are citizens to whom is denied the greatest and the first blessing of the constitution under which you live. If the truth must be told, the Tory party is the turbulent party of this nation.

Ibid. pp. 228-41.

3. FOREIGN POLICY

76. W. E. GLADSTONE: Speech in the House of Commons, 7 May 1877

Sir, there is before us not one controversy, but two. There is the controversy between Russia and Turkey; there is the controversy between Turkey and her revolted subjects. I think the Government and their supporters out-of-doors in the Press are committing a great error in this—that it is the first of these two controversies—that between Russia and Turkey, which, after all, is only symptomatic—to which they address their minds. In my opinion, the other is the deeper and more important. The other is a controversy which can have no issue but one, and I do not hesitate to say that the cause of the revolted subjects of Turkey against their oppressors is as holy a cause as ever animated the breast, or as ever stirred the hand of man. Sir, what part are we to play in regard to it? . . .

Sir, there were other days, when England was the hope of freedom. Wherever in the world a high aspiration was entertained, or a noble blow was struck, it was to England that the eyes of the oppressed were always turned—to this favourite, this darling home of so much privilege and so much happiness, where the people that had built up a noble edifice for themselves would, it was well known, be ready to do what in them lay to secure the benefit of the same inestimable boon for others. You talk to me of the established tradition and policy in regard to Turkey. I appeal to an established tradition, older, wiser, nobler far—a tradition not which disregards British interests, but which teaches you to seek the promotion of those interests in obeying the dictates of honour and of justice. And, Sir, what is to be the end of this? Are we to dress up the fantastic ideas some people entertain about this policy, and that policy in the garb of British interests, and then, with a new and base idolatry, to fall down and worship them? Or are we to look, not at the sentiment, but at the hard facts of the case, which Lord Derby told us fifteen years ago—namely, that it is the populations of those countries that will ultimately possess them—that will ultimately determine their abiding condition? It is to this fact, this law, that we should look.

Gladstone's Speeches, ed. A. Tilney Bassett (1916), pp. 582-3.

77. W. E. GLADSTONE: Speech in the House of Commons, 30 July 1878

The doctrine of the Government is that something was to be done. But something was done. The Sultan was already under obligations to Europe to execute reforms in Asiatic Turkey by the Treaty of 1856. If we wished to give effect to that obligation, why did not we invoke the authority of Europe? Is it not higher and stronger than ours? Do we mean to set up our own authority as greater than that of Europe? Do you think that we have a monopoly of humanity? Has our conduct, with regard to Turkey, been such as to show that the care of the subject-populations has been our interest alone, or has been more studiously propagated by us than by other Powers of Christendom? Do you think that intervention in the Sultan's affairs is prejudicial and unwise when it is attempted by others, but beneficent and wise when done by you single-handed? Now, suppose that the Sultan had made an agreement with Russia, to do, in a certain portion of his territory, that which he has agreed with you to do in far the larger part of it. Suppose a Russian Minister had said—'We are going to reform the Judicature, the police, the finances, the Civil Service of Turkey, and stop the progress of corruption in Constantinople.' Would you have commended Russia for taking that course? Would you have allowed Russia to take that course? No, nor yet to do a tenth part of what you have done. You would have inflamed the country and called out your Reserves, and adopted your military measures. Sir, the whole tendency of what Her Majesty's Government has done is to establish one law for others, and another for themselves. . . .

[After discussing the methods by which the Government had secured Cyprus from the Turkish Government, Mr. Gladstone concluded:]

This to my mind, Sir, is a most serious matter. I think we have lost greatly by the conclusion of this [Cyprus] Convention; I think we have lost very greatly indeed the sympathy and respect of the nations of Europe. I do not expect or believe that we shall fall into that sort of contempt which follows upon weakness. I think it to be one of the most threadbare of all the weapons of Party warfare when we hear, as we sometimes hear, on the accession of a new Government, that before its accession the Government had been despised all over the world, and that now, on the contrary, she has risen in the general estimation, and holds her proper place in the Councils of Nations. This England of ours is not so poor and so weak a thing as to depend upon the reputation of this or that Administration; and the world knows pretty well of what stuff she is made. I am not quite sure, however, that the world has the same clear and strong conviction with respect to the standard of our moral action as it has with respect to the standard of our material strength. Now, I am desirous that the standard of our material strength shall be highly and justly estimated by the other nations of Christendom; but I believe it to be of still more vital consequence that we should stand high in their estimation as the lovers of truth, of honour, and of openness in all our proceedings, as those who know how to cast aside the motives of a narrow selfishness, and give scope to considerations of broad and lofty principle. I value our insular position, but I dread the day when we shall be reduced to a moral insularity. I desire that sympathy should be cherished with every country, be its name what it may; and I fear that the conclusion of this Convention will be injurious to the action of that sympathy. The proceedings have all along been associated with a profession as to certain British interests, which although I believe them to be perfectly fictitious and imaginary, have yet been pursued with as much zeal and eagerness, as if they had been the most vital realities in the world. This setting up of our interests, out of place, in an exaggerated form, beyond their proper sphere, and not merely the setting up of such interests, but the mode in which they have been pursued has greatly diminished, not, as I have said, the regard for our material strength, but the estimation of our moral standard of action, and consequently our moral position in the world. If that be so, Sir, with respect to Foreign countries, with respect to Parliament, I believe the case to be graver still.

Ibid. pp. 536-7 and 549-50.

78. W. E. GLADSTONE: Speech at the Foresters' Hall, Dalkeith, 26 November 1879

[This speech and Nos. 79 and 80 were all delivered during Gladstone's Midlothian election campaign of 1879–80.]

Go from South Africa to the mountains of Central Asia. Go into the lofty hills of Afghanistan, as they were last winter, and what do we there see? I fear a yet sadder sight than was to be seen in the land of the Zulus. . . . You have seen during last winter from time to time that from such and such a village attacks had been made upon the British forces, and that in consequence the village had been burned. Have you ever reflected on the meaning of those words? . . . Those hill tribes had committed no real offence against us. We, in the pursuit of our political objects, chose to establish military positions in their country. If they resisted, would not you have done the same? And when, going forth from their villages they had resisted, what you find is this, that those who went forth were slain, and that the village was burned. Again, I say, have you considered the meaning of these words? The meaning of the burning of the village is, that the women and the children were driven forth to perish in the snows of winter. Is not that a terrible supposition? Is not that a fact which . . . rouses in you a sentiment of horror and grief, to think that the name of England, under no political necessity, but for a war as frivolous as ever was waged in the history of man, should be associated with consequences such as these? . . .

Remember the rights of the savage, as we call him. Remember that the happiness of his humble home, remember that the sanctity of life in the hill villages of Afghanistan among the winter snows, is as inviolable in the eye of Almighty God as can be your own. Remember that He who has united you together as human beings in the same flesh and blood has bound you by the law of mutual love; that that mutual love is not limited by the shores of this island, is not limited by the boundaries of Christian civilisation; that it passes over the whole surface of the earth, and embraces the meanest along with the greatest in its unmeasured scope.

Political Speeches in Scotland, November and December 1879, by W. E. Gladstone (Rev. edn., Edinburgh, 1880), pp. 91-4.

79. W. E. GLADSTONE: Speech at Penicuik, 25 March 1880

It is said by Admiral Martin, and very truly, that there is no doubt, under the British Government, the material condition of the inhabitants of Cyprus will be decidedly improved. I have no doubt of that whatever; but experience shows us that mankind are not governed solely by what relates to their material condition. . . . We became in 1815 protectors—Gt. Britain acquired the protectorate of the Ionian Islands. We did much good in these islands. We improved the roads; we improved the police; we promoted equal laws; we favoured religious toleration. We did many things that were right, but yet the people said to us: 'This may be all very well; but we are Greeks and we want to be united to the people of our own blood.' And therefore, instead of gratitude and attachment, a condition of things most disgraceful and painful arose in the Ionian Islands; and in the Ionian Islands this shameful power of banishing men without trial, for any cause approved by the head of the British Government, was unfortunately, to our great disgrace, very long in use. It was abandoned a short time before we gave up the Protectorate, but what I want to point out to you is, that these national affinities inspire feelings which are part of our nature, which are a good and an honourable part of our nature—that it is natural, legitimate and right for people of a given race to be associated with their brethren of that race. . . .

Now the bulk of the people of Cyprus are Greeks—and rely upon it that if matters continue as they are, Greek sympathies, with the opening and extending emancipation of the East of Europe—Greek sympathies will prevail in the island; and instead of earning, even by the benefits you may confer on them, gratitude and attachment in the form of a disposition to continue in political connection with you, the more you improve their condition the quicker will be the development of this strong sentiment of nationality, and the more earnest the desire of the Greeks of Cyprus to be united with the free Greeks of the rest of the world. . . .

I asked you what you thought of the quality of mercy. . . . General Roberts has sent home an account of the Afghans whom he has executed, and I find among these Afghans that some were executed for the offence of inciting their fellow-countrymen to resist; they are not merely slain in action, but they are executed for that offence. I am not going to censure General Roberts. Such is the necessity of his position that I will not take into my hands the office of judging him. But I say, is not this monstrous, that we should place ourselves in such a position that when the Afghan discharges the first duty of a patriot—namely to endeavour to bring his countrymen to resist the foreign invader—that is to be treated as a sin, and is to be visited, not merely by the chances of war, but by an ignominious death, even after resistance has ceased?

I know not, I cannot answer for the interior of other men's minds, but I have striven and will strive to lay these things before you as I see them, and I will close by saying, what was the profession with which the Government entered this war? They said that they wished to have an Afghanistan independent, strong and friendly. As to the independence of Afghanistan, Afghanistan has forfeited, by treaty extorted by necessity from its ruler, all independence; for the whole of its foreign relations are given over into the hands of England. As to its strength, it was a country, it was a nation, it was a unity: it is now a chaos. One sovereign has been driven out of it, to perish by disease and anxiety: another sovereign is a prisoner in our hands; and there is no ruler from one end of the land to the other that can call it his own. So much for the strength of Afghanistan that you said you desired; so much for the independence of Afghanistan that the Ministers said they would secure. As to the friendliness of Afghanistan, carry away with you from this room, this night, the recollection of the burning words of General Roberts, that every Afghan regards with natural hatred the foreign invader of his native land.

Ibid. pp. 287-96.

80. W. E. GLADSTONE: Speech at Loanhead, 22 March 1880

[In this speech Gladstone sets out the policy which he believes ought to have been followed in the Eastern Crisis of 1875-8.]

The Powers of Europe in the course of 1876 had shown a great and general desire to meet the necessities of the case in the East, to stop the excesses and abuses which had led to the rebellions in Bosnia and Herzegovina, and to take effectual securities against the repetition of those horrors which have covered with everlasting infamy the name of the Turks in Bulgaria. . . . Now, what I presumed at that time to teach was this, that what is called autonomy—self-government, practical self-government—ought to be given to those provinces. . . . The Sultan might have remained as the head of the Empire containing these provinces. He might have received from them by arrangement, effected under the sanction of Europe, most liberal contributions towards the expenses of his Government; but the essential part of it was this, that the people should have, not the management of the affairs of the Turkish Empire, but the management of their own local affairs. . . .

Local self-government was what was asked for these provinces. It was not the first time it had been conferred in the Turkish Empire. What were called the Danubian Principalities and, again, the Principality of Servia, had earned this privilege for themselves, and had prospered, thriven under it—given no trouble to Europe, had become the seat of contentment and tranquillity simply by the granting of this concession. We contended that if Europe—united Europe—told Turkey you must act up to this point; you must give to Bulgaria, to Bosnia, to Herzegovina what you have given to Servia, what you have given to Roumania, that the Turk would have done it. . . . And never were the means of peaceful and bloodless coercion so fully and indisputably in the hands of any Power, as were then in the hands of the European Powers applicable against Turkey, had Turkey been obstinately determined to persist.

Turkey would undoubtedly have lost the power of appointing pashas and governors and policemen in those three provinces. Instead of perpetuating danger, bloodshed, disquiet and disgrace, she would have had peaceful relations with them. Ceasing to suffer from her, they would have ceased to entertain hostile sentiments to her, and, in fact, although giving up a portion of the despotic power which she might abuse, she would have retained all that was valuable to her, and would have made the populations of those provinces feel that to be under the Sultan was to give them a kind of shelter for the growth of their local and practical liberties. . . . What would have been the conse-quence of that policy as far as Russia was concerned? Simply this, that Russia would have acted as one of the six Powers of Europe; that, great as would have been the boon conceded to the populations of the three provinces, they would have received that boon from the hands of the

Powers without distinction. Whatever gratitude they felt, whatever sentiments of dependence might be in them, would have been a sentiment directing itself towards those six Powers alike. Russia, as Russia, would have gained nothing by the transaction; Turkey, as Turkey, would have avoided the terrible loss she has incurred.

Now, let us recollect what happened. This policy which I have described was discarded with contempt as a visionary scheme invented by the enemies of Turkey, and so the 'friends of Turkey' got the upper hand, and what did the 'friends of Turkey' do? They stood by and they encouraged her by side-long representations given by our ambassadors in Constantinople, encouraged her to rush into that terrible war with Russia. The friends of Turkey, as they called themselves, had the upper hand, and what have they done for her, what are the proofs of friendship they have left her? Why, they have left her mangled and mutilated, invaded on every side, with the Powers of Europe now all entitled to interfere in the concerns of Turkey. They have left her deprived of all those three provinces that I have described—that is to say, deprived of what would have been taken from her under the other policy. Seven millions of people in Roumania, and in Servia, and in Montenegro, over whom she claimed sovereignty, are completely separated from her. That is one of the results the friends of Turkey brought about for her. . .

But I have still to draw your attention to the other subject—the aggrandizement of Russia. Now, recollect that if the Powers in 1876 had acted together, and had together obtained from Turkey certain boons for the inhabitants of those three provinces, by which the concessions of Turkey would have been limited, the boon would have been given by the six Powers of Europe, not by one of them in particular. But that concert of Europe was broken up, and Russia found herself in the condition of considering whether she should make solitary war upon Turkey or not. It is not for me to decide whether Russia was right or wrong in making that war. I wish to point out to you that by the result of that war Russia has obtained a great aggrandizement. . . . In the first place, she has so completely conquered the military power of Turkey that it is hardly possible, in the nature of things, that Turkey should ever make another serious military struggle against her. In the second place, Russia has obtained military fame by that war, the amount of which no man can reasonably undervalue. . . . But that was not all. We have also given her territory. Russia has got territory now that she did not possess in 1876—territory which has brought her again to the bank of the Danube—it having from the first been one of the main objects of the Crimean War to drive her back from the bank of the Danube. . . .

I ask, to whom is due that aggrandizement? I ask, is it due to the men who in 1876 wanted to settle this Turkish question without giving to Russia any opportunity of acquiring upon any pretence one inch of territory; or is it due to the men who rejected that settlement? . . . The port of Batoum in the Black Sea, the fortress of Kars in Armenia, other fortresses in Armenia and a considerable portion of Armenia were in the same manner secured to Russia as the results of this war, which we left to Russia the opportunity to make because we refused to act in concert with the rest of the Powers of Europe in telling Turkey what she must do. . . .

Now in my opinion it is quite right that we should regard Russia in the East and toward the Black Sea with jealousy; because I am quite sure that if England were in that position we should have great inclination to extend ourselves southwards; therefore I think it possible that the Russians may have a similar disposition. Now I am myself deeply anxious to check that extension by legitimate means—not by violence, but by legitimate means. In my opinion, there is one means of checking it which is legitimate, and which is effectual: and that is, to grant to the inhabitants of these provinces what the Roumanians and the Servians have now got, and what I admit Bulgaria has now got practically—power of self-government; under which, instead of holding life, liberty, property and everything that is valuable upon earth at the mercy of a lawless superior, they might have the means of securing for themselves the blessing of law and order, and passing their lives in peaceful industry. If you do that, that is the true way to exclude Russia. If you give those people freedom and the benefits of freedom—the peace, the order, the prosperity that follow upon freedom—that is the way to make a barrier against despotism. Fortresses may be levelled to the ground; treaties may be trodden under foot—the true barrier against despotism is in the human heart and in the human mind. Give to people that inestimable boon of the reasonable liberties which will enable them to secure the main purposes of life, then you may trust them to defend those liberties; and in those people you will have a far more effectual ally against the aggressive tendencies of Russia, of Austria, or of anybody else, than in all the treaties and all the fortresses of the world. But what have we done? We left those people to their fate. After the horrors that were enacted in Bulgaria, we allowed the Bulgarians to understand that we were willing to write on their behalf any number of idle remonstrances, but that to use the peremptory language which united Europe was justified in using was a course we could not join in, and on the contrary, that we disapproved of it. That being so, we left to Russia the place of the deliverer. Russia stepped into that place, and by stepping into it, achieved, at great cost to herself, the deliverance of those provinces; and, you cannot conceal it from yourselves, she has won the affections of those provinces. The name of our free country has become odious in those provinces. . . . And then those who have done it are not ashamed to cast upon their opponents, whose policy would entirely have prevented it, the charge of aggrandizing the Russians. . . .

(The Prince Consort wrote) in 1860, at a time when great uneasiness had been excited with respect to France on account of her plans for the annexation of Savoy: 'I cannot, however, say that any other Power is trusted, or that they mutually trust each other; and this will continue to be the case so long as no common accord is established, and that is only to be achieved under the guidance and fostering care of England.' Those words of the Prince Consort are, in my judgment, most true and most wise words. Their substance consists in these two principles—first of all, that our main hope for putting down disturbances, aggrandize-ments and selfish schemes in Europe depends upon maintaining the 'common accord' or what is commonly called the concert of Europe; and, secondly, that the high office of bringing Europe into concert, and keeping Europe in concert, is an office specially pointed out for our country to perform. But why is it pointed out for our country to perform—why is it that we should hope so far to disarm jealousy, so far to inspire confidence into the general mind of Europe, as to induce the inhabitants and Governments of the various European countries to accord to us a kind of moral leadership? Why are they to accord to us that advantage? Gentlemen, they never will accord to us that advantage until they see that we are free from selfish aims in Europe—including the Mediterranean. . . . The happy conditions in which we live as an island, large enough for power, but safe from territorial contact with those States, and therefore under no fear of suffering mischief from them, and tempted by no hopes to do them mischief—that happy condition, so long as we are believed to be disinterested in Europe, secures for us the noblest part that any Power was ever called upon to play. . . . But how can that part be performed by a Power which pursues selfish aims in the dark? . . . These are selfish aims, and the Power that entertains and prosecutes these aims must forever renounce and forswear all hope of rising to the noble function that the Prince Consort pointed out—the bringing about the 'common accord' of Europe, embodying in one organ the voice of civilised mankind in the actings and fostering care of England.

Ibid. pp. 210-22.

81. W. E. GLADSTONE: *England's Mission* (*The Nineteenth Century*, September 1878)

The honour to which recent British policy is entitled is this: that from the beginning of the Congress to the end, the representatives of England, instead of taking the side of freedom, emancipation and national progress, took . . . the side of servitude, of reaction and of barbarism. With a zeal worthy of a better cause, they laboured to reduce the limits within which the populations of European Turkey are to be masters of their own destinies; to keep as much as they could of direct Turkish rule; and to enfeeble as much as they could the limitations upon that rule. Nor was this only to restrain or counterwork the influence of Russia. For, upon the record, they have done more than any other Power to assist Russia in despoiling Roumania of her Bessarabian territory; and they have worked energetically against Greece, which represented the only living anti-Russian force in the Levant. . . . The honour which the Government have earned for us at Berlin, is that of having used the name and influence, and even, by their preparations, the military power of England, to set up the principles of Metternich, and to put down the principles of Canning. We, who have helped Belgium, Spain, and Portugal to be free, we who led the way in the establishment of free Greece, and gave no mean support to the liberation and union of Italy, have at Berlin wrought actively to limit everywhere the area of self-government, and to save from the wreck as much as possible of a domination which has contributed more than any other that ever existed to the misery, the debasement, and the extermination of mankind. . . .

For a vigorous, that is to say, a narrow, restless, blustering, and self-asserting foreign policy, no Ministry has ever been punished in this country. . . . A vigorous foreign policy exhibits all the advantages of a good and available political speculation. First, by forcing upon the public mind a stronger excitement, it produces a comparative indifference to the humdrum detail of legislation, and effectually covers all domestic shortcomings. . . . Secondly, instead of asserting that on the views of a party, a vigorous foreign policy asserts what are presumptively claims and interests of the nation, and thus sheds a halo round its acts. Thirdly, in thus appealing to the self-love and pride of the community, it is pretty certain to carry its influence and driving power for a time beyond the circle of its sworn followers, and to enlist the support of all those good citizens who, from the shilling gallery and elsewhere, enthusiastically applaud the lines—

'Methought upon one pair of English legs
Did march three Frenchmen.'

But last, and best of all, as they are contending, forsooth, on behalf of the greatness of England, it follows that they are enabled at once to place all opponents in the category of contenders for its littleness. All those who will not be put off by their devices . . . are at once condemned . . . as men who prefer their party to their country, as friends of the foreigner, and as conspirators against the greatness of the Empire. . . .

Territorial aggrandisement, backed by military display, is the *cheval de bataille* of the Administration. Empire is greatness; leagues of land are empire; your safety is measured by the fear you strike into other nations; trade follows the flag; he that doubts is an enemy to his country. . . .

It is very disagreeable for an Englishman to hint to Englishmen that the self-love and pride which all condemn in individuals, have often lured nations to their ruin or their loss; that they are apt to entail a great deal of meanness, as well as a great deal of violence; that they begin with a forfeiture of respect abroad, and end even in the loss of self-respect; that their effect is to destroy all sobriety in the estimation of human affairs, and to generate a temperament of excitability which errs alternately on the side of arrogance, and of womanish and unworthy fears. For the performance of this disagreeable duty, we are entitled to look to the Queen's Government, which ought in foreign affairs invariably to play the part of moderator. . . . The doctrines of national self-restraint, of the equal obligations of States to public law, and of their equal rights to fair construction as to words and deeds, have [however] been left to unofficial persons. The Government, not uniformly nor consistently, but in the main and on the whole, have opened up and relied on an illegitimate source of power, which never wholly fails: they had appealed, under the prostituted name of patriotism, to exaggerated fears, to imaginary interests, and to the acquisitiveness of a race which has surpassed every other known to history in the faculty of appropriating to itself vast spaces of the earth, and establishing its supremacy over men of every race and language. Now I hold that to stimulate these tendencies, to overlook the proportion between our resources and our obligations, and above all to claim anything more than equality of rights in the moral and political intercourse of the world, is not the way to make England great, but to make it both morally and materially little.

The Nineteenth Century, September 1878.

4. IRELAND

82. JOHN BRIGHT: Speech at Dublin, 30 October 1866

Now, if it were possible, would it not be worth while to change the sentiments and improve the condition of the Irish cultivators of the soil? If we were to remove the State Church, there would still be a Church, but it would not be a supremacy Church. The Catholics of Ireland have no idea of saying that Protestantism in its various forms shall not exist in their island. There would still be a Church, but it would be a free Church of a section of a free people. . . .

Who objects to this? The men who are in favour of supremacy, and the men who have a fanatical hatred of what they call Popery. To honest and good men of the Protestant Church and of the Protestant faith there is no reason whatever to fear this change. What has the voluntary system done in Scotland? What has it done amongst the Nonconformists of England? What has it done amongst the population of Wales? and what has it done amongst the Catholic population of your own Ireland? In my opinion, the abolition of the Established Church would give Protestantism itself another chance. I believe there has been in Ireland no other enemy of Protestantism so injurious as the Protestant State Establishment. . . . One effect of the Established Church has been this, the making Catholicism in Ireland not only a faith but a patriotism, for it was not likely that any member of the Catholic Church would incline in the slightest degree to Protestantism so long as it presented itself to his eyes as a wrongdoer and full of injustice in connection with the government of his country.

But if honest Protestantism has nothing to fear from the changes that I would recommend, what has the honest landowner to fear? The history of Europe and America for the last one hundred years affords scarcely any picture more painful than that which is afforded by the landowners of this kingdom. The Irish landowner has been different from every other landowner, for the bulk of his land has only been about half cultivated, and he has had to collect his rents by a process approaching the evils of civil war. His property has been very insecure—the sale of it sometimes has been rendered impossible. The landowner himself has often been hated by those who ought to have loved him. He has been banished from his ancestral home by terror, and not a few have lost their lives without the sympathy of those who ought to have been their protectors and their friends. . . .

What is the first remedy which you would propose? Clearly this—that which is the most easily applicable and which would most speedily touch the condition of the country. It is this—that the property which the tenant shall invest or create in his farm shall be secured to the tenant by law. I believe that if Parliament were fairly to enact this it would make a change in the whole temper of the country. I recollect in the year 1849 being down in the county of Wexford. I called at the house of an old farmer of the name of Stafford, who lived in a very good house, the best farm-house, I think, that I had seen since leaving Dublin. He lived on his own farm, which he had bought fifteen years before. The house was a house which he had himself built. He was a venerable old man, and we had some very interesting conversation with him. I asked how it was he had so good a house? He said the farm was his own, and the house was his own, and, as no man could disturb him, he had made it a much better house than was common for the farmers of Ireland. I said to him, 'If all the farmers of Ireland had the same security for the capital they laid out on their farms, what would be the result?' The old man almost sprang out of his chair, and said, 'Sir, if you will give us that encouragement, we will *bate* the hunger out of Ireland.' It is said that all this must be left to contract between the landlord and the tenant; but the public, which may be neither landlord nor tenant, has a great interest in this question; and I maintain that the interests of the public require that Parliament should secure to the tenant the property which he has invested in his farm. But I would not stop here.

There is another, and what I should call a more permanent and far-reaching remedy for the evils of Ireland, and those persons who stickle so much for political economy I hope will follow me in this. The great evil of Ireland is this—that the Irish people—the Irish nation—are dispossessed of the soil, and what we ought to do is to provide for, and aid in, their restoration to it by all measures of justice. Why should we tolerate in Ireland the law of primogeniture? Why should we tolerate the system of entails? Why should the object of the law be to accumulate land in great masses in few hands, and to make it almost impossible for persons of small means, and tenant-farmers, to become possessors of land? If you go to other countries—for example, to Norway, to Denmark, to Holland, to Belgium, to France, to Germany, to Italy, or to the United States, you will find that in all these countries those laws of which I complain have been abolished, and the land is just as free to buy and sell, and hold and cultivate, as any other description of property in the kingdom. No doubt your Landed Estates Court and your Record of Titles Act were good measures, but they were good because they were in the direction that I want to travel farther in.

But I would go farther than that; I would deal with the question of absenteeism. I am not going to propose to tax absentees; but if my advice were taken, we should have a Parliamentary Commission empowered to buy up the large estates in Ireland belonging to the English nobility, for the purpose of selling them on easy terms to the occupiers of the farms and to the tenantry of Ireland. . . . What you want is to restore to Ireland a middle-class proprietary of the soil; and I venture to say that if these estates could be purchased and could be sold out farm by farm to the tenant occupiers in Ireland, that it would be infinitely better in a conservative sense, than that they should belong to great proprietors living out of the country.

Speeches by John Bright, M.P., ed. by J. H. T. Rogers (1868), vol. i, pp. 361-76.

83. JOHN BRIGHT: Speech in the House
of Commons, 1 April 1868

The sword has scarcely ever been out of the hand of the governing power in Ireland. And if a fair, simple, and unadorned narrative were given of the transactions of this Parliament with Ireland with regard to its different enactments, coercive restrictions, suspensions of the Habeas Corpus Act, and so forth, it would form a narrative which would astonish the world and would discredit us. Sir, I am afraid it is not too much to say that, in support of this supremacy, many victims have perished on the scaffold in Ireland, and that the fields of Ireland have been more than once drenched with the blood of her people. But, after all this is done, we are not a bit more secure.

It is no matter what Government sits on the bench opposite. The right hon. gentleman the member for South Lancashire was there two years ago, and on that occasion, by the consent of his colleagues, the then Home Secretary had to introduce the Bill for the suspension of the Habeas Corpus Act. Now you are on that side of the House, and you have to do the same. Nobody says it is not necessary. I am not prepared to say it has not been necessary at other times. But surely if this be necessary it shows that the Union is not very secure in Ireland. In fact, Sir, the suspension of the Habeas Corpus Act has become so common that it causes almost no remark. The measure is introduced into the House. An Irish member makes a feeble protest against it, and it is passed, and we suspend the liberties of one of the three kingdoms from year to year. And the Prime Minister has the courage—I might almost use another word—he has the courage to say there is no crisis, and that things are going on very much as usual, and that the House of Commons is not required to do much or care much for that country.

What you have in Ireland is this. There is anarchy, which is subdued by force, and after centuries of rule, we have got no farther. We have not reconciled Ireland to us, we have done none of those things which the world says we ought to have done; and at this moment—in the year 1868—we are discussing the question whether it is possible to make any change with reference to the Established Church in Ireland which will bring about a better state of feeling between the people and the Imperial Government. Sir, I am afraid that there has been very little statesmanship and very much neglect, and I think we ought to take shame to ourselves, and try to get rid of some of our antiquated prejudices on this matter, and look at it as men whose vision is not impaired by the passionate feelings which have so often prevailed in this country with regard to this question.

Ibid. pp. 420-37.

84. W. E. GLADSTONE: Speech in the House of Commons, 8 April 1886

[Gladstone's speech was made in introducing the First Home Rule Bill.]

It is felt on both sides of the House, unless I am much mistaken, that we have arrived at a stage in our political transactions with Ireland where two roads part, one from the other, not soon probably to meet again. . . .

We concur entirely in that conclusion, . . . and our intention is, Sir, to propose to the House of Commons that which, as we think, if happily accepted, will liberate Parliament from the restraints under which of late years it has ineffectually struggled to perform the business of the country; will restore legislation to its natural, ancient, unimpeded course; and will, above all, obtain an answer—a clear, we hope, and definite answer—to the question whether it is or is not possible to establish good and harmonious relations between Great Britain and Ireland on the footing of those free institutions to which Englishmen, Scotchmen, and Irishmen are alike unalterably attached. . .

The first point to which I would call your attention is this, that whereas exceptional legislation—legislation which introduces exceptional provisions into the law—ought itself to be in its own nature essentially and absolutely exceptional, it has become for us not exceptional, but habitual. We are like a man who, knowing that medicine may be the means of his restoration to health, endeavours to live upon medicine. Nations, no more than individuals, can find a subsistence in what was meant to be a cure. But has it been a cure? Have we attained the object which we desired, and honestly desired to attain? No, Sir, agrarian crime has become, sometimes upon a larger and sometimes upon a smaller scale, as habitual in Ireland as the legislation which has been intended to repress it. . . .

But the agrarian crime in Ireland is not so much a cause as it is a symptom. It is a symptom of a yet deeper mischief of which it is only the external manifestation. That manifestation is mainly threefold. In the first place, with certain exceptions for the case of winter juries, it is impossible to depend in Ireland upon the finding of a jury in a case of agrarian crime according to the facts as they are viewed by the Government, by the Judges, and by the public, I think, at large. That is a most serious mischief, passing down deep into the very groundwork of civil society. It is also, Sir, undoubtedly a mischief that, in cases where the extreme remedy of eviction is resorted to by the landlord, these cases of eviction, good, bad, and indifferent as to their justification, stand pretty much in one and the same discredit with the rural population of Ireland, and become, as we know, the occasion of transactions that we all deeply lament. Finally, Sir, it is not to be denied that there is great interference in Ireland with individual liberty in the shape of intimidation. . . .

The consequence of that is to weaken generally the respect for law, and the respect for contract, and that among a people who, I believe, are as capable of attaining to the very highest moral and social standard as any people on the face of the earth. . . .

Nothing has been more painful to me than to observe that, in this matter, we are not improving, but, on the contrary, we are losing ground. Since the last half-century dawned, we have been steadily engaged in extending, as well as in consolidating, free insititutions. I divide the period since the Act of Union with Ireland into two—the first from 1800 to 1832, the epoch of what is still justly called the great Reform Act; and, secondly, from 1833 to 1885. I do not know whether it has been as widely observed as I think it deserves to be that, in the first of these periods—thirty-two years—there were no less than eleven years in which our Statute Book was free throughout the whole year from repressive legislation of an exceptional kind against Ireland. But in the fifty-three years since we advanced far in the career of Liberal principles and actions—in those fifty-three years from 1833 to 1885—there were but two years which were entirely free from the action of this special legislation for Ireland. Is not that of itself almost enough to prove that we have arrived at the point where it is necessary that we should take a careful and searching survey of our position? . . .

If coercion is to be the basis for legislation, we must no longer be seeking, as we are always laudably seeking, to whittle it down almost to nothing at the very first moment we begin, but we must, like men, adopt it, hold by it, sternly enforce it, till its end has been completely attained—with what results to peace, good will, and freedom I do not now stop to enquire. Our ineffectual and spurious coercion is morally worn out. . . .

I can, indeed, conceive and in history we may point to circumstances in which coercion of that kind, stern, resolute, consistent, might be, and has been, successful. But it requires, in my judgment, two essential conditions, and these are—the autocracy of Government, and the secrecy of public transactions. With those conditions, that kind of coercion to which I am referring might possibly succeed. But will it succeed in the light of day, and can it be administered by the people of England and Scotland against the people of Ireland by the two nations which, perhaps, above all others upon earth—I need hardly except America—best understand and are most fondly attached to the essential principles of liberty? . . .

This I will say, that the people of England and Scotland will never resort to that alternative until they have tried every other. Have they tried every other? Well, some we have tried, to which I will refer. I have been concerned with some of them myself. But we have not yet tried every alternative, because there is one—not unknown to human experience—on the contrary, widely known to various countries in the world where this dark and difficult problem has been solved by the comparatively natural and simple, though not always easy, expedient of stripping law of its foreign garb, and investing it with a domestic character. I am not saying that this will succeed; I by no means beg the question at this moment; but this I will say, that Ireland, as far as I know, and speaking of the great majority of the people of Ireland, believes it will succeed, and that experience elsewhere supports that conclusion. The case of Ireland, though she is represented here not less fully than England or Scotland, is not the same as that of England or Scotland. England by her own strength, and by her vast majority in this House, makes her own laws just as independently as if she were not combined with two other countries. . . . Scotland, wisely recognized by England, has been allowed and encouraged in this House to make her own laws as freely and as effectually as if she had a representation six times as strong. The consequence is that the mainspring of law in England is felt by the people to be English; the mainspring of law in Scotland is felt by the people to be Scotch; but the mainspring of law in Ireland is not felt by the people to be Irish, and I am bound to say that it cannot be felt to be Irish in the same sense as it is English and Scotch. The net results of this statement which I have laid before the House because it was necessary as the groundwork of my argument, are these—in the first place, I admit it to be little less than a mockery to hold that the state of law and of facts conjointly, which I have endeavoured to describe, conduces to the real unity of this great, noble, and world-wide Empire. In the second place, something must be done, something is imperatively demanded from us to restore to Ireland the first conditions of civil life—the free course of law, the liberty of every individual in the exercise of every legal right, the confidence of the people in the law, and their sympathy with the law, apart from which no country can be called, in the full sense of the word, a civilized country, nor can there be given to that country the blessings which it is the object of civilized society to attain. . . .

Sir, I do not deny the general good intentions of Parliament on a variety of great and conspicuous occasions, and its desire to pass good laws for Ireland. But let me say that, in order to work out the purposes of Government, there is something more in this world occasionally required than even the passing of good laws. . . . The passing of many good laws is not enough in cases where the strong permanent instincts of the people, their distinctive marks of character, the situation and history of the country, require not only that these laws should be good, but that they should proceed from a congenial and native source, and besides being good laws should be their own laws. . . .

The principle that I am laying down I am not laying down exceptionally for Ireland. It is the very principle upon which, within my recollection, to the immense advantage of the country, we have not only altered, but revolutionized our method of governing the Colonies. I had the honour to hold office in the Colonial Department fifty-one years ago. At that time the Colonies were governed from Downing Street. It is true that some of them had Legislative Assemblies; but with these we were always in conflict. . . . All that has changed. England tried to pass good laws for the Colonies at that period; but the Colonies said—'We do not want your good laws; we want our own.' We admitted the reasonableness of that principle, and it is now coming home to us from across the sea. We have to consider whether it is applicable to the case of Ireland. Do not let us disguise this from ourselves. We stand face to face with what is termed Irish nationality. Irish nationality vents itself in the demand for local autonomy, or separate and complete self-government in Irish, not in Imperial, affairs. Is this an evil in itself? Is it a thing that we should view with horror or apprehension? . . . Sir, I hold that it is not. . . .

I say that the Irishman is as capable of loyalty as another man—I say that if his loyalty has been checked in its development, why is it? Because the laws by which he is governed do not present themselves to him, as they do to us in England and Scotland, with a native and congenial aspect. . . .

I ask that in our case we should practise, with firm and fearless hand—what we have so often preached—the doctrine which we have so often inculcated upon others—namely, that the concession of local self-government is not the way to sap or impair, but the way to strengthen and consolidate unity. . . . I ask that we should apply to Ireland that happy experience which we have gained in England and in Scotland, where the course of generations has now taught us, not as a dream or a theory, but as practice and as life, that the best and surest foundation we can find to build upon is the foundation afforded by the affections, the convictions, and the will of the nation.

Gladstone's Speeches, ed. by A. Tilney Bassett
(1916), pp. 602-44.

85. W. E. GLADSTONE: Speech in the House of Commons, 17 February 1888

[On 9 September 1887, on the occasion of a prosecution against William O'Brien, one of the leaders of the National League, a crowd gathered at Mitchelstown, County Cork. During the meeting there was a scuffle with the police, who opened fire. Three people were killed.]

The right hon. gentleman was especially indignant with me because in the recess I had telegraphed to some correspondent the words 'Remember Mitchelstown.' . . . I never in my life uttered words by letter or telegram which I more rejoice to allude to, or which I am better contented to have employed than the words 'Remember Mitchelstown.' . . . It was time I should say 'Remember Mitchelstown' —particularly when Mitchelstown might have become what is called a prerogative instance. . . . I tell the right hon. gentleman frankly that I am of opinion that he has become by clear implication, and by his own deliberate act, a breaker of the law. (Cheers.) He broke the law by authoritative assent and approval bestowed upon those who had wantonly and repeatedly, and with fatal consequences, broken it. He not only did this, but he did it under circumstances where that authoritative approval, conveyed to the mind of the police, would naturally, excusably, almost necessarily, have pointed out to them that that was to be a model and the rule of their conduct. It was in the interests of law and order that I denounced conduct like this.

[Mr. Gladstone then went on to deal with certain cases in which arbitrary methods of arrest and treatment in prison had occurred.]

I wish to point out that at the moment when this gentleman, whose wife was in danger, was naturally anxious to repair to his home, a new charge was brought against him (as he was going out of the court on bail), a new sentence of a month was passed, his right of appeal was taken away, and he was prevented, not only from preparing his defence in the first case, but also from repairing to his home, where not only difficulty and pain but actual danger threatened him. Is that the sort of administration of the Act of last year which the Government are prepared to defend? Is it thus that Ireland is to be reconciled? Is it thus that the Irish nation is to be converted? Is it in this House of Commons—the most ancient and noblest of all the temples of freedom in the world—that such operations as these are to be either passed over in silence or defended? . . .

The Plan of Campaign is an interference with the law; it is, in truth, a substitute, without authority, for the law. Far be it from me to deny that, necessarily, such a Plan in the abstract is an evil. It is something more; it is a sign of deeper evils; it is a sign that the law itself is not doing its work, and that the conditions of legality do not exist; it is a warning to set about restoring them. This is not the only case where extra-legal combination and anti-legal combination have been brought into existence, sometimes with the effect, sometimes with the purpose, of mitigating social disorder. You will recollect the Swing riots, sheer and gross offences against the law in England. But these offences had the most powerful and important effects in bringing about wide, sweeping, essential reforms of the law, which without them possibly would never, probably would not at the time, have been obtained. . . . Such is the condition of man and the imperfection of institutions that sometimes things which are evils in themselves are the cure and mitigation of greater evils.

[Mr. Gladstone argued that there was no established connection between the Plan of Campaign or the National League and agrarian rise in Ireland: that, on the contrary, both were working in the interests of quiet and order, and that the Government's plan to suppress them was not only a failure, but entirely misconceived.]

Will the Government for ever continue to deal with signs and never look at the substance? Will it for ever deal with external symptoms, and never search out the source and seat of the malady? There are many things said by the Government in debate, but there is one thing they and their supporters most rarely say. We never hear them express a confidence that they will be able to establish a permanent resistance to Home Rule. . . . I do not disguise for myself the strength of the combination that is against us. . . . They have nearly the whole of the wealth of the country; they have nearly the whole of the men of social station in the country; they have a vast preponderance in all the elements of social strength. . . . There is therefore, I do not doubt, ample power to interpose delay before this great question shall be settled. But, Sir, delay on a subject of this kind,—a controversy between nations—is no obvious or unmixed good. You are happily free at this moment from the slightest shadow of foreign complications. You have at this moment the constitutional assent of Ireland, pledged to you in the most solemn form, for the efficacy of the policy I am considering (Home Rule). The day may come when your condition may not be so happy. I do not expect, any more than I desire, these foreign complications. Still, it is unwise to shut them wholly out of view. What we have to fear is rather this, that if resistance to the national voice of Ireland be pushed too far, those who now guide the mind of the nation may gradually lose their power and be supplanted by ruder and more dangerous agencies. Nay, it may happen that these very institutions, the National League and the Plan of Campaign, which would vanish into thin air upon a rational and early settlement of the Irish question, may drive such a deep root into the soil, may acquire such a mastery, if not over the understanding, over the feelings and passions of the people, that these institutions may grow to dangerous power. It is possible that having themselves been brought, perhaps having been forced, into existence by bad government, that they may acquire a strength that will enable them hereafter to offer the most serious hindrances to government which is good. . . .

For 700 years, with Ireland practically unrepresented, with Ireland prostrate, with the forces of this great and powerful island absolutely united against her—for these 700 years you have tried and failed to do that which you are now trying to do with Ireland fully represented in your Parliament, with Ireland herself as a people raised to a position which is erect and strong, and with the mind even of England so divided that if you look to the elections of the last twelve months, the majority of the nation have voted in favour of the concession of her desires. How long is this to continue? I would venture to ask hon. gentlemen opposite, under such circumstances as these, is your persistence in this system of administration—I will not say just, because that I know you will contest, but is it wise; is it politic, is it hopeful; and above all is it conservative? Or will you not now at length bethink yourselves of change, and consent to administer and finally to legislate for Ireland as you legislate for England and Scotland, in conformity with the constitutionally expressed wishes of the profound and permanent convictions of its people, and will you thus at last consent to present to the world the blessed spectacle of a truly and not a nominally united Empire?

Coercion in Ireland, a reprint of Mr. Gladstone's speech in the House of Commons, 17 February 1888.

PART V

THE NEW LIBERALISM

86. T. H. GREEN: *Liberal Legislation or Freedom of Contract*, a Lecture given at Leicester, 1881

[T. H. Green (1836–82), the leading representative of the English idealist school of philosophy, was a Fellow of Balliol, 1860–78, and then, until his death in 1882, Whyte Professor of Moral Philosophy.]

We shall probably all agree that freedom, rightly understood, is the greatest of blessings; that its attainment is the true end of all our efforts as citizens. But when we thus speak of freedom, we should consider carefully what we mean by it. We do not mean merely freedom to do as we like irrespectively of what it is that we like. We do not mean a freedom that can be enjoyed by one man or one set of men at the cost of a loss of freedom to others. When we speak of freedom as something to be so highly prized, we mean a positive power or capacity of doing or enjoying something worth doing or enjoying, and that, too, something that we do or enjoy in common with others. We mean by it a power which each man exercises through the help or security given him by his fellow-men, and which he in turn helps to secure for them. When we measure the progress of a society by its growth in freedom, we measure it by the increasing development and exercise on the whole of those powers of contributing to social good with which we believe the members of the society to be endowed; in short, by the greater power on the part of the citizens as a body to make the most and best of themselves. Thus, though of course there can be no freedom among men who act not willingly but under compulsion, yet on the other hand the mere removal of compulsion, the mere enabling a man to do as he likes, is in itself no contribution to true freedom. In one sense no man is so well able to do as he likes as the wandering savage. He has no master. There is no one to say him nay. Yet we do not count him really free, because the freedom of savagery is not strength, but weakness. The actual powers of the noblest savage do not admit of comparison with those of the humblest citizen of a law-abiding state. He is not the slave of a man, but he is the slave of nature. Of compulsion by natural necessity he has plenty of experience, though of restraint by society none at all. Nor can he deliver himself from that compulsion except by submitting to this restraint. So to submit is the first step in true freedom, because the first step towards the full exercise of the faculties with which man is endowed. But we rightly refuse to recognise the highest development on the part of an exceptional individual or exceptional class, as an advance towards the true freedom of.man, if it is founded on a refusal of the same opportunity to other men. The powers of the human mind have probably never attained such force and keenness, the proof of what society can do for the individual has never been so strikingly exhibited, as among the small groups of men who possessed civil privileges in the small republics of antiquity. The whole framework of our political ideas, to say nothing of our philosophy, is derived from them. But in them this extra-ordinary efflorescence of the privileged class was accompanied by the slavery of the multitude. That slavery was the condition on which it depended, and for that reason it was doomed to decay. There is no clearer ordinance of that supreme reason, often dark to us, which governs the course of man's affairs, than that no body of men should in the long run be able to strengthen itself at the cost of others' weakness. The civilisation and freedom of the ancient world were shortlived because they were partial and exceptional. If the ideal of true freedom is the maximum of power for all members of human society alike to make the best of themselves, we are right in refusing to ascribe the glory of freedom to a state in which the apparent elevation of the few is founded on the degradation of the many. . . .

If I have given a true account of that freedom which forms

the goal of social effort, we shall see that freedom of contract,
freedom in all the forms of doing what one will with one's
own, is valuable only as a means to an end. That end is
what I call freedom in the positive sense: in other words,
the liberation of the powers of all men equally for contributions to a common good. No one has a right to do what he
will with his own in such a way as to contravene this end.
It is only through the guarantee which society gives him
that he has property at all, or, strictly speaking, any right
to his possessions. This guarantee is founded on a sense of
common interest. Every one has an interest in securing to
every one else the free use and enjoyment and disposal of
his possessions, so long as that freedom on the part of one
does not interfere with a like freedom on the part of others,
because such freedom contributes to that equal development
of the faculties of all which is the highest good for all. This is
the true and the only justification of rights of property. . . .

Our modern legislation then with reference to labour, and
education, and health, involving as it does manifold interference with freedom of contract, is justified on the ground
that it is the business of the state, not indeed directly to
promote moral goodness, for that, from the very nature of
moral goodness, it cannot do, but to maintain the conditions
without which a free exercise of the human faculties is
impossible. . . .

Now we shall probably all agree that a society in which
the public health was duly protected, and necessary education duly provided for, by the spontaneous action of individuals, was in a higher condition than one in which the
compulsion of law was needed to secure these ends. But we
must take men as we find them. Until such a condition of
society is reached, it is the business of the state to take the
best security it can for the young citizens' growing up in
such health and with so much knowledge as is necessary for
their real freedom. . . .

And the question is whether without these laws the
suffering classes could have been delivered quickly or slowly
from the condition they were in. Could the enlightened
self-interest or benevolence of individuals, working under a
system of unlimited freedom of contract, have ever brought

them into a state compatible with the free development of the human faculties? No one considering the facts can have any doubt as to the answer to this question. Left to itself, or to the operation of casual benevolence, a degraded population perpetuates and increases itself. Read any of the authorised accounts, given before royal or parliamentary commissions, of the state of the labourers, especially of the women and children, as they were in our great industries before the law was first brought to bear on them, and before freedom of contract was first interfered with in them. Ask yourself what chance there was of a generation, born and bred under such conditions, ever contracting itself out of them.

Works of T. H. Green, ed. by R. L. Nettleship,
vol. iii (1888), pp. 370-6.

87. HERBERT SPENCER: *The Coming Slavery*
(1884)

[Herbert Spencer (1820–1903) was the popular philosopher of the great scientific movements of the second half of the nineteenth century. His belief in the process of evolution produced a highly individualist theory of government which stood in sharp contrast to that of T. H. Green (No. 86).]

The extension of this policy (of interference), causing extension of corresponding ideas, fosters everywhere the tacit assumption that Government should step in whenever anything is not going right. 'Surely you would not have this misery continue!' exclaims some one, if you hint a demurrer to much that is now being said and done. Observe what is implied by this exclamation. It takes for granted, first, that all suffering ought to be prevented, which is not true; much suffering is curative, and prevention of it is prevention of a remedy. In the second place, it takes for granted that every evil can be removed; the truth being that with the existing defects of human nature, many evils can only be thrust out of one place or form into another place or form—often being increased by the change. The exclamation also implies the unhesitating belief, here especially concerning us, that evils of all kinds should be dealt with by the State. There does not occur the inquiry whether there are at work other agencies capable of dealing with evils, and whether the evils in question may not be among those which are best dealt with by these other agencies. And obviously, the more numerous governmental interventions become, the more confirmed does this habit of thought grow, and the more loud and perpetual the demands for intervention. . . .

But the governing agency would be a master which he and others made and kept constantly in check; and one which therefore would not control him or others more than was needful for the benefit of each and all.

To which reply the first rejoinder is that, even if so, each member of the community as an individual would be a slave to the community as a whole. Such a relation has habitually existed in militant communities, even under quasi-popular forms of government. In ancient Greece the accepted principle was that the citizen belonged neither to himself nor to his family, but belonged to his city—the city being with the Greek equivalent to the community. And this doctrine, proper to a state of constant warfare, is a doctrine which socialism unawares re-introduces into a state intended to be purely industrial. The services of each will belong to the aggregate of all; and for these services, such returns will be given as the authorities think proper. So that even if the administration is of the beneficent kind intended to be secured, slavery, however mild, must be the outcome of the arrangement.

A second rejoinder is that the administration will presently become not of the intended kind, and that the slavery will not be mild. The socialist speculation is vitiated by an assumption like that which vitiates the speculations of the 'practical' politician. It is assumed that officialism will work as it is intended to work, which it never does. The machinery of Communism, like existing social machinery, has to be framed out of existing human nature; and the defects of existing human nature will generate in the one the same evils as in the other. The love of power, the selfishness, the injustice, the untruthfulness, which often in comparatively short time bring private organisations to disaster, will inevitably, where their effects accumulate from generation to generation, work evils far greater and less remediable; since, vast and complex and possessed of all the resources, the administrative organisation once developed and consolidated, must become irresistible. . . .

It would need but a war with an adjacent society, or some internal discontent demanding forcible suppression, to at once transform a socialistic administration into a grinding tyranny like that of ancient Peru; under which the mass of the people, controlled by grades of officials, and leading lives that were inspected out-of-doors and in-doors, laboured for the support of the organisation which regulated them, and were left with but a bare subsistence for themselves. . . .

The foregoing discussions have, I think, shown that the dictates of utility, and, consequently, the proper actions of governments, are not to be settled by inspection of facts on the surface, and acceptance of their *prima facie* meanings; but are to be settled by reference to, and deduction from, fundamental facts. The fundamental facts to which all rational judgments of utility must go back, are the facts that life consists in, and is maintained by, certain activities; and that among men in a society, these activities, necessarily becoming mutually limited, are to be carried on by each within the limits thence arising, and not carried on beyond those limits; the maintenance of the limits becoming, by consequence, the function of the agency which regulates society. If each, having freedom to use his powers up to the bounds fixed by the like freedom of others, obtains from his fellow-men as much for his services as they find them worth in comparison with the services of others—if contracts uniformly fulfilled bring to each the share thus determined, and he is left secure in person and possessions to satisfy his wants with the proceeds; then there is maintained the vital principle alike of individual life and of social life. Further, there is maintained the vital principle of social progress; inasmuch as, under such conditions, the individuals of most worth will prosper and multiply more than those of less worth. So that utility, not as empirically estimated but as rationally determined, enjoins this maintenance of individual rights; and, by implication, negatives any course which traverses them.

Here, then, we reach the ultimate interdict against meddling legislation. Reduced to its lowest terms, every proposal to interfere with citizens' activities further than by enforcing their mutual limitations, is a proposal to improve life by breaking through the fundamental conditions to life. When some are prevented from buying beer that others may be prevented from getting drunk, those who make the law assume that more good than evil will result from interference with the normal relation between conduct and consequences, alike in the few ill-regulated and the many well-regulated. A government which takes fractions of the incomes of multitudinous people, for the purpose of sending to the colonies some who have not prospered here, or for building better industrial dwellings, or for making public libraries and public museums, etc., takes for granted that, not only proximately but ultimately, increased general happiness will result from transgressing the essential requirement to general happiness—the requirement that each shall enjoy all those means to happiness which his actions, carried on without aggression, have brought him. In other cases we do not thus let the immediate blind us to the remote. When asserting the sacredness of property against a private transgressor, we do not ask whether the benefit to a hungry man who takes bread from a baker's shop, is or is not greater than the injury inflicted on the baker: we consider, not the special effects, but the general effects which arise if property is insecure. But when the State exacts further amounts from citizens, or further restrains their liberties, we consider only the direct and proximate effects, and ignore the indirect and distant effects which are caused when these invasions of individual rights are continually multiplied. We do not see that by accumulated small infractions of them, the vital conditions to life, individual and social, come to be so imperfectly fulfilled that the life decays.

Herbert Spencer, *Man versus The State*
(1909), pp. 27-90.

88. D. G. RITCHIE: *The Principles*
of State Interference
(1891)

[D. G. Ritchie (1853–1903) was a Fellow of Jesus College, Oxford, 1878–94, and then Professor of Logic and Metaphysics at St. Andrews University until his death.]

Underlying all these traditions and prejudices there is a particular metaphysical theory—a metaphysical theory which takes hold of those persons especially who are fondest of abjuring all metaphysics; and the disease is in their case the more dangerous since they do not know when they have it. The chief symptom of this metaphysical complaint is the belief in the abstract individual. The individual is thought of, at least spoken of, as if he had a meaning and significance apart from his surroundings and apart from his relations to the. community of which he is a member. It may be quite true that the significance of the individual is not exhausted by his relations to any given set of surroundings; but apart from all these he is a mere abstraction—a logical ghost, a metaphysical spectre, which haunts the habitations of those who have derided metaphysics. The individual, apart from all relations to a community, is a negation. You can say nothing about him, or rather it, except that it is not any other individual. Now, along with this negative and abstract view of the individual there goes, as counterpart, the way of looking at the State as an opposing element to the individual. The individual and the State are put over against one another. Their relation is regarded as one merely of antithesis. Of course, this is a point of view which we can take, and quite rightly for certain purposes; but it is only one point of view. It expresses only a partial truth; and a partial truth, if accepted as the whole truth, is always a falsehood. Such a conception is, in any case, quite inadequate as a basis for any profitable discussion of the duties of Government.

It is this theory of the individual which underlies Mill's famous book on *Liberty*. Mill, and all those who take up his attitude towards the State, seem to assume that all power gained by the State is so much taken from the individual; and conversely, that all power gained by the individual is gained at the expense of the State. Now this is to treat the two elements, power of the State and power (or liberty) of the individual, as if they formed the debit and credit sides of an account book; it is to make them like two heaps of a fixed number of stones, to neither of which you can add without taking from the other. It is to apply a mere quantitative conception in politics, as if that were an adequate 'category' in such matters. The same thing is done when society is spoken of as merely 'an aggregate of individuals.' The citizen of a State, the member of a society of any sort, even an artificial or temporary association, does not stand in the same relation to the whole that one number does to a series of numbers, or that one stone does to a heap of stones. Even ordinary language shows us this. We feel it to be a more adequate expression to say that the citizen is a member of the body politic, than to call him merely a unit in a political aggregate. . . .

Life Mr. Spencer defines as adaptation of the individual to his environment; but, unless the individual manages likewise to adapt his environment to himself, the definition would be more applicable to death.

It must not be supposed that we wish to blind ourselves to the many real difficulties and objections which there are in the way of remedying and preventing evils by direct State action. If assured that the end is good, we must see that the means are sufficient and necessary, and we must be prepared to count the cost. But, admitting the real difficulties, we must not allow imaginary difficulties to block the way. In the first place, as already said, State action does not necessarily imply the direct action of the central government. Many things may be undertaken by local bodies which it would be unwise to put under the control of officials at a distance. 'Municipalisation' is, in many cases, a much better 'cry' than 'Nationalisation.' Experiments may also be more safely tried in small than in large areas, and local bodies may profit by each other's experience. Diffusion of power may well be combined with concentration of information. 'Power', says J. S. Mill, 'may be localised, but knowledge to be most useful must be centralised.' Secondly, there are many matters which can more easily be taken in hand than others by the State as at present constituted. Thus the means of communication and locomotion can in every civilised country be easily nationalised or municipalised, where this has not been done already. With regard to productive industries, there may appear greater difficulty. But the process now going on by which the individual capitalist more and more gives place to enormous joint-stock enterprises, worked by salaried managers, this tendency of capital to become 'impersonal', is making the transition to management by government (central or local) very much more simple, and very much more necessary, than in the days of small industries, before the 'industrial revolution' began. The State will not so much displace individual enterprise, as substitute for the irresponsible company or 'trust' the responsible public corporation. Thirdly, and lastly, be it observed that the arguments used against 'government' action, where the government is entirely or mainly in the hands of a ruling class or caste, exercising wisely or unwisely a paternal or 'grandmotherly' authority—such arguments lose their force just in proportion as government becomes more and more genuinely the government of the people by the people themselves. The explicit recognition of popular sovereignty tends to abolish the antithesis between 'the Man' and 'the State.' The State becomes, not 'I' indeed, but 'we.' The main reason for desiring more State action is in order to give the individual a greater chance of developing all his activities in a healthy way. The State and the individual are not sides of an antithesis between which we must choose; and it is possible, though, like all great things, difficult for a democracy to construct a strong and vigorous State, and thereby to foster a strong and vigorous individuality, not selfish nor isolated, but finding its truest welfare in the welfare of the community. Mr. Spencer takes up the formula 'from status to contract' as a complete philosophy of history. Is there not wanting a third and higher stage in which there shall be at once order and progress, cohesion and liberty, socialistic—but, *therefore*, rendering possible the highest development of all such individuality as constitutes an element in well-being? Perhaps then Radicalism is not turning back to an effete Toryism, but advancing to a further and positive form, leaving to the Tories and the old Whigs and to Mr. Spencer the worn-out and cast-off creed of its own immaturity.

D. G. Ritchie, *Principles* ...... (1902),
pp. 11-12, 62-5.

89. J. A. HOBSON: *The Crisis of Liberalism*
(1909)

[J. A. Hobson (1858–1940) was a prolific writer on political and economic subjects. His most famous work was *Imperialism* (No. 111), but, in his economic writings, he also anticipated parts of the work of J. M. Keynes.]

The Liberals of this country as a party never committed themselves either to the theory or the policy of this narrow 'laissez-faire' individualism; they never conceived liberty as something limited in quantity, or purely negative in character. But it is true that they tended to lay an excessive emphasis upon the aspect of liberty which consists in absence of restraint, as compared with the other aspect which consists in presence of opportunity; and it is this tendency, still lingering in the mind of the Liberal Party, that to-day checks its energy and blurs its vision. A more constructive and a more evolutionary idea of liberty is needed to give the necessary *elan de vie* to the movement; and every cause of liberation, individual, class, sex, and national, must be recharged with the fresh enthusiasm of this fuller faith.

Liberalism will probably retain its distinction from Socialism, in taking for its chief test of policy the freedom of the individual citizen rather than the strength of the State, though the antagonism of the two standpoints may tend to disappear in the light of progressive experience. But it will justify itself by two great enlargements of its liberative functions. In seeking to realise liberty for the individual citizen as 'equality of opportunity' it will recognise that, as the area and nature of opportunities are constantly shifting, so the old limited conception of the task of Liberalism must always advance. . . . We must fearlessly face as our first, though not our only question, What is a free Englishman to-day? If we answer this question faithfully, we shall recognise that it comprises many elements of real liberty and opportunity which have not been won for the people as a whole. Is a man free who has not equal opportunity with his fellows of such access to all material and moral means of personal development and work as shall contribute to his own welfare and that of his society? Such equal opportunity at least implies an equal access to the use of his native land as a workplace and a home, such mobility as will enable him to dispose of his personal energies to the best advantage, easy access to that factor of capital or credit which modern industry recognises as essential to economic independence, and to whatever new form of industrial power, electric or other, may be needed to co-operate with human efforts. A man is not really free for purposes of self-development in life and work who is not adequately provided in all these respects, and no small part of constructive Liberalism must be devoted to the attainment of these equal opportunities.

But all such distinctively economic liberties are evidently barren unless accompanied by a far more adequate realisation of spiritual and intellectual opportunity than is contained in our miserably meagre conception of popular education. For education in the large meaning of the term is the opportunity of opportunities, and the virtual denial to the majority of the people of any real share of the spiritual kingdom which is rightly theirs must remain for all true Liberals an incessant challenge to their elementary sense of justice, as well as the most obvious impediment both to the achievement and the utilisation of every other element of personal liberty. It is this truth that also underlies the great struggle against militarism and imperialism which assumes so many shapes upon the stage of politics, and which, driven to the last resort, will always be disclosed as the antagonism between physical and moral force, as the guardian and promoter of civilisation. The practical interpretation and realisation of moral and intellectual liberty for the people as the most urgent and fruitful of all tasks of Liberalism, though standing first in order of importance, cannot, however, be detached in political endeavour from the other more material liberties. It is the peril, as it is the glory, of Liberalism that it is required to drive several teams abreast along the road of progress.

Finally, though Liberals must ever insist that each enlargement of the authority and functions of the State must justify itself as an enlargement of personal liberty, interfering with individuals only in order to set free new and larger opportunities, there need remain in Liberalism no relics of that positive hostility to public methods of co-operation which crippled the old Radicalism. When society is confronted, as it sometimes will be, by a breakdown of competition and a choice between private monopoly and public enterprise, no theoretic objections to the State can be permitted to militate against public safety.

J. A. Hobson, *The Crisis of Liberalism* (1909),
pp. 92-5.

90. L. T. HOBHOUSE: *Liberalism*
(1911)

[L. T. Hobhouse (1864–1929) was a philosopher and journalist. He was associated with the *Manchester Guardian* for most of his working life, but was also the Martin White Professor of Sociology at the University of London, 1907–29.]

For the moment we have only to deal with those actions of State which compel all citizens, or all whom they concern, to fall in with them and allow of no divergence. This kind of coercion tends to increase. Is its extension necessarily an encroachment upon liberty, or are the elements of value secured by collective control distinct from the elements of value secured by individual choice, so that within due limits each may develop side by side?

We have already declined to solve the problem by applying Mill's distinction between self-regarding and other-regarding actions, first because there are no actions which may not directly or indirectly affect others, secondly because even if there were they would not cease to be matter of concern to others. The common good includes the good of every member of the community, and the injury which a man inflicts upon himself is matter of common concern, even apart from any ulterior effect upon others. If we refrain from coercing a man for his own good, it is not because his good is indifferent to us, but because it cannot be furthered by coercion. The difficulty is founded on the nature of the good itself, which on its personal side depends on the spontaneous flow of feeling checked and guided not by external restraint but by rational self-control. To try to form character by coercion is to destroy it in the making. Personality is not built up from without but grows from within, and the function of the outer order is not to create it, but to provide for it the most suitable conditions of growth. Thus, to the common question whether it is possible to make men good by Act of Parliament, the reply is that it is not possible to compel morality, because morality is the act or character of a free agent, but that it is possible to create the conditions under which morality can develop, and among these not the least important is freedom from compulsion by others. . . .

Where, then, is the sphere of compulsion, and what is its value? The reply is that compulsion is of value where outward conformity is of value, and this may be in any case where the non-conformity of one wrecks the purpose of others. We have already remarked that liberty itself only rests upon restraint. Thus a religious body is not, properly speaking, free to march in procession through the streets unless people of a different religion are restrained from pelting the procession with stones and pursuing it with insolence. We restrain them from disorder not to teach them the genuine spirit of religion, which they will not learn in the police court, but to secure to the other party the right of worship unmolested. The enforced restraint has its value in the action that it sets free. But we may not only restrain one man from obstructing another—and the extent to which we do this is the measure of the freedom we maintain—but we may also restrain him from obstructing the general will; and this we have to do whenever uniformity is necessary to the end which the general will has in view. The majority of employers in a trade we may suppose would be willing to adopt certain precautions for the health or safety of their workers, to lower hours or to raise the rate of wages. They are unable to do so, however, as long as a minority, perhaps as long as a single employer, stands out. He would beat them in competition if they were voluntarily to undertake expenses from which he is free. In this case, the will of a minority, possibly the will of one man, thwarts that of the remainder. It coerces them, indirectly, but quite as effectively as if he were their master. If they, by combination, can coerce him no principle of liberty is violated. It is coercion against coercion, differing possibly in form and method, but not in principle or in spirit. Further, if the community as a whole sympathizes with the one side rather than with the other, it can reasonably bring the law into play. Its object is not the moral education of the recusant individuals. Its object is to secure certain conditions which it believes necessary for the welfare of its members, and which can only be secured by an enforced uniformity.

It appears, then, that the true distinction is not between self-regarding and other-regarding actions, but between coercive and non-coercive actions. The function of State coercion is to override individual coercion, and, of course, coercion exercised by any association of individuals within the State. It is by this means that it maintains liberty of expression, security of persons and property, genuine freedom of contract, the rights of public meeting and association, and finally its own power to carry out common objects undefeated by the recalcitrance of individual members. Undoubtedly it endows both individuals and associations with powers as well as with rights. But over these powers it must exercise supervision in the interests of equal justice. Just as compulsion failed in the sphere of liberty, the sphere of spiritual growth, by the mere absence of supervisory restriction, men are able directly or indirectly to put constraint on one another. This is why there is no intrinsic and inevitable conflict between liberty and compulsion, but at bottom a mutual need. The object of compulsion is to secure the most favourable external conditions of inward growth and happiness so far as these conditions depend on combined action and uniform observance. The sphere of liberty is the sphere of growth itself. There is no true opposition between liberty as such and control as such, for every liberty rests on a corresponding act of control. The true opposition is between the control that cramps the personal life and the spiritual order, and the control that is aimed at securing the external and material conditions of their free and unimpeded development.

L. T. Hobhouse, *Liberalism* (1911), pp. 142-7.

2. THE EXTENSION OF DEMOCRACY

91. HERBERT SAMUEL: *Liberalism*
(1902)

For how can there be true self-government if restrictions, whether formal or informal, written or unwritten, are allowed to limit the people's free choice of their representatives? What liberty of election is there when all men of small income, however able, upright and earnest, however closely their convictions may tally with those of the electors, are barred from candidature; when political associations are compelled to seek their candidates within a small circle of rich men, and to accept—notoriously a frequent case— some dilettante politician, some landowner or capitalist whose views on important points are not their own, some questionable financier or some lawyer more ambitious than reliable, solely because there is no other available member of their party who possesses the necessary means? What hope is there of adequate social reform when the Lower Chamber is so composed that it can only approach industrial questions from the outside and never from the inside, can only know the needs of the people by information at second-hand and never learn them by actual experience; when a class spirit pervades it, leading it to deal with progressive legislation like an unwilling servant, idle whenever the master's eye is not on him, careless of details, obeying rather the letter than the spirit of the orders he has received? And finally, what freedom of career is there when this road is closed; when the poor man, however capable, sees the higher

positions in the State arbitrarily denied to him, when the
nation blindly repulses from the Parliament and from the
Ministry all talent that is not combined with wealth? The
House of Commons is the most conspicuous theatre of public
action, and gives the widest scope for useful work. To enter
it is one of the most honourable ambitions that a British
subject can form. An injustice is done to the majority of
the nation, if its doors, opened wide to the rich, are left
scarcely ajar for the poor.

Such are the grave abuses that attach to the present system
and such the reasons that lead Liberals to demand the grant
of a moderate salary to Members of Parliament, together
with the payment of the official expenses of elections from
public funds.

Herbert Samuel, *Liberalism* (1902), pp. 92-5.

92. Sir HENRY CAMPBELL-BANNERMAN:
Speech to the National Liberal Federation at Plymouth,
7 June 1907

['The quarrel' had resulted from the tactics of the House of Lords
during the first eighteen months of the Campbell-Bannerman Ministry's
life. In 1906 an Education Bill and a Plural Voting Bill had been killed
in the Lords, and in 1907 four land reform bills had been either mutilated
or destroyed.]

The quarrel was forced upon us, and it is because we are
in earnest about our legislation and intend to find a way of
getting it through, and because we do not regard politics as a
mere game played for the amusement of two parties in the
State, that we propose to bring this matter to a serious and
decisive test. And remember another thing: these successive
blows at the authority of the House of Commons, directed
though they were at particular measures, were part of the
general scheme for discrediting—not this Government, that
was a small affair—but discrediting any Liberal Government,
and impressing the country with the view that a Liberal
Ministry, be it ever so powerful, ever so united, is impotent
to carry its measures. You observe the brilliant idea. They
first make our work well-nigh impossible and then hold us

up to the contempt of the country as bunglers and impostors. And what is the sequel to that? What are they hoping and praying for in their Primrose lodge and tariff reform camp meetings? It is this, that the House of Lords by these tactics will set Protection on its feet again, and drive the electors in a fit of disgust back into the fold where for twenty long years they have been shepherded and fleeced. That is the game, and it may be exceedingly clever; but there is one thing I have learned in my Parliamentary experience . . . it is not cleverness which pays in the long run. The people of this country are a straightforward people. They like honesty and straightforwardness of purpose. They may laugh at it and they may be amused by it and they may in a sense admire it, but they do not like cleverness! You may be too clever by half. Sir, they are reckoning without their host. There is one thing they have overlooked. His Majesty's Government have no intention to play the part referred to them in this nice ·little game, and when I hear those gusts of mirthless laughter arising from the Opposition benches whenever the question of the House of Lords is referred to, I feel sorry that the relics of a once great and respectable party, as the Conservative party was, are so engulfed in their petty tactics, so deluded by the flippant habit of mind which has become popular among them, as to be totally oblivious to the gravity of the issue which stands at their door.

I am addressing you to-night under a deep sense of responsibility; for the very existence of Liberalism as a force in the State and as an instrument of progress in the times to come depends upon the outcome of the struggle upon which we are now embarking. If there is to be no place for self-respecting Liberalism in this country, if Liberalism with the country behind it cannot enforce its policy, then is it not better that we should go down in the assertion of our rights rather than linger on as a shadow of a Government, strong, perhaps, in numbers, strong, perhaps, also it may be, in good intentions, but withal without authority or power? I ask you now to turn to the constitutional issue involved in this controversy. And I will tell you at once that, in my opinion, the Lords have abused their powers within the Constitution, and that in assigning to them their proper place, as it is our purpose to do—and a very good, useful, and honourable place it is—so far from attacking the Constitution or setting up a revolution, it is we who are defending, it is the Lords who are straining the Constitution. Remember that we are forced into this struggle by the circumstances which surround and confront us; it is the climax of a series of attacks upon the rights and liberties of the Commons. Therefore, if the immediate causes of the deadlock and confusion were withdrawn, we should none the less be bound to go forward. What is the doctrine of the Constitution? That doctrine is not as you might infer from the action of the peers, it is not that there are two Chambers exercising co-ordinate authority and equal powers. The peers themselves put forward no such claim. In terms they admit the predominance of the House of Commons, although their practice at times belies their profession. The last word, the ultimate supremacy, rests with the House of Commons. That is the accepted constitutional doctrine, and what we have to do is to see that the relations between the two Houses are so arranged as to define the limits within which the power which the Constitution has conferred upon the Lords may be properly exercised. . . . We must give the House of Lords to understand that, whilst we are perfectly ready to legislate with due deliberation and give every weight to their representations, the British people must be masters in their own house. . . . Above all things, remember, as you go into this struggle, that the greatest instrument of liberty, justice, and progress in this world is in your keeping and that it is yours to see that the efficiency of this great instrument of Parliamentary Government is not soiled and blunted any longer in the misuse to which it has been subjected.

The Times, 8 June 1907.

93. DAVID LLOYD GEORGE: Speech at
Newcastle, 9 October 1909

[The 'Bill' was the Finance Bill, the Lloyd George Budget of 1909, which was to be rejected by the House of Lords on its second reading on 30 November 1909.]

Well, now, we are going to send the Bill up—all the taxes or none. What will the Lords do? I tell you frankly it is a matter which concerns them far more than it concerns us. . . .

But still this is the great Constitutional party, and if there is one thing more than another better established about the British Constitution it is this, that the Commons, the Commons alone, have the complete control of supply and ways and means; and what our fathers established through centuries of struggle and of strife—even of bloodshed—we are not going to be traitors to.

Who talks about altering or meddling with the Constitution? The Constitutional party—the great Constitutional party. As long as the Constitution gave rank and possession and power to the Lords it was not to be interfered with. As long as it secured even their sports from intrusion and made interference with them a crime; as long as the Constitution enforced royalties and ground rents and fees and premiums and fines, and all the black retinue of exaction; as long as it showered writs and summonses and injunctions and distresses and warrants to enforce them, then the Constitution was inviolate. It was something that was put in the same category as religion, that no man should touch with rude hands, something that the chivalry of the nation ought to range itself in defence of. But the moment the Constitution looks round; the moment the Constitution begins to discover that there are millions of people outside park gates who need attention, then the Constitution is to be torn to pieces.

Let them realise what they are doing. They are forcing a revolution, and they will get it. The Lords may decree a revolution, but the people will direct it. If they begin, issues will be raised that they little dream of. Questions will be asked which are now whispered in humble voices, and answers will be demanded then with authority. The question will be asked whether five hundred men, ordinary men chosen accidentally from among the unemployed, should override the judgement of millions of people who are engaged in the industry which makes the wealth of the country.

That is one question. Another will be, Who ordained that a few should have the land of Britain as a perquisite? Who made ten thousand people owners of the soil, and the rest of us trespassers in the land of our birth? Who is it who is responsible for the scheme of things whereby one man is engaged through life in grinding labour to win a bare and precarious subsistence for himself, and when at the end of his days, he claims at the hands of the community he served a poor pension of eight pence a day, he can only get it through a revolution; and another man who does not toil receives every hour of the day, every hour of the night while he slumbers, more than his poor neighbour receives in a whole year of toil? Where did the table of that law come from? Whose finger inscribed it? These are the questions that will be asked.

D. Lloyd George, *Better Times* (1910), pp. 173-5.

94. H. H. ASQUITH: Speech at the Albert Hall, 10 December 1909

The immediate, the actively provoking cause of what is rightly called a constitutional crisis is the entirely new claim put forward by the House of Lords, not only to meddle with, but, in effect, to control and to mould our national finances. . . . This year, by one stroke, they have taken upon themselves to shatter the whole fabric of the year's taxation. This, I repeat, is a new and entirely unexpected danger to popular liberties. Two years ago it was as undreamt of as would have been, as it is to-day, the revival by an arbitrary Minister of the veto of the Crown. . . .

We are indeed . . . suddenly confronted with no less than three constitutional innovations. In the first place we have the claim of the Upper House, not as an archaic legal survival, but as a living and effective right, to control the levying of taxation. In the second place we have the claim of the same House, a body which cannot itself be dissolved, to compel a dissolution of the popular Chamber. And, lastly, as a consequence and a corollary of the other two, we have the assertion of its power to make or unmake the Executive Government of the Crown. Every one of these revolutionary pretensions we shall withstand for all we are worth. The result is what at first sight seems rather like a paradox. We, the progressive party, find ourselves here to-day, in the first place, occupying Conservative and con-stitutional ground, defending the liberties which have been transmitted to us from the past against invasions and usurpa-tions which have for the first time received the official countenance of the Tory party. What has been done once may be done again. I do not say that it will be. But I do say this, that it becomes our first duty to take effective steps to make its recurrence impossible. We shall therefore demand authority from the electorate to translate the ancient and unwritten usage into an Act of Parliament, and to place upon the Statute-book the recognition, explicit and complete, of the settled doctrine of our Constitution, that it is beyond the province of the House of Lords to meddle in any way, to any degree, or for any purpose, with our national finance. . . .

So far we are on the defensive. But at the same time and by the same action the House of Lords has not indeed raised but has hurried on a larger issue still. I tell you quite plainly and I tell my fellow-countrymen outside that neither I nor any other Liberal Minister supported by a majority in the House of Commons is going to submit again to the rebuffs and the humiliations of the last four years. We shall not assume office, and we shall not hold office, unless we can secure the safeguards which experience shows us to be necessary for the legislative utility and honour of the party of progress. . . . I myself, and I believe a large majority of the Liberal party, are in favour of what is called a bicameral system. I see nothing inconsistent with democratic principle or practice in a Second Chamber as such. On the contrary, I see much practical advantage that might result from the existence side by side with the House of Commons of a body, not, indeed, of co-ordinate authority, but suitable in its numbers and by its composition to exercise impartially in regard to our ordinary legislation the powers of revision, amendment, fuller deliberation, and, subject to proper safeguards, of delay. . . . Those are both useful and dignified functions. Yes, gentlemen, but we have got to deal with a present and an immediate necessity. . . . Our present position gives us all the drawbacks, with few, if any, of the advantages of a Second Chamber. For what is our actual Second Chamber? It is a body which has no pretensions or qualifications to be the organ or the interpreter of the popular will. It is a body in which one party in the State is in possession of a permanent and overwhelming majority. It is a body which, as experience has shown, in temper and in action is frankly and nakedly partisan. It is a body which does not attempt to exercise any kind of effective control over the legislation of the other House when its own party is in a majority there. It is a body which, when the conditions are reversed, however clear and emphatic the verdict of the country has been, sets itself to work to mutilate and to destroy democratic legislation, and even in these last days it lays a usurping hand on democratic finance. That is a plain, literal, unvarnished picture of what everyone knows to be the fact.

We are going to ask the country to give us authority to apply an effective remedy to these intolerable conditions. Here, again, what is to be done is to be done by Act of Parliament. The time for unwritten convention has unhappily gone by. We are not proposing the abolition of the House of Lords or setting up a Second Chamber, but we do ask, and we are going to ask the electors to say, that the House of Lords shall be confined to the proper functions of a Second Chamber, which I enumerated to you a few moments ago. The absolute veto which it at present possesses must go. The powers which it claims from time to time of, in effect, compelling us to choose between a dissolution and so far as legislative projects are concerned—legislative sterility—that power must go also. The people, in future, when they elect a new House of Commons, must be able to feel, what they cannot feel now, that they are sending to

Westminster men who will have the power not merely of proposing and debating, but of making laws. The will of the people, as deliberately expressed by their elected representatives, must, within the limits of a single Parliament, be made effective.

H. H. Asquith, *The Three Capital Issues.*
A speech .... 10 December 1909
(Liberal Publication Dept.).

95. L. T. HOBHOUSE: *Liberalism*
(1911)

Thus individuals will contribute to the social will in very varying degrees, but the democratic thesis is that the formation of such a will, that is, in effect, the extension of intelligent interest in all manner of public things, is in itself a good, and more than that, it is a condition qualifying other good things. Now the extension of interest is not to be created by democratic forms of government, and if it neither exists nor can be brought into existence, democracy remains an empty form and may even be worse than useless. On the other hand, where the capacity exists the establishment of responsible government is the first condition of its development. Even so, it is not the sole condition. The modern State is a vast and complex organism. The individual voter feels himself lost among the millions. He is imperfectly acquainted with the devious issues and large problems of the day, and is sensible how little his solitary vote can affect their decision. What he needs to give him support and direction is organisation with his neighbours and fellow-workers. He can understand, for example, the affairs of his trade union, or, again, of his chapel. They are near to him. They affect him, and he feels that he can affect them. Through these interests, again, he comes into touch with wider questions—with a Factory Bill or an Education Bill— and in dealing with these questions he will now act as one of an organised body whose combined voting strength will be no negligible quantity. Responsibility comes home to him, and to bring home responsibility is the problem of all government. The development of social interest—and that is democracy—depends not only on adult suffrage and the supremacy of the elected legislature, but on all the intermediate organisations which link the individual to the whole. This is one among the reasons why devolution and the revival of local government, at present crushed in this country by a centralised bureaucracy, are of the essence of democratic progress.

The success of democracy depends on the response of the voters to the opportunities given them. But, conversely, the opportunities must be given in order to call forth the response. The exercise of popular government is itself an education. In considering whether any class or sex or race should be brought into the circle of enfranchisement, the determining consideration is the response which that class or sex or race would be likely to make to the trust. Would it enter effectively into the questions of public life, or would it be so much passive voting material, wax in the hands of the less scrupulous politicians? The question is a fair one, but people are too ready to answer it in the less favourable sense, on the ground of the actual indifference or ignorance which they find or think they find among the unenfranchised. They forget that in that regard enfranchisement itself may be precisely the stimulus needed to awaken interest, and while they are impressed with the danger of admitting ignorant and irresponsible, and perhaps corruptible voters to a voice in the government, they are apt to overlook the counterbalancing danger of leaving a section of the community outside the circle of civic responsibility. The actual work of government must affect, and also it must be affected by, its relation to all who live within the realm. To secure good adaptation it ought, I will not say to reflect, but at least to take account of, the dispositions and circumstances of every class in the population. If any one class is dumb, the result is that Government is to that extent uninformed. It is not merely that the interests of that class may suffer, but that, even with the best will, mistakes may be made in handling it, because it cannot speak for itself. Officious spokesmen will pretend to represent its views, and will obtain, perhaps, undue authority merely because there is no way of bringing them to book. So among ourselves does the press constantly represent public opinion to be one thing while the cold arithmetic of the polls conclusively declares it to be another. The ballot alone effectively liberates the quiet citizen from the tyranny of the shouter and the wire-puller.

L. T. Hobhouse, *Liberalism* (1911), pp. 231-5.

3. SOCIAL REFORM

96. JOSEPH CHAMBERLAIN:
Speech at Hengler's Circus, Hull, 5 August 1885

Everywhere the reforms to which the resolution has made reference are casting their shadows before; everywhere in the country I see a quickening of political life; everywhere there is discussion and hope and expectation. Gentlemen, it will be dangerous to disappoint that hope. It will be impossible to stifle that discussion; and if there are any people who imagine that the enfranchisement of two millions of citizens can have taken place, and that these men intend to make no use of the privilege which has been conferred upon them, they will have a rude awakening. They are not wise men, they are not the true friends of the institutions of this country, who will not bring impartial minds to the consideration of the new problems that are calling for solution. . . .

I have always had a deep conviction that when the people came to govern themselves, and when the clamour of vested interests and class privileges was overborne by the powerful voice of the whole nation, that then the social evils which disgrace our civilisation, and the wrongs which have cried vainly for redress, would at last find a hearing and a remedy. . . . I do not want you to think that I suggest to you that legislation can accomplish all that we desire, and above all, I would not lead you into wild and revolutionary projects. . . . But, on the other hand, I want you not to accept as final or as perfect, arrangements under which millions of your fellow-countrymen are subject to untold privations and misery, with the evidence all around them of accumulated wealth and unbounded luxury. . . . I believe that the great evil with which we have to deal is the excessive inequality in the distribution of riches. Ignorance, intemperance, immorality and disease—these things are all interdependent and closely connected; and although they are often the cause of poverty they are still more frequently the consequence of destitution. . . . It is not our duty, it is not our wish, to pull down and abase the rich, although I do not think that the excessive aggregation of wealth in a few hands is any advantage to anybody. But our object is to elevate the poor, to raise the general condition of the people.

The Radical Platform, Speeches by the Rt. Hon.
J. Chamberlain, M.P. (1885), pp. 2-4.

97. JOSEPH CHAMBERLAIN:
Speech at the Public Hall, Warrington, 8 September 1885

. . . There is not a single Liberal candidate who has not accepted some one or more points of the Radical programme. It is therefore perfectly futile and ridiculous for any political Rip Van Winkle to come down from the mountain on which he has been slumbering, and to tell us that these things are to be excluded from the Liberal programme. The world has moved on whilst these dreamers have been sleeping, and it would be absurd to ignore the growth of public opinion, and the change in the situation which the Reform Acts have produced.

I do not wish you to think that I desire to rest my case upon political necessity alone. If we cannot convince our allies of the justice and reasonableness of our views, then, with whatever reluctance, we must part company; we will fight alone; we will appeal unto Caesar; we will go to the people from whom we come and whose cause we plead; and, although the verdict may be delayed, I, for my part, have not one shadow of doubt as to the ultimate decision. We have been looking to the extension of the franchise in order to bring into prominence questions which have been too long neglected. The great problem of our civilisation is still unsolved. We have to account for and to grapple with the mass of misery and destitution in our midst, co-existent as it is with the evidence of abundant wealth and teeming prosperity. It is a problem which some men would put aside by reference to the eternal laws of supply and demand, to the necessity of freedom of contract, and to the sanctity of every private right of property. But, gentlemen, these phrases are the convenient cant of selfish wealth. . . . These are no answers to our questions. I quite understand the reason for timidity in dealing with this question so long as Government was merely the expression of the will of a prejudiced and limited few. . . . But now that we have a Government of the people by the people, we will go on and we will make it for every man his natural rights—his right to existence, and to a fair enjoyment of it. I shall be told tomorrow that this is Socialism. . . . Of course, it is Socialism. The Poor-Law is Socialism. The Education Act is Socialism. The greater part of municipal work is Socialism, and every kindly act of legislation by which the community has sought to discharge its responsibilities and its obligations to the poor is Socialism, but it is none the worse for that. Our object is the elevation of the poor, of the masses of the people—a levelling up, by which we shall do something to remove the excessive inequality in social life which is now one of the greatest dangers. . . . I do not pretend that for every grievance a remedy will be found. We must try experiments as we are bound to do . . . and if we fail, let us try again and again until we succeed.

Ibid. pp. 22-3.

98. W. E. GLADSTONE:
Speech at the Opening of new Reading and Recreation Rooms at Saltney, 26 October 1889

We live at a time when there is a disposition to think that the Government ought to do this and that, and that the Government ought to do everything. There are things which the Government ought to do, and does not do, I have no doubt. In former periods the Government have neglected much, and possibly even now they neglect something. But there is a danger on the other side. If the Government takes into its hand that which the man ought to do for himself, it will inflict upon him greater mischiefs than all the benefits he will have received or all the advantages that would accrue from them. The essence of the whole thing is, that the spirit of self-reliance, the spirit of true and genuine manly independence, should be preserved in the minds of the people, in the minds of the masses of the people, in the minds of every member of that class. If he loses his self-reliance, if he learns to live in a craven dependence upon wealthier people rather than upon himself, you may depend upon it he incurs mischiefs for which no compensation can be made.

The Speeches of W. E. Gladstone (1892),
vol. x, p. 132.

99. LORD ROSEBERY:
Speech at Chesterfield, 16 December 1901

Now, having shown these facts, what is the advice I have to offer you? The first piece is this, that you have to clean your slate. It is six years now since you were in office. It is sixteen years since you were in anything like power. During that time the world has not stood still. It does seem to me that under these circumstances the primary duty of the Liberal party is to wipe its slate clean and consider very carefully what it is going to write on it in future. Now, there will be some who will not agree with that advice, for I will tell you a secret. There are a great many Tory Liberals in the Liberal party. There is a Toryism in Liberalism, as great and as deep, unconscious though it be, as any in the Carlton Club. There are men who sit still with the fly-blown phylacteries of obsolete policies bound round their foreheads, who do not remember that, while they have been mumbling their incantations to themselves, the world has been marching and revolving, and that if they have any hope of leading or guiding it they must march and move with it too. . . . You may ask me what is the line of policy and what are the measures to which I should apply the axioms which I have laid down, and which I am happy to see have received the meed of your approval. Well, it is a little difficult to put oneself in the place of proposing measures. One can only do that by imagining oneself responsible Minister at this moment, and any so wild a flight of imagination I can scarcely conceive. But my watchword if I were in office at this moment would be summed up in one single word—the word 'efficiency.' If we have not learned from this war that we have greatly lagged behind in efficiency we have learned nothing, and our treasure and our lives are thrown away unless we learn the lessons which the war has given us.

> Lord Rosebery, *National Policy*. A speech
> delivered .... 16 December 1901,
> authorised edn. (1902).

100. WINSTON S. CHURCHILL:
Speech at St. Andrew's Hall, Glasgow,
11 October 1906

Something more is needed if we are to get forward. There lies the function of the Liberal Party. Liberalism supplies at once the higher impulse and the practicable path; it appeals to persons by sentiments of generosity and humanity; it proceeds by course of moderation. By gradual steps, by steady effort from day to day, from year to year, Liberalism enlists hundreds of thousands upon the side of progress and popular democratic reform whom militant Socialism would drive into violent Tory reaction. That is why the Tory Party hate us. That is why they, too, direct their attacks upon the great organisation of the Liberal Party, because they know it is through the agency of Liberalism that society will be able in the course of time to slide forward, almost painlessly—for the world is changing very fast—on to a more even and a more equal foundation. That is the mission which lies before Liberalism. The cause of the Liberal Party is the cause of the left-out millions; and because we believe that there is in all the world no other instrument of equal potency and efficacy available at the present time for the purposes of social amelioration, we are bound in duty and in honour to guard it from all attacks, whether they arise from violence or from reaction.

There is no necessity to-night to plunge into a discussion of the philosophical divergencies between Socialism and Liberalism. It is not possible to draw a hard-and-fast line between individualism and collectivism. You cannot draw it either in theory or in practice. That is where the Socialist makes a mistake. Let us not imitate that mistake. No man can be a collectivist alone or an individualist alone. He must be both an individualist and a collectivist. The nature of man is a dual nature. The character of the organisation of human society is dual. Man is at once a unique being and a gregarious animal. For some purposes he must be collectivist, for others he is, and he will for all time remain, an individualist. . . . No view of society can possibly be complete which does not comprise within its scope both collective organisation and individual incentive. The whole tendency of civilisation is, however, towards the multiplication of the collective functions of society. The ever-growing complications of civilisation create for us new services which have to be undertaken by the State, and create for us an expansion of the existing services. There is a growing feeling, which I entirely share, against allowing those services which are in the nature of monopolies to pass into private hands. There is a pretty steady determination, which I am convinced will become effective in the present Parliament, to intercept all future unearned increment which may arise from the increase in the speculative value of land. There will be an ever-widening area of municipal enterprise. I go farther; I should like to see the State embark on various novel and adventurous experiments. I am delighted to see that Mr. Burns is now interesting himself in afforestation. I am of opinion that the State should increasingly assume the position of the reserve employer of labour. I am very sorry we have not got the railways of this country in our hands. We may do something better with the canals, and we are all agreed, every one in this hall who belongs to the Progressive Party, that the State must increasingly and earnestly concern itself with the care of the sick and the aged, and, above all, of the children. I look forward to the universal establishment of minimum standards of life and labour, and their progressive elevation as the increasing energies of production may permit. I do not think that Liberalism in any circumstances can cut itself off from this fertile field of social effort, and I would recommend you not to be scared in discussing any of these proposals just because some old woman comes along and tells you they are Socialistic. If you take my advice, you will judge each case on its merits. Where you find that State enterprise is likely to be ineffective, then utilise private enterprises, and do not grudge them their profits.

W. S. Churchill, *Liberalism and the Social Problem*
(1909), pp. 78-81.

101. DAVID LLOYD GEORGE: Speech at Swansea, 1 October 1908

What is the work still waiting the Liberal Party in this country? It is to establish complete religious equality in our institutions. There is no religious equality so long as men of capacity and character are debarred from competing for teacherships in 14,000 State schools because they cannot conscientiously conform to the doctrines of some dominant sect. There is no religious equality as long as one sect whose dogmas, in Wales at any rate, are repudiated by the vast majority of the people, is able to pose as the official exponent of the faith of the Welsh people, and to enjoy all the privileges, emoluments, and endowments attached to that position. I place the establishment of complete religious equality in the forefront, because it lies in the domain of conscience . . . and nothing can save a people afflicted by such institutions from the spirit of bondage but an incessant protest against them. . . .

The same observations apply to the question of civil equality. We have not yet attained it in this country—far from it. You will not have established it in this land until the child of the poorest parent shall have the same opportunity for receiving the best education as the child of the richest. . . . It will never be established so long as you have five hundred men nominated by the lottery of birth to exercise the right of thwarting the wishes of the majority of forty millions of their countrymen in the determination of the best way of governing the country. I hope no prospect of a temporary material advantage will blind the people of this country to the permanent good for them of vindicating in the laws and institutions of the land these great principles, which lie at the root of freedom and good government for the people.

On the other hand, I think there is a danger that Liberals may imagine that their task begins and ends there. If they do so, then they will not accomplish even that task.

British Liberalism is not going to repeat the fate of Continental Liberalism. The fate of Continental Liberalism should warn them of that danger. It has been swept on one side before it had well begun its work, because it refused to adapt itself to new conditions. The Liberalism of the Continent concerned itself exclusively with mending and perfecting the machinery which was to grind corn for the people. It forgot that the people had to live whilst the process was going on, and people saw their lives pass away without anything being accomplished. British Liberalism has been better advised. It has not abandoned the traditional ambition of the Liberal Party to establish freedom and equality; but side by side with this effort it promotes measures for ameliorating the conditions of life for the multitude.

The old Liberals in this country used the natural discontent of the people with the poverty and precariousness of the means of subsistence as a motive power to win for them a better, more influential, and more honourable status in the citizenship of their native land. The new Liberalism, while pursuing this great political ideal with unflinching energy, devotes a part of its endeavour also to the removing of the immediate causes of discontent. It is true that men cannot live by bread alone. It is equally true that a man cannot live without bread. . . . It is a recognition of that elemental fact that has promoted legislation like the Old Age Pensions Act. It is but the beginning of things. . . . Poverty is the result of a man's own misconduct or misfortune. In so far

as he brings it on himself, the State cannot accomplish much.
It can do something to protect him. In so far as poverty is
due to circumstances over which the man has no control,
then the State should step in to the very utmost limit of its
resources, and save the man from the physical and mental
torture involved in extreme penury. . . . The aged we have
dealt with during the present Session. We are still confronted
with the more gigantic task of dealing with the rest—the
sick, the infirm, the unemployed, the widows, and the
orphans. No country can lay any real claim to civilisation
that allows them to starve. Starvation is a punishment that
society has ceased to inflict for centuries on its worst criminals,
and at its most barbarous stage humanity never starved
the children of the criminal. . . . Is it just, is it fair, is it
humane, to let them suffer privation? I do not think the
better-off classes, whose comfort is assured, realise the
sufferings of the unemployed workmen. What is poverty?
Have you felt it yourselves? If not, you ought to thank God
for having been spared its sufferings and temptations. Have
you ever seen others enduring it? Then pray God to forgive
you if you have not done your best to alleviate it. By poverty
I mean real poverty, not the cutting down of your establishment, not the limitation of your luxuries. I mean the poverty
of the man who does not know how long he can keep a roof
over his head, and where he will turn to find a meal for
the pinched and hungry little children who look to him for
sustenance and protection. That is what unemployment
means.

D. Lloyd George, *Better Times* (1910),
pp. 49-54.

102. L. T. HOBHOUSE: *Liberalism*
(1911)

By sternly withholding all external supports we should
teach the working classes to stand alone, and if there were
pain in the disciplinary process there was yet hope in the
future. They would come by degrees to a position of economic independence in which they would be able to face the

risks of life, not in reliance upon the State, but by the force of their own brains and the strength of their own right arms.

These views no longer command the same measure of assent. On all sides we find the State making active provision for the poorer classes and not by any means for the destitute alone. We find it educating the children, providing medical inspection, authorizing the feeding of the necessitous at the expense of the ratepayers, helping them to obtain employment through free Labour Exchanges, seeking to organise the labour market with a view to the mitigation of unemployment, and providing old age pensions for all whose incomes fall below thirteen shillings a week, without exacting any contribution. Now, in all this, we may well ask, is the State going forward blindly on the paths of broad and generous but unconsidered charity? Is it and can it remain indifferent to the effect on individual initiative and personal or parental responsibility? . . . Are we, in fact—for this is really the question—seeking charity or justice?

We said above that it was the function of the State to secure the conditions upon which mind and character may develop themselves. Similarly we may say now that the function of the State is to secure conditions upon which its citizens are able to win by their own efforts all that is necessary to a full civic efficiency. It is not for the State to feed, house, or clothe them. It is for the State to take care that the economic conditions are such that the normal man who is not defective in mind or body or will can by useful labour feed, house, and clothe himself and his family. The 'right to work' and the right to a 'living wage' are just as valid as the rights of person or property. That is to say, they are integral conditions of a good social order. A society in which a single honest man of normal capacity is definitely unable to find the means of maintaining himself by useful work is to that extent suffering from malorganisation. There is somewhere a defect in the social system, a hitch in the economic machine Now, the individual workman cannot put the machine straight. He is the last person to have any say in the control of the market. It is not his fault if there is overproduction in his industry, or if a new and cheaper process has been introduced which makes his particular skill, perhaps the product of years of application, a drug in the market. He does not direct or regulate industry. He is not responsible for its ups and downs, but he has to pay for them. That is why it is not charity but justice for which he is asking. Now, it may be infinitely difficult to meet his demand. To do so may involve a far-reaching economic reconstruction. The industrial questions involved may be so little understood that we may easily make matters worse in the attempt to make them better. All this shows the difficulty in finding means of meeting this particular claim of justice, but it does not shake its position as a claim of justice. A right is a right none the less though the means of securing it be imperfectly known; and the workman who is unemployed or underpaid through economic malorganisation will remain a reproach not to the charity but to the justice of society as long as he is to be seen in the land.

If this view of the duty of the State and the right of the workman is coming to prevail, it is owing partly to an enhanced sense of common responsibility, and partly to the teaching of experience. In the earlier days of the Free Trade era, it was permissible to hope that self-help would be an adequate solvent, and that with cheap food and expanding commerce the average workman would be able by the exercise of prudence and thrift not only to maintain himself in good times, but to lay by for sickness, unemployment, and old age. The actual course of events has in large measure disappointed these hopes. It is true that the standard of living in England has progressively advanced throughout the nineteenth century. It is true, in particular, that, since the disastrous period that preceded the Repeal of the Corn Laws and the passing of the Ten Hours Act, social improvement has been real and marked. Trade Unionism and co-operation have grown, wages upon the whole have increased, the cost of living has diminished, housing and sanitation have improved, the death rate has fallen from about twenty-two to less than fifteen per thousand. But with all this improvement the prospect of a complete and lifelong economic independence for the average workman upon the lines of individual competition, even when supplemented and guarded by the collective bargaining of the Trade Union, appears exceedingly remote. The increase of wages does not appear to be by any means proportionate to the general growth of wealth. The whole standard of living has risen; the very provision of education has brought with it new needs and has almost compelled a higher standard of life in order to satisfy them. As a whole, the working classes of England, though less thrifty than those of some Continental countries, cannot be accused of undue negligence with regard to the future. The accumulation of savings in Friendly Societies, Trade Unions, Co-operative Societies, and Savings Banks shows an increase which has more than kept pace with the rise in the level of wages; yet there appears no likelihood that the average manual worker will attain the goal of that full independence, covering all the risks of life for self and family, which can alone render the competitive system really adequate to the demands of a civilised conscience.

L. T. Hobhouse, *Liberalism* (1911), pp. 157-64.

103. C. P. SCOTT:
Leading article in the *Manchester Guardian*, 8 July 1912

As a result of the three-cornered contests in the two constituencies it is quite possible that while Liberalism and Labour are snapping and snarling at each other the Conservative dog may run away with the bone. That would be lamentable, but it might have its compensations if it led to a somewhat deeper consideration of the whole question of the relations of the two divisions of the party of progress. And first we must ask whether they are properly described as two divisions of the same army, or whether they ought rather to be regarded as quite separate armies pursuing distinct ends which might at any time bring them into direct and necessary antagonism. Few Liberals will hesitate as to the answer to be given to this question. They are in too complete accord with the essential aims of Labour, with its deep social sympathies, its demand for justice to the disinherited classes, its advocacy of international co-operation and a pacific policy in all external relations as the condition of internal reform, its steady refusal to permit the burden of taxation to be replaced on the means of subsistence of the poor by any cajoleries of tariffmongers—they see too clearly in all this the very life and temper of the only Liberalism worthy of the name to doubt for a moment that they have here not possible enemies but real and trustworthy friends. Tories may shriek of confiscation and parade the Socialist bogey, but the working men of England are not Socialists in any revolutionary sense, and it will be time enough for Liberals to refuse to co-operate cordially with those who most directly represent them when, if ever, the danger arises. For the present most Liberals will agree that, judged by their action in the House of Commons, the Labour members have shown themselves so far perhaps the very best Liberals in that assembly. Towards such a party the natural attitude of Liberals would seem to be one not of jealousy or hostility but of frank and intimate co-operation. Their aims are in substance our aims, their strength is our strength. In combination with them we can achieve great things; but any real antagonism would bring disaster to both.

C. P. Scott, 1846–1932. The Making of the
'Manchester Guardian' (1946), pp. 203-4.

4. THE GOVERNMENT AND THE NATIONAL ECONOMY

104. H. H. ASQUITH:
Speech at Cinderford, 8 October 1903

I should very much like to know how you are going to raise nine millions by a tax on foreign manufactures unless you treat as manufactures for the purpose of the tax articles like paper, leather, cement, and many forms of unwrought iron, which are just as much the raw materials of industries as iron ore or raw wood. All roads converge to the same point. You cannot have retaliation effectively as against your principal foreign competitors without ultimately taxing raw materials and food. Preference admittedly you cannot have without ultimately taxing food, and, as I have endeavoured to show, you cannot have it logically and consistently without also taxing raw materials. The moment you try to put *ad valorem* duties on manufactures, you lead to the same conclusion. Among the things imported into this country, of those on which no further British capital or labour is to be expended the proportion is so insignificant that it would not yield you any substantial revenue at all. By whatever way you approach it you come to the same goal. This is a proposal to tax British industry, to tax the food of the people, and thereby to diminish their wages, to tax the raw material out of which our wealth is made. It is a scheme which is based upon unfounded assumptions and unproved inferences. There is no ground whatever for saying either that British trade, as a whole, is stagnant or decaying, or that the Empire can only by maintained by reverting to fiscal devices which were tried and found wanting in the old days of Protection. Free influx of food and of raw materials, from every possible source of supply, into this country is not only as essential, but is more essential to our national strength and prosperity than it was in the days of Cobden and Peel.

Do not, however,—and this shall be my final word—do not let it be supposed that because we are driven to defend the citadel of free trade we, therefore, think that all is for the best and are content with a policy of folded hands. That there are disquieting features in our industrial as in our social conditions no honest observer, certainly no member of the party of progress, will be found to deny. We have seen industries, in which we ought to have maintained our supremacy, falling behind, and in some cases entirely taken away from us by our competitors. Defective knowledge, inferior processes, lack of flexibility or versatility, a stubborn industrial conservatism, these are the real enemies of British trade and have done us infinitely more harm than all the tariffs and all the dumping syndicates that were ever created. Better education, better training, better methods, a larger outlook, these are our primary needs—and it says little for our political sagacity that we should allow our minds to be diverted from them by quarrels as to the quantum of dogmatic theology that is to be administered to little children, or by attempts to revive the buried fallacies of Protection.

True it is also, that in spite of the continuous growth of our national prosperity, we still have with us the unemployed, the ill-fed, the aged poor; but here, again, let us look to natural and not to artificial remedies. Instead of raising the price of bread let us try to raise the standard of life. Temperance, better housing, the tenure and taxation of land, these are matters as to which we have allowed our legislation to fall deplorably into arrear. To take up the task in a spirit of faith and of resolute purpose is, I hope and believe, the mission of the Liberal Party in a Liberal Parliament.

All Sides of the Fiscal Controversy, ed. by T. C. Gilmour (1903), pp. 72-3.

105. SIR HENRY CAMPBELL-BANNERMAN: Speech at Bolton, 15 October 1903

Why are we free-traders? They say that it is a shibboleth. Well, a shibboleth is a test, and I am not sure that it is not somewhat of a test. It is a test of the patriotism, and the good sense, and the insight of a man which side he takes in a controversy such as this. But they talk of it as an obsolete shibboleth, and I am under the impression that they think a shibboleth means a doctrine, and this is only a way of trying to discredit and get rid of a doctrine which is inconvenient to them. Then they say we are worshippers of Cobden. Yes, we are admirers of Cobden. But we are not free-traders because of Cobden. On the other hand, we revere Cobden and Peel and Gladstone because of what they did for free trade, nor is it any condition of our belief in free trade that other countries should follow our example. The thing is good for us, good for this free country, good for every man, whatever his calling or station in the country may be. We are satisfied that it is right because it gives the freest play to individual energy and initiative and character and the largest liberty both to producer and consumer. We say that trade is injured when it is not allowed to follow its natural course, and when it is either hampered or diverted by artificial obstacles. We are not willing to substitute for a system which safeguards the interests of the whole community and maintains the purity of Parliamentary government a system of out-relief based upon favouritism and involving the transformation of healthy trades giving strength to the community into parasitic industries sapping its vitality. We do not wish to promote the creation of monopolies and privilege which protection invariably does. We are Liberals. We believe in free trade because we believe in the capacity of our countrymen. That at least is why I oppose protection root and branch, veiled and unveiled, one-sided or reciprocal. I oppose it in any form. . . . Men will say—they are saying —are you satisfied with the condition of the country, with the standard of well-being of the people? Here is Mr. Chamberlain advocating protection and putting everything else aside for it; here is Mr. Balfour lagging and limping lamely after him along the same path: tariffs are to them the divine remedy for the woes that afflict the State. It may be said, if you Liberals reject their remedy have you any remedy of your own, or do you think no remedy is required? I answer, No, Sir, emphatically; no, we are not content. We do not put forward free trade as being in itself a full remedy because we are satisfied with free trade and with the increase in our collective wealth that has accompanied it, and it must not be thought that we are not as determined as ever to deal with the impediments to the wholesome dis-tribution of wealth, whether they arise from bad laws, bad customs, bad institutions, bad social conditions, or from careless and extravagant administration.

The Times, 16 October 1903.

106. DAVID LLOYD GEORGE:
Speech at Bedford, 11 October 1913

Landlordism is the greatest of all monopolies in this land. Not only is it the greatest of all monopolies, it is the least controlled of all monopolies. I want to know the reason why, and I think the time has come to inquire. . . . I wonder how many people there are who realise what gigantic powers those who own the land possess upon the life of the nation.

The Sovereign of this Empire has no power over his subjects comparable to the power which the landlord has over his subjects. What can he do? The landowner can devastate the countryside. He can sweep every cottage away and convert it into a wilderness. He can do what no foreign invader is permitted to do now by the laws of civilised warfare— destroy cottages and drive the peasantry away to exile, convert the land into a desert. He can do more than a foreign enemy. Even in the old barbarous days of warfare, the moment the invader had retired the peasants returned to their homes, rebuilt their cottages, tilled their land, and the country assumed its normal appearance of industry and of thrift. Landlordism can by legal process not merely ordain a wilderness, it can maintain a wilderness. . . .

The workman is worse off than he used to be. There was a time when he had an interest in the land—a freehold interest. The labourer was a freeholder in the land. He had his commons. There he could graze a cow to give him butter and milk for himself and his children. There was a little patch where he could raise corn to feed them. There he had his poultry, his geese, his pigs—a patch of land where he could raise green produce for his table. He was a gentleman. He was independent. He had a stake in the country. His title was as ancient and apparently as indefeasible as that of the lord of the manor. Where has it gone to? Stolen! Landlord Parliaments have annexed Naboth's vineyard. There is now occasionally a little garden. Sometimes, as a matter of grace, he has a little row of potatoes, but he has no longer a right in the soil as his fathers had. He has been converted from a contented, well-fed, independent peasant to a hopeless, underpaid, landless drudge on the soil.

His wages are less to-day in proportion to their purchasing power than they were in the reign of Henry the Seventh. That is what we have done with him, and the land system is responsible for it. The labourer has no real access to the owner of the soil, and the responsibility must lie with the owner. . . . Land ownership is not merely an ownership; it is a stewardship. How idle it is to talk about the ownership of land as if it were something you were putting your money in and had no responsibility for! Land ownership has always through its history been established, maintained, and continued as stewardship for the State of that particular plot of British soil. It is enforced by ownership. Ownership is its condition. Ownership is its reward. In essence it is a trust. The landowners of England are responsible not merely for the farmers that till their soil, but for the labourers as well. . . .

It is not enough to deal with the state of things temporarily and tentatively. You must deal with it thoroughly. You must do what business-men do. When a business gets into a thoroughly bad condition through long years of mismanagement, it is no use tinkering here and mending there. You must recast it and put it on a thoroughly good basis and deal boldly with it. . . . I will give you a few of the directions in which this can be accomplished. The best labour and abundance of the best labour must be drawn to the land by first of all securing for the labourer a real living wage— and better conditions as to hours and otherwise. He must be given a decent, comfortable home to bring up his family in, and where he can rest after his toil. We must also give him a measure of land that will at least enable him to provide himself and his family with all the vegetables they need for their table. In Ireland by law an acre of land has been secured for each cottage. Hours of labour must be so ordered that leisure shall be left him for cultivating his garden.

You must secure for him a ladder of progress, something that will give him a prospect. There is the garden—that is the first step. There ought to be an allotment for those who are a little more enterprising. Those who are still more enterprising ought to be able to look forward to a small holding—ten, twenty, thirty, and up to fifty acres—and then the most enterprising and capable of all amongst them might look forward to taking their position among the substantial farmers in the community. That is for the labourer—a living wage, fair hours of labour, and for all of them a decent home, gardens, prospect of allotments, small holdings—that is the first condition of any safe, secure, beneficial land reform.

What next? . . . The cultivator, large or small, must be completely protected against confiscation of the improvements effected by him in the conditions of the land, whether such confiscation takes the form of capricious eviction or increase in the rent, on his own improvement, or the destruction of his crops by game. One more. Every effort must be made to equip the cultivator for his task, by instruction, by expert advice, and by other means. The cultivator must be assisted to get his produce to the market without paying excessive tolls to anyone, and without unnecessary delay, difficulty and expense in collection. . . .

The present system of rating, in so far as it discourages improvement by either owner or cultivator, and rewards the indolent or unenterprising or overcrowding owner who declines to put his land to the best use, must be reconsidered and recast. Greater and wider facilities must be given to the State for the acquisition of land, whether for immediate or prospective use, and the land must be acquired on terms which are fair to the community as well as to the owner. . . . There ought to be provision made for dealing with cases where the owner has either not the power or the means or the disposition to spend the necessary capital on buildings, draining, or other expenditure for the best equipment of his land.

And last of all—and this is the point—the powerful aid of the State, both by legislation, by administration, and by finance, must be invoked to carry these purposes—all of them—into effective operation. . . .

Walking along the principal streets of our great cities you will see displayed advertisements calling attention to the allurements of Canada, Australia, and New Zealand, for British labour. There you will find a picture of a nice home, with most beautiful surroundings. . . . Do you know when the land question will be settled in England, and Scotland and Wales? It will be when similar advertisements, setting forth the attractions of settlement on British soil will be displayed in some of the most prominent windows of the streets of every city and town in the land.

D. Lloyd George, *The Rural Land Problem.*
A speech delivered .... on 11 October
1913 (Liberal Publication Dept.).

107. DAVID LLOYD GEORGE:
Speech at Middlesbrough, 8 November 1913

I am not going to dwell on the effects of overcrowding. You know them just as well as I do. It is impossible to bring up a healthy, vigorous, and strong race of men and women under these conditions. It is a national weakness as well as a national disgrace. . . . Men do not live under these conditions of their own free will and choice. Why are they not altered? . . . In my judgement the great municipalities of this country have struggled manfully in very difficult circumstances to meet these conditions. What are their difficulties? The first difficulty they have to encounter is the price of land—the extravagant compensation they have to pay before they can move any step in the direction of reform; and the second difficulty is the pressing burden of rates. . . .

You have got a ring, a dense ring, of impenetrable greed compressing the town and crushing it in, until at its very heart you get a hard slum. We want to shatter that ring, so that the town shall have lungs and expand. . . . You have a great city in this county, the city of Leeds. A short time ago they wanted to acquire land for the purpose of their waterworks. They wanted to construct two reservoirs about thirty miles from the town. It was very essential for the life of the county. They applied to a great landowner who is a member of the House of Lords. He has two great estates in the neighbourhood. I believe he paid for one of them £25 an acre. He paid for the other £21 an acre, and this includes the land, good and bad, and buildings as well. That is what he paid. It is not what the Leeds Corporation paid. The Leeds Corporation applied for 394 acres on the edge of the moorland—not good agricultural land, not fairly good; most of it was bad. It was twenty miles from the nearest town of any size. Therefore it was not building land. What did he demand for it? I ought to explain that the rent was about 12/- an acre. He demanded £500 an acre. He demanded a huge sum of money because the construction of the waterworks would disturb the game on the rest of the property. . . . The arbitrators were summoned and they awarded two hundred years' purchase for that land, which was twenty miles removed from the nearest town of any size, on the edge of the moorland. Two hundred years' purchase they had to pay for acquiring land for the purpose of discharging the most elementary duty of a municipality—to provide water for the people. He paid rates on the basis of twelve shillings an acre. . . . Here is a case in Hastings. The Hastings Corporation had to buy land for an essential purpose. It was rated at £3 an acre, the price was £2000 an acre, which they paid. This was 677 years' purchase. Edinburgh has a more moderate case, they paid 384 years' purchase for their land. . . .

[Mr. Lloyd George then went on to discuss rating problems, suggesting that the National Exchequer should bear a bigger burden of the expense of local services and that there should be a reform of the rating system.]

There is another thing I want to say about rates. There are people who do not contribute now who ought. I gave you a case, the case of the noble Lord who sold 394 acres of his land. He was paying on the basis of twelve shillings an acre—he was probably paying about half-a-crown an acre. It is about time he should pay on the value he charges other people. The worst of the present system is that the moment a man neglects his property he escapes rates; the moment a man begins to improve his property he is fined as a ratepayer. A shopkeeper extends his premises, a great workshop is erected, the rate assessor comes down and says: 'Information has been laid against you, sir, that you have extended your works, that you are providing more employment for hundreds of workmen; are you guilty or not guilty?' He says: 'I cannot deny it.' Then says the assessor: 'I fine you £50 or £100 a year as long as you live, and don't do it again.' And he goes on to a moorland near Leeds, not a building in sight, not a plough on the land, no sign of one. Then he says, 'This is all right, no improvements here.' He meets the proprietor and says, 'What are you doing with this land?' The proprietor says, 'I am holding it up until Leeds people want water, then I am going to charge them 800 years' purchase for disturbing my pheasants.' The rate collector takes him by the hand and says, 'It is such men as you who make the greatness of our country; we will only put you down at twelve shillings an acre. We have to put something down.'

He goes home, feeling that he has done his duty. But somebody meets him in the street and says, 'Have you heard that Mr. Brown has added a bathroom to his house?' He says, 'I don't believe it; I will go there at once.' He goes and says, 'Is this true what I hear about you, that you have put on a new bathroom at your house?' Mr. Brown says, 'I am sorry', and the official replies, '£2 added to your assessment, sir.' And he walks home past a slum district, and says, 'No baths here, anyway.' The proprietor reassures him on the spot. 'No improvements about my property, it is not worth as much as it was years ago.' He takes him by the hand and says, 'Well done, thou good and faithful servant, go and write quickly thy assessment down by 15 per cent.' You think I am caricaturing. That is the rating system of England. . . .

Now I will summarise what we are going to do. . . . The first step will be the organisation of a complete survey, a national survey by the Imperial Government, of the whole of the housing accommodation of this island. Note will be taken of every inadequacy, of every defect, every insufficiency in housing accommodation—everything which leads to overcrowding and all its evils. There will be an inventory of all the slums, the insanitary character of dwellings, the lack of air, and light, and space, the absence of any means of healthy recreation, the deficiency of transport arrangements . . . in fact the survey will be complete and searching. And that survey will be the basis of all future operations against slums and overcrowded houses.

There will be facilities for the erection of new houses and transport, the removal of the existing difficulties in the way of town improvement, the extravagant prices of land, the heavy rates, the injustice in our rating assessments, and the restrictions on the purchase of land by municipalities. And then, when we come to the poor residuum of the population who, if you gave them a new house, could not pay for it, who, working hard and incessantly, cannot earn enough to pay for it, we propose to deal with that by extending our wages boards so far as to give the people who labour a fair day's wage for a fair day's work. And then there is the still larger problem of casual labour—the people who can only get a job for a day or two. That problem we hope to solve by opening up the resources of the land. . . .

I have told you something about the conditions of things in our great cities. It is hardly credible that in a great rich land like ours there should be so many people with hunger and pain haunting their lives. . . . I have a deep conviction that by a sustained effort we can eliminate for ever out of the life of this nation the waste, the disorganisation, the intemperance, the injustice, the wrong which is responsible for so much human wretchedness. There is a vast amount of human misery in this country which is preventable, and let no man be deceived by tranquillities, unless we exert ourselves to remove these evils the despair they create will rest on our souls.

> D. Lloyd George, *The Urban Land Problem.* Speeches
> delivered . . . . at Middlesbrough on 8 November
> 1913 (Liberal Publication Dept.).

108. L. T. HOBHOUSE: *Liberalism*
(1911)

In destroying the last relics of this system economic individualism has laid the basis of great material advances, but at great cost to the happiness of the masses. The ground problem in economics is not to destroy property, but to restore the social conception of property to its right place under conditions suitable to modern needs. This is not to be done by crude measures of redistribution, such as those of which we hear in ancient history. It is to be done by distinguishing the social from the individual factors in wealth, by bringing the elements of social wealth into the public coffers, and by holding it at the disposal of society to administer to the prime needs of its members.

The basis of property is social and that in two senses. On the one hand, it is the organised force of society that maintains the rights of owners by protecting them against thieves and depredators. In spite of all criticism many people still seem to think of the rights of property as though they were conferred by Nature or by Providence upon certain fortunate individuals, and as though these individuals had an unlimited right to command the State, as their servant, to secure them by the free use of the machinery of law in the undisturbed enjoyment of their possessions. They forget that without the organised force of society their rights are not worth a week's purchase. . . .

This brings us to the second sense in which property is social. There is a social element in value and a social element in production. In modern industry there is very little that the individual can do by his unaided efforts. Labour is minutely divided; and in proportion as it is divided it is forced to be co-operative. Men produce goods to sell, and the rate of exchange, that is, price, is fixed by relations of supply and demand, the rates of which are determined by complex social forces. In the methods of production every man makes use, to the best of his ability, of the whole available means of civilisation, of the machinery which the brains of other men have devised, of the human apparatus which is the gift of acquired civilisation. Society thus provides conditions or opportunities of which one man will make much better use than another, and the use to which they are put is the individual or personal element in production which is the basis of the personal claim to reward. To maintain and stimulate this personal effort is a necessity of good economic organisation, and without asking here whether any particular conception of Socialism would or would not meet this need, we may lay down with confidence that no form of Socialism which should ignore it could possibly enjoy enduring success. On the other hand, an individualism which ignores the social factor in wealth will deplete the national resources, deprive the community of its just share in the fruits of industry and so result in a one-sided and inequitable distribution of wealth. Economic justice is to render what is due not only to each individual but to each function, social or personal, that is engaged in the performance of useful service, and this due is measured by the amount necessary to stimulate and maintain the efficient exercise of that useful function. This equation between function and sustenance is the true meaning of economic equality. . . .

The central point of Liberal economics, then, is the equation of social service and reward. This is the principle that every function of social value requires such remuneration as serves to stimulate and maintain its effective performance; that every one who performs such a function has the right, in the strict ethical sense of that term, to such remuneration and to no more; that the residue of existing wealth should be at the disposal of the community for social purposes. Further, it is the right, in the same sense, of every person capable of performing some useful social function that he should have the opportunity of so doing, and it is his right that the remuneration he receives for it should be his property, *i.e.* that it should stand at his free disposal, enabling him to direct his personal concerns according to his own preferences. These are rights in the sense that they are conditions of the welfare of its members which a well-ordered State will seek by every means to fulfil. But it is not suggested that the way of such fulfilment is plain, or that it could be achieved at a stroke by a revolutionary change in the tenure of property or the system of industry. It is, indeed, implied that the State is vested with a certain overlordship over property in general and a supervisory power over industry in general, and this principle of economic sovereignty may be set side by side with that of economic justice as a no less fundamental conception of economic Liberalism. For here, as elsewhere, liberty implies control. But the manner in which the State is to exercise its controlling power is to be learnt by experience and even in large measure by cautious experiment. We have sought to determine the principle which should guide its action, the ends at which it is to aim. The systematic study of the means lies rather within the province of economics; and the teaching of history seems to be that progress is more continuous and secure when men are content to deal with problems piecemeal than when they seek to destroy root and branch in order to erect a complete system which has captured the imagination.

It is evident that these conceptions embody many of the ideas that go to make up the framework of Socialist teaching, though they also emphasise elements of individual right and personal independence, of which Socialism at times appears oblivious. The distinction that I would claim for economic Liberalism is that it seeks to do justice to the social and individual factors in industry alike, as opposed to an abstract Socialism which emphasises the one side and an abstract Individualism which leans its whole weight on the other. . . . Thus in economics we avoid the confusion of liberty with competition, and see no virtue in the right of a man to get the better of others. At the same time we are not led to minimise the share of personal initiative, talent, or energy in production, but are free to contend for their claim to adequate recognition.

L. T. Hobhouse, *Liberalism* (1911), pp. 188-212.

5. IMPERIALISM AND THE BOER WAR

109. Sir WILLIAM HARCOURT:
Speech at West Monmouthshire, 31 May 1899

What is this Imperialism which, in the slang of the day, is paraded as the highest form of patriotism? I laugh sometimes when I hear myself and others denounced as 'Little Englanders.' I confess I did not know that there was a 'Little England' to belong to. I always thought that England was the greatest, the most extensive, the most powerful, the most famous nation in the world; that it was one of which any man might be proud to be a citizen and have no cause to be dissatisfied. Little England, forsooth! Where is it? If I desire (which I do not) to be a Little Englander, I must cease to be a British citizen, because being a British citizen I am necessarily a Great Englander, a citizen of a great Empire. . . .

But what does that Imperialism you hear so much about mean? If it means pursuing a policy which is the wisest and best for that great Empire to which we belong, of course we are all Imperialists in that sense. But then remains the practical question—what is the policy of Imperialism? It is a policy which has its first regard to the consolidation of the vast dominions, the countless millions, and the varied interests which compose our unequalled Empire, the development of their resources, the lightening of their burdens, the fostering of their natural growth, the relief of distress within it, and the raising of the standard of all sorts and conditions of men who are the subjects of the Queen. That is Imperialism as I inderstand it. That is a policy which makes the Empire great and keeps it so.

There is another and exactly opposite view of imperial policy. It is to postpone and subordinate all these objects to vanity, to the acquisition of fresh populations, the adoption of additional burdens—that is the extensionists' theory, and the extensionists, it seems to me, are extremely like what in currency are called the inflationists, who are of opinion that the more paper you issue the more wealth you create and the more prosperity you will have. Well, I am not an inflationist in currency and I am not an extensionist. In my judgement, at least, it is a greater and a wiser policy to cultivate an Empire than to boom an Empire. . . .

To these ends (the ends of the Imperialists) the principal genius of administration and the energies of Parliament are directed. Social reforms are neglected. Indeed Mr. Chamberlain told us, in a scornful tone, that to talk of their social reforms was merely 'parochial' and that what we ought to occupy ourselves with is this inflated Imperialism. Now, what is the end of that? It means that the Empire is committed to land speculators, to mining syndicates, and that they are to determine the limits of the Empire and the methods of its administration. They are not particular— all know that—as to the methods to be employed. 'Expansion, at any rate, at whatever cost, and by whatever means.' That is the sleeping genie. Well, sometimes I think it might be better if it took a little more sleep.

A. G. Gardiner, *Life of Sir William Harcourt*
(London, 1923), vol. ii, pp. 496-7.

110. J. L. HAMMOND: *Colonial and Foreign Policy*,
in *Liberalism and the Empire*
(1900)

A main cause of the precipitate abandonment of their tradition by many Liberals is to be found in a fatalism, a doctrine contemned by strenuous men and strenuous times, which has lately been erected with solemn honours into a political principle. It is not only amongst Conservatives that the new divinity claims its votaries. The pseudo-scientific jargon of 'manifest destiny,' 'inevitable development,' and the like—the vocabulary of men who see finality in each fugitive phase and phenomenon of public affairs—has invaded almost every school of political thought. . . . The assumptions of Imperialist determinism have no greater claim to scientific accuracy than any of the predictions hazarded with no less assurance in the past which history has turned to ridicule. . . .

But the futility of this practice is of small consequence in comparison with its vicious results. If war is imminent, we are warned that no human power can stop it. When war breaks out, Providence and the enemy must divide the blame. If a conflict is inevitable, diplomacy becomes a mere incident, or, rather, well-timed irritation becomes a diplomatic art; and it is the business of a statesman, recognising that he cannot avoid a struggle, to arrange to provoke it at the moment most convenient to his own country. . . . Thus, fatalism becomes a narcotic administered to the public conscience by the advocates of aggrandisement. . . . But the whole temper of fatalism is foreign to the Liberal spirit. If Liberals are content with a moral somnolence, it is no wonder they have little taste for a creed which insists on nothing so strongly as the duty of developing just the active sense of responsibility that fatalism saps. Ulysses' bow was useless to men who were unable to draw it. The faith of Mr. Gladstone sits ill upon a listless indifference to its great and vivifying principles. All the native fire and inspiration is gone out of his creed when it is invoked by Liberals who understand by Liberalism a disorderly collection of miscellaneous

enthusiasms rather than an established attitude to the fundamental moralities of politics. For all idealism belongs to
robust and virile natures; and the temper which governed
the foreign policy associated with the name of Liberal during
the nineteenth century was, above and before all things,
idealist. . . .

The Liberals who made the foreign policy of England
during a great part of the century, and whose doctrines, as
we believe, supply the true solution of our modern problems,
were distinguished by three great principles. They believed
in morality between nations, they respected and cherished
the best instincts of a true nationalism, and they held that
England could not cut herself off from the highest interests
of Europe. Each of these principles is attacked by
Imperialism. . . . None of these Liberal principles are to
be found in the new ideal of national conduct and the new
moral canon presented by Imperialism. The moral syllogism
which it applies to politics runs thus: The British Empire is
the greatest blessing known to mankind. Whatever helps to
extend the Empire is good. Therefore, although a particular
course of action may be immoral, in the sense that it is
a breach of faith, or that it is an attack upon national
rights, or that it implies violence, it becomes not merely
innocent, but positively virtuous, if it helps to extend the
Empire. . . .

But the contrast between the Liberal and the Imperialist
positions might be put in another form: The Liberal believes
that the greatness of the British Empire imposes a special
obligation to act with self-control and moderation; the
Imperialist sees in it an authority for disregarding the
restraints which he would recognise as binding on a State
less powerful and less beneficent. There are certain things,
argues the Liberal, which our very strength makes it at once
impolitic and unchivalrous for the British Empire to do.
Great Britain's position is such, argues the Imperialist, that
she must not be held to her word, or hampered by conven-
tions like other people; she acts as the right hand of
Providence in regenerating the world, and no technical
obstacles must be allowed to interfere with her mission of
carrying from continent to continent the energies of a just

and sublime civilization, the art of a new and divine ordinance.

Liberalism and the Empire (1900), pp. 161-71.

111. J. A. HOBSON: *Imperialism*
(1902)

Modern British colonialism has been no drain upon our material and moral resources, because it has made for the creation of free white democracies, a policy of informal federation, of decentralisation, involving no appreciable strain upon the governmental faculties of Great Britain. Such federation, whether it remains informal with the slight attachment of imperial sovereignty which now exists, or voluntarily takes some more formal shape, political or financial, may well be regarded as a source of strength, political and military.

Imperialism is the very antithesis of this free, wholesome colonial connection, making, as it ever does, for greater complications of foreign policy, greater centralisation of power, and a congestion of business which ever threatens to absorb and overtax the capacity of parliamentary government.

The true political nature of Imperialism is best seen by confronting it with the watchwords of progress accepted in the middle of the nineteenth century by moderate men of both great parties in the State, though with interpretations varying in degree—peace, economy, reform, and popular self-government. Even now we find no formal abandonment of the principles of government these terms express, and a large section of professed Liberals believe or assert that Imperialism is consistent with the maintenance of all these virtues. . . .

The political effects, actual and necessary, of the new Imperialism, as illustrated in the case of the greatest of imperialist Powers, may be thus summarised. It is a constant menace to peace, by furnishing continual temptations to further aggression upon lands occupied by lower races and by embroiling our nation with other nations of rival imperial ambitions; to the sharp peril of war it adds the chronic danger and degradation of militarism, which not merely wastes the current physical and moral resources of the nation, but checks the very course of civilisation. It consumes to an illimitable and incalculable extent the financial resources of a nation by military preparation, stopping the expenditure of the current income of the State upon productive public projects and burdening posterity with heavy loads of debt. Absorbing the public money, time, interest and energy on costly and unprofitable work of territorial aggrandisement, it thus wastes those energies of public life in the governing classes and the nations which are needed for internal reforms and for the cultivation of the arts of material and intellectual progress at home. Finally, the spirit, the policy, and the methods of Imperialism are hostile to the institutions of popular self-government, favouring forms of political tyranny and social authority which are the deadly enemies of effective liberty and equality.

J. A. Hobson, *Imperialism* (1938 edn.), pp. 125-6, 152.

112. SIR HENRY CAMPBELL-BANNERMAN:
Speech at Stirling, 26 October 1901

The cardinal fact upon which the whole problem turns is that this is of the nature of a civil war. We are not fighting with a foreign foe whom we are to thrash and over-come and vanquish and punish, and then abandon him and turn our back upon him. These men are to be our neigh-bours—nay, they are to be our fellow-citizens. Whatever be their faults, whatever be their offences in the present or in the past against us, if we are to stay in South Africa at all, they will be there; and not only so, but they are indis-tinguishable from the great majority of our own citizens in our own colonies. . . . Now any one who rightly appreciates these facts, what will he say are to be our objects in the war which we have undertaken in South Africa? The first ought to be to impose upon our antagonists our military superiority. But the second is to impress upon them our ultimate and essential friendliness towards them. . . .

Are the elements to be found for a settlement in the conditions to which you have now reduced South Africa?

The whole country in the two belligerent States outside the mining towns is a howling wilderness. The farms are burned, the country is wasted; the flocks and herds are either butchered or driven off; the mills are destroyed; furniture and implements of agriculture are smashed. These things are what I have termed methods of barbarism. I adhere to the phrase. I cannot improve upon it. If these are not the methods of barbarism, what methods does barbarism employ? . . . In time of war, things are not done in a rosewater sort of way; but the universal treatment of a whole country in this way, and the sweeping of women and children into camps is a process for which I venture to say nothing can furnish justification. When the war is happily ended and we set about the Constitution of this Arcadia, the fifty thousand prisoners of war will, of course, return to what by some sort of irony we may perhaps be permitted to call their home. These are the materials for your new self government. They will meet the hundred thousand women and children or the survivors of them. There will not be many children at the present rate. They will meet them, and in what sort of mind towards the British Empire will these men be when the husband meets the wife and hears her story, when the brother meets the sister, when the father asks in vain for his child? . . .

Hitherto I have spoken of the belligerent States. Now, what of the old Colony of the Cape? To what condition has the statesmanship of the Government brought it? . . . The Constitution is suspended. . . . Martial law, which is in other words no law, nothing but the arbitrary rule of soldiers, who know nothing of law, prevails from end to end of the country. We have reason to fear that martial law is but a form of undeclared war upon the Dutch population. With all the ordinary guarantees of civil rights suspended, no man is safe in property, in liberty or in life. The independent Press is silenced. So severe are the restrictions on news, that we have only partial information; but we have enough to know that hundreds of men, not Dutch only, but many British, have been arrested, thrown into gaol, deported to a distance from their homes, tried and condemned by these military tribunals on the evidence, it may be, of spiteful neighbours or political opponents. Why, with what indignation would we denounce such proceedings in other countries. . . . Have these Ministers of ours not learned that it is not by the suppression of civil rights, not by harshness, not by coercion and force in any form, that a free people can be kept quiet and contented? . . .

The Government . . . have revived old enmities and created new ones, they have sown seeds of lasting discord, and when they, by-and-by, lay down in discredit their responsibilities, they will leave a new Ireland in the Southern Seas to be a weakness and a difficulty to the Empire. . . . How true are the words of Mr. Burke in his famous speech on the conciliation of the American colonies. . . . Mr. Burke in this great speech urged a further objection to force—he was objecting to applying force in any case of this kind—and that was that you impair the object by your very endeavour to preserve it. The thing you fought for is not the thing you recover, but depreciated, small, wasted and consumed in the contest. You may preserve your authority in South Africa, but it will be depreciated, and lessened, and wasted, and consumed. Is it too late even now to hope for counsels of moderation and a statesmanship which shall revert to the great traditions which have bound Great Britain and her Colonies together?

Speeches of Sir H. Campbell-Bannerman (1908), pp. 77-83.

6. ARMAMENTS

113. SIR HENRY CAMPBELL-BANNERMAN: Speech at the Albert Hall, 21 December 1905

We Liberals, let us not forget it, are the heirs of a great and inspiring tradition. That tradition was founded in days when public opinion was opposed to any attempt to regulate differences by an appeal to the reason and conscience of mankind. Mr. Gladstone defied the public opinion of his day. He took his stand on higher ground, and by referring the Alabama dispute to arbitration he established a precedent of priceless value to mankind. . . . I rejoice that since that time the principle of arbitration has made great strides, and that to-day it is no longer counted weakness for any of the Great Powers of the world to submit those issues which would once have been referred to the arbitrament of self-assertion and of passion to a higher tribunal. . . .

I hold that the growth of armaments is a great danger to the peace of the world. A policy of huge armaments keeps alive and stimulates and feeds the belief that force is the best, if not the only, solution of international differences. It is a policy that tends to inflame old sores and to create new sores. And I submit to you that as the principle of peaceful arbitration gains ground it becomes one of the highest tasks of a statesman to adjust those armaments to the newer and happier condition of things. What nobler role could this great country assume than at the fitting moment to place itself at the head of a league of peace, through whose instrumentality this great work could be effected?

Sir H. Campbell-Bannerman, *Liberal Policy*.
A speech delivered . . . 21 December
1905 (Liberal Publication Dept.).

114. Debate on the Army Estimates, House of Commons, 28 February 1907

W. P. BYLES (Salford N.) . . . There was another class of members who were not military men at all and had no love of militarism. They represented a large number of people outside the House—men and women who believed that the greatness of England rested, not on the science of war, but on the arts of peace. . . . He thought the whole conception of our military system was out of all proportion to what was really necessary if only they cultivated a friendly policy with the nations of the earth instead of destroying one another. . . .

What did we want a striking force for? Whom did we want to strike? Why did we not shake hands instead of striking at all? . . . There were some who held what was called the 'menagerie theory', that they were kept from one another by barred cages and that they were ready to fly at one another's throats the moment they got loose. He did not believe in any such theory. . . .

He had for years addressed crowded meetings of poor men and women, and he had told them that when a Liberal Government was in power it could run the country on £100,000,000; but that, after ten years of Tory rule, it cost £150,000,000. . . . He told them also that for every shilling the Liberal Government took out of their pockets for the Army and other purposes the Tories had been taking eighteen pence, and that when a democratic Government came into power again they would restore things as they formerly were. It was on those pledges that he got his seat and it was on those pledges that he was supporting the present Government. He therefore expressed sincere disappointment that such an enormous proposal should have been put before the House in the second session of the present Parliament. . . .

The burden of the peace charges in this country was worse, because it was more permanent, than an occasional war. It was like the case of a man who paid a high premium for insurance. It was better to run the risk of a fire. . . . Fifty years ago Mr. Disraeli had said there was a niche in the temple of Fame for the ruler or Minister who would be the first to grapple with the question of military expenditure. He wished his right hon. friend would occupy that niche. He had hoped that the right hon. gentleman would in his proposals have shown a greater desire for the reduction of armaments.

Parliamentary Debates, House of Commons,
4th Series, clxx, cols. 325-7.

115. Sir EDWARD GREY:
Speech in the House of Commons, 29 March 1909

I will, in conclusion, submit to the House the general views on which I approach this great problem. There are those who like and those who dislike naval and military expenditures; there are those who like the martial spirit and those who dislike it. Well, Sir, the martial spirit, I should be the last to deny, has its place, and its proper place, in the life of a nation. . . . That I sympathise with entirely, but I would ask the people to consider to what consequences the growth of armaments has led? The great countries of Europe are raising enormous revenues, and something like half of them is being spent on naval and military prepara- tions. You may call it national insurance, that is perfectly true, but it is equally true that half the national revenue of the great countries of Europe is being spent on what is, after all, preparations to kill each other. Surely the extent to which this expenditure has grown really becomes a satire and a reflection on civilisation. Not in our generation, perhaps, but if it goes on at the present rate at which it has recently increased, sooner or later I believe it will submerge that civilisation. . . . Sooner or later, if it goes on at this rate, it must lead to national bankruptcy.

Is it to be wondered that the hopes and aspirations of the best men in the leading countries are devoted to trying to find some means of checking it. Surely that is a statement of the case in which, however attached a man may be to what I may call the martial spirit, he may at least see that the whole of Europe is in the presence of a great danger. But, Sir, no country alone can save that. If we alone, among the Great Powers, gave up the competition and sank into a position of inferiority, what good should we do? None whatever—no good to ourselves, because we cannot realise great ideals of social reform at home when we are holding our existence at the mercy, the caprice if you like, of another nation. That is not feasible. If we fall into a position of inferiority our self-respect is gone, and it removes that enterprise which is essential both to the material success of industry and to the carrying out of great ideals, and you fall into a state of apathy. We should cease to count for anything amongst the nations of Europe, and we should be fortunate if our liberty was left and we did not become the conscript appendage of some stronger Power. That is a brutal way of stating the case, but it is the truth. It is disagreeable that it should be so, but in matters like this I know of no safe way except to look at what is disagreeable frankly in the face, and to state it, if necessary, in its crudest form.

Speeches on Foreign Affairs, 1904-1914, by Sir Edward
Grey, ed. P. Knaplund (1931), pp. 142-3.

116. SIR EDWARD GREY:
Speech in the House of Commons, 13 March 1911

If you are to have these great burdens of force piled up in times of peace, as it has been in the last generation, it will become intolerable. There are those who think it will lead to war precisely because it is becoming intolerable. I hear it said that as the burden grows it will be felt so strongly that some nation will seek relief in war. I think it is much more likely that the burden will be dissipated by internal revolution. . . . But it does not follow from that that one nation can, as the hon. members who moved and seconded this Resolution suggested, put a stop to the rivalry by dropping out of the race. If one nation, and especially a nation of this kind, dropped out of the competition, I do not believe we should be serving the purpose of which I have been speaking by reducing the general rivalry. On the contrary, it might very well be that if one nation dropped out of the competition it might momentarily give a spurt of expenditure in some other.

The hon. member for Merthyr Tydvil (J. Keir Hardie) spoke not more strongly than I have spoken of the growing feeling there was against this policy of expenditure, and he spoke of the Socialist vote. Yes, but that growing feeling must find its expression and make itself felt not in one country alone but in countries simultaneously. He spoke of the growth of the Socialist vote, but it had no effect on the passing of the German Navy Estimates the other day. And until that feeling has reached greater power in the nations generally than it has at the present time, we shall not reap the benefit of it.

Parliamentary Debates, House of Commons,
5th Series, xxii, cols. 1985-6.

117. SIR JOHN BRUNNER, President of the National Liberal Federation: Speech at the 35th Annual Meeting, Leeds, 26 November 1913

The Prime Minister . . . has told you, in public speech at the Mansion House but a few days ago, that it is your duty to take counsel together to secure a saner and more fruitful appropriation of the vast sums we are pouring out in preparing for war. I hate this gross, growing, mad expenditure. Sir Edward Grey told us in the House of Commons that the hideous expenditure of Christendom in preparing for war will, if not checked, submerge civilisation. I warn you to resist the secret international organisation of the makers of war material in Germany, France, Italy, Russia, Turkey, America, Canada and England, whose object is to promote suspicion and misunderstanding. I warn you that the daily Press of all these countries will be suborned in the future, as it has been in the past, and induced to publish statements inciting to international hatred. It is a devil's business. I warn you that the Governments of these countries, our own included, may be influenced, as they have already been influenced, by these statements of the Press. Our answer to Mr. Asquith is that he himself, as the head of the Government, has already indicated other saner and more fruitful appropriations of these vast sums, and we shall promise him our united, ardent support in their adoption. We are for peace, we are intent upon securing ample food, wholesome houses, the cultivation of health in body and mind. We desire the blessings of civilisation for every home and every family. With all the warmth of my heart, with all the force of my mind, I commend to you the final Resolution which will come before this meeting:

'That this Council views with grave anxiety the continued growth in armaments, which, unless checked, must inevitably lead to an increase in taxation. The Council expresses its most earnest hope that, in view of the conspicuous improvement in the relations between Great Britain and foreign Powers, no opportunity will be lost in continuing to press forward friendly negotiations with these Powers, in order that an end may be put to suspicion and misunderstanding, the most fruitful causes of the disastrous rivalry in armaments between the nations of Europe. . . .'

Annual Report of the National Liberal Federation
for 1913, pp. 47-8, 62.

7. FOREIGN POLICY

118. Debate on the Foreign Office Estimates, House of Commons, 22 July 1909

(A)

J. M. ROBERTSON (Tyneside). If the policy of the Foreign Secretary has committed this country to an alliance with France in a European war, irrespective of the merits of the case, I think that would be a departure from Liberal traditions. A great deal has been said on the traditions of Liberal foreign policy. What is the Liberal tradition as to foreign policy? (Cries of 'Non-intervention' and 'Freedom'.) To say that Liberal foreign policy is freedom is to use the idlest of rhetoric. The practical tradition of Liberal foreign policy is non-intervention in foreign affairs. (An Hon. Member: 'Was that Palmerston's policy?') Palmerston's is exactly a case which is to be rejected as really representative of Liberal tradition. If any man is to be taken as representative of Liberal foreign policy, it is Richard Cobden. . . . The only consistent attitude is to denounce intervention, whether democratic or anti-democratic. If England learned any lesson from the French Revolution, it was that neither side does well to interfere.

(B)

ARTHUR PONSONBY (Stirling Burghs). I think it would be nothing short of a calamity if this debate terminated without a single voice being raised from the Liberal side of the House in protest against the visit of the Czar. . . . The very large body of Liberal opinion in this country will feel very strongly the contrast between the tone of the speech of the right hon. gentleman today (Sir E. Grey) and the ringing tones of Mr. Gladstone. The strength of our diplomacy, the force of our opinion in the councils of Europe, depends on the detached, disinterested, humanitarian views we have taken in upholding the freedom of downtrodden peoples. Take, for instance, the history of the last fifty years, whether in Italy, in the Lebanon, Bulgaria, Armenia or Macedonia. I am afraid the modern idea is to disapprove the humanitarian view and sympathetic attitude of those who appreciate the liberties of the people and to put in its place the force of Empire and of armaments. If anybody thinks that our diplomacy is strengthened by the number of our Dreadnoughts, I fancy they will find themselves very much mistaken. Throughout the last half-century it has been to our credit that the greatest success we have had has been our strong feeling of humanitarianism and our desire to uphold the views of people who are downtrodden.

Parliamentary Debates, House of Commons,
5th Series, viii, (A), cols. 717-18; (B), cols. 729-30.

119. SIR EDWARD GREY:
Speech in the House of Commons, 27 November 1911

Now let me say a word upon the general aspects of what I consider is the proper foreign policy of this country, and what the foreign policy of the Government has been. It is said to be, and in a sense that is quite true, a continuation of the policy of the Government in which Lord Lansdowne was Secretary for Foreign Affairs. Some years ago we had constant trouble and friction with France and Russia. Everybody remembers it. . . . The relations have been changed from those of friction and difficulty into relations of friendship, and it is well that it has been so, because in different parts of the world British interests touch and rub against French and Russian interests. . . .

In addition to that, our friendship with France and Russia is in itself a guarantee that neither of them will pursue a provocative or aggressive policy towards Germany, who is their neighbour and ours. Any support we would give France and Russia in times of trouble would depend entirely on the feeling of Parliament and public feeling here when the trouble came, and both France and Russia know perfectly well that British public opinion would not give support to provocative or aggressive action against Germany. . . .

Now let me say this: German strength is, by itself, a

guarantee that no other country will desire or seek a quarrel with Germany. That is one side of the shield of which Germans may well be proud, but I think it ought to be remembered by German public opinion that there is another side to the shield, and that is if a nation has the biggest army in the world, and if it has a very big navy, and is going on building a still bigger navy, then it must do all in its power to prevent what would otherwise be the natural apprehensions in the minds of others. . . . All we or the other neighbours of Germany desire is to live with her on equal terms.

There is one foreign policy different to the one which I have been endeavouring to sketch to the House, and it seems to me to be advocated in some quarters of the country. It seems to me to be simply disastrous. It is that we should give it to be understood that in no circumstances, however aggressively, provocatively, or wantonly, a friend of ours was attacked, we should give our friend any assistance whatever. That would be an attempt to revert to what was once called a policy of 'splendid isolation.' It would deprive us of the possibility of having a friend in Europe, and it would result in the other nations of Europe, either by choice or by necessity, being brought into the orbit of a single diplomacy from which we should be excluded. The ideal of splendid isolation contemplated a balance of power in Europe to which we were not to be a party, and from which we were to be able to stand aside in the happy position of having no obligations and being able to take advantage of any difficulties which arose in Europe from friction between opposing Powers. That policy is not a possible one now. Any single Power that attempted to adopt that policy in Europe to-day would be felt as a public nuisance, and if we were that single Power, one result would be that in the course of a few years we should be building warships not against a two-Power standard, but probably against the united navies of Europe. As a matter of fact that policy, which would be disastrous, is not a policy. It is the negation of a policy, and if it were accompanied, as I suppose it would be accompanied, with constant criticisms of individual members of the House about the internal affairs and proceedings of other Governments, constant pressure upon the Secretary of State for Foreign Affairs of the day to interfere and make representations about matters which do not directly concern us, then I say that the disastrous consequences of such an attitude of mingled interferences and drift would soon become apparent in an expenditure on armaments even greater than the present expenditure, and sooner or later the very peace that people desired to preserve would topple over. Such an attitude would not even gain us the friendship of Germany.

> *Speeches on Foreign Affairs, 1904–1914*, by Sir Edward Grey, ed. P. Knaplund (1931), pp. 162-6.

120. Debate in the House of Commons, 14 December 1911

[These speeches were made in an adjourned debate on a Question proposed on the 27 November 1911 by Sir E. Grey, 'That the Foreign Policy of His Majesty's Government be now considered.']

(A)

JOSIAH WEDGWOOD (Newcastle-under-Lyme). The foreign policy of the Government is not a Liberal foreign policy. It is not merely a continuation, but it is an accentuation, of the foreign policy of our predecessors. We have this question of the balance of power raised to a sort of fetish which the whole of the Foreign Office staff and the Foreign Secretary as well worship, and our foreign policy seems to feed the balance of the scales with slices of the Congo or of Morocco. When it is not a question of the balance of power the one other thing that seems to affect our Foreign Office policy is that of material British interest. The pursuit of these two aims . . . was not the Liberal foreign policy, and never has been until now. It is entirely antagonistic to the tradition of Canning and Palmerston and Gladstone. When the people of this country sent this Government to power in 1906 and again in 1910 it was with the idea of having the old Gladstonian and Palmerstonian traditions carried out in Liberal foreign policy as well as in Liberal domestic policy. We do not always want to be interfering in petty details,

in tapping the barometer on every particular question to see
whether the Foreign Office is moving on Liberal lines. . . .
But we think we have a genuine right to say to Liberal
Ministers, we expect broad Liberal principles to be followed.
. . . I am perfectly certain I speak not only for Liberals,
but for a large number of Conservatives, when I say that
the majority of Englishmen place the moral results of our
foreign policy above the material results, and that they are
more anxious for justice between foreign nations and freedom
in foreign nations than they are for commercial treaties or
extra concessions in Africa or Asia or Arabia. I am quite
certain the British people would rather have the influence
of the British Foreign Office directed towards the extension
of justice than the extension of territory. This being, as I
think it is, the universal opinion of Liberals throughout the
country, and the opinion of all that is best of the Conservatism
of the country as well, I think it right to ask the Government
what they have done in this direction. How have they influenced politics in any corner of the world on Liberal lines?
How have they increased the ideas of justice between man
and man? How have they increased principles of freedom
among the peoples of the world? . . .

If you look to any part of the world where there have
been difficulties in the last six years I think you will find it
difficult to lay your finger upon one spot . . . from China
to Peru, where the influence of the Liberal Government has
made anything better or influenced things in the slightest
degree in a Liberal direction. . . .

If you go back to the Government of Mr. Gladstone in
1892 or 1880, or to Palmerston and Gladstone in 1860 to
1872, in every case you find the influence of the Government
directed towards freedom, and you find on the map of
Europe some recording testimony of their work for freedom
and liberty and justice. It is only in the case of this Government that you cannot point to anything . . . The fact of
the matter is that the Foreign Office itself and the whole
traditions of the Foreign Office and its staff are far too
aristocratic in tone and illiberal in principle. They are not
in touch or in sympathy with Liberalism—they do not want
what we want. . . . You have throughout the whole of

this particular Department Conservative sympathies which are directed towards perpetuating the old ideas of foreign policy of the previous Conservative Government, and I do not see how there is any hope of the Liberal Government making foreign policy Liberal as long as they allow the Conservative tendencies of the Foreign Office staff to remain unchanged. . . .

The other day there was a cartoon in *Punch* showing the Secretary of State for Foreign Affairs seated at a table with cards in his hand, and interfering Radicals looking over his shoulder, and he is supposed to say: 'How do you expect I can play the game successfully if I show my cards?' I think that cartoon accurately illustrates the Foreign Office view of diplomacy. They think they are playing a game with cards at which nobody is allowed to look. The game they are playing is a very silly game: it is a game of concession hunters and land grabbers. . . . It is about time the people of England and Germany insisted upon knowing what it is these diplomatists are playing at. They are playing, not a national game, but merely a plutocratic financial game. It is a game, not of national honour, but of national dishonour.

(B)

J. G. Swift MacNeill (S. Donegal). I say in the plainest possible terms, after an experience of twenty-five years in this House, that Parliament might as well not exist so far as foreign affairs or foreign relations are concerned. . . . The hon. gentleman spoke with a very natural horror at the idea that we were drifting into war last July. He might have said that we were drifting into war quite unknown to ourselves . . . , even while Parliament was sitting. Why was not Parliament told? Why were not the people given some stake in the interests affecting themselves? Are they to be treated like children? . . . Until what I have described as the cult of mystery is abolished in the Foreign Office really we are being led blindfold. . . .

According to theory the slightest railway or turnpike Bill may be investigated in every line and syllable by this House, but treaties involving the greatest international obligations, treaties involving precious human lives, can be signed, sealed, and delivered, yet the people who are responsible for them know nothing whatever about them. They are ept in leading-strings by superior persons.

You would not endure that for a moment in regard to some petty Bill. Why do you endure it in matters which affect your children's children? . . . There is a continuity of foreign policy and that foreign policy is deposited in the breasts of a certain distinct caste of statesmen like the Egyptian priests. I remember the late leader of the Opposition making a strong attack on the Radical party opposite. He had something unpleasant to say about every member of the Cabinet, but he excepted the Foreign Secretary, because the Foreign Secretary was carrying out the policy of Lord Lansdowne, and because there should be no discussion on these things. They were too high and mighty altogether for the poor ordinary man. I do not think so, and I do not believe the people of England think so. I do not think the representatives of the people are just to themselves or to their constituencies, if they do not see that at least we know, if this country is to go to war, the why and wherefore of it, and also if this country is to sign treaties.

Parliamentary Debates, House of Commons, 5th Series, xxxii, (A), cols. 2620-5; (B), cols. 2585-93.

121. *The Manchester Guardian*: Leading Article, 1 August 1914

There is in our midst an organised conspiracy to drag us into the war should the attempts of the peace-makers fail. . . . The objects of the conspirators are now openly avowed. We are to join in, not under certain conditions or in defence of this or that British interest which may happen to be threatened, but in any case. We are to do so for three reasons. The first is that we are bound in our own interests to maintain the balance of power in Europe. The second is that we are the protectors of the neutrality of Belgium. The third, that we are in honour bound to stand by our friends. Each of these reasons must be considered separately and tried not by tests of self-interest alone, but also by the highest standards of British honour. For we seek no peace except with honour intact.

The Balance of Power, as a doctrine of English policy, was responsible for the long feud with France in the 18th century, culminating in the war with Revolutionary France. It made the National Debt. It lost England the great lead that it had obtained in constitutional liberties and condemned us to the worst period of reaction in our history. . . . Its revival has been the work of the last seven to eight years and, we deeply regret to think, has been coincident with the access to power of the Liberal Government. We do not say that it has been its doing. The doctrine has at all times been the greatest enemy of progress. . . . But even if we admired the doctrine as much as we in fact detest it, it supplies no reason why we should take the side of Russia against Germany. If Russia wins, there will be the greatest disturbance of the Balance of Power that the world has ever seen. The whole condition of our continued existence as an Asiatic Power will have to be revised, and over all the world, wherever we come into contact with Russia, we shall have a repetition of the self-effacement which we have witnessed in Persia. The victory of Germany, on the other hand, would in effect be a victory for the principle of the Balance of Power. If we believe in this principle—which we do not— then we might be for intervention on the side of Germany. Because we do not believe in it we are able, without the least misgiving, to counsel neutrality as the right policy for this country.

Then we are to side with Russia against Germany because we are guarantors of the neutrality of Belgium, which, it is assumed, is in danger from Germany and from her alone. *The Times* has quoted the authority of Gladstone for this proposition. Now it is quite true that during the Franco-Prussian war Lord Granville concluded treaties with both France and Germany guaranteeing the neutrality of Belgium. Article 3 of both treaties declares that they are to remain in force during the continuance of the war and for twelve months afterwards. Both treaties have, therefore, expired. But it will be said there are the earlier treaties of the 'forties in which we, in common with most of the Great Powers, guaranteed Belgian neutrality. Are we not bound by those? Let the great Lord Derby answer for us. He was asked in 1867 whether we were bound by a similar collective guarantee in the case of Luxembourg. He said No. 'We are bound in honour—you cannot place a legal construction on it—to see, in concert with others, that these arrangements are maintained. But if the other Powers join with us it is certain that there will be no violation of neutrality. If they, situated exactly as we are, decline to join, we are not bound single-handed to make up the deficiency. Such a guarantee has obviously rather the character of a moral sanction to the arrangements which it defends than that of a contingent liability to make war. It would, no doubt, give a right to make war, but would not necessarily impose the obligation.' And that is the view taken by most international lawyers. We are, therefore, absolutely free; there is no entanglement in Belgium.

Then is it honour that we must fight for? No, for honour's sake we must keep the peace. There are, as Mr. Asquith and Sir E. Grey have both told us, no engagements with European Powers that should take away our perfect freedom of choice. . . . Being free as regards Europe, we are not free as regards our own people, but must decide in favour of neutrality. For if we decide differently then we violate dozens of promises made to our own people, promises to seek peace, to protect the poor, to husband the resources of the country, to promote peaceful progress.

The Manchester Guardian (1 August 1914).

122. SIR EDWARD GREY:
Speech in the House of Commons, 3 August 1914

I come first to the question of British obligations. I have assured the House that if any crisis such as this arose, we should come before the House of Commons and be able to say to the House that it was free to decide what the British attitude should be, that we should have no secret engagement which we should spring upon the House, and tell the House

that, because we had entered into that engagement, there
was an obligation of honour upon the country. . . .

What the Prime Minister and I said to the House was
perfectly justified, that, as regards our freedom to decide in
a crisis what our line should be, whether we should intervene
or whether we should abstain, the Government remained
prefectly free and, *a fortiori*, the House of Commons remains
perfectly free. . . .

For many years we have had a long-standing friendship
with France. . . . But how far that friendship entails
obligation, let every man look into his own heart and his
own feelings and construe the extent of the obligation for
himself. I construe it myself as I feel it, but I do not wish to
urge upon anyone else more than their feelings dictate as to
what they should feel about the obligation. The House,
individually and collectively, may judge for itself. . . . The
French fleet is in the Mediterranean, and has for some years
been concentrated there because of the feeling of confidence
and friendship which has existed between our two countries.
My own feeling is that if a foreign fleet, engaged in a war
which France had not sought and in which she had not
been the aggressor, came down the English Channel and
bombarded and battered the undefended coast of France,
we could not stand aside and see this going on with our arms
folded, looking on dispassionately, doing nothing. . . .

But I also want to look at the matter without sentiment
and from the point of view of British interests, and it is on
that that I am going to base and justify what I am presently
going to say to the House. . . .

We have great and vital interests in the independence—
and integrity is the least part—of Belgium. . . . Mr.
Gladstone said: 'We have an interest in the independence
of Belgium which is wider than that which we may have in
the literal operation of the guarantee. It is found in the
answer to the question whether, under the circumstances of
the case, this country, endowed as it is with influence and
power, would quietly stand by and witness the perpetration
of the direst crime that ever stained the pages of history, and
thus become participators in the sin.' . . .

I ask the House, from the point of view of British

interests, to consider what may be at stake. If France is beaten in a struggle of life and death, beaten to her knees, loses her position as a Great Power, becomes subordinate to the will and power of one greater than herself—if that were to happen, if Belgium fell under the same dominating influence, and then Holland, and then Denmark, then would not Mr. Gladstone's words come true,[1] that just opposite to us there would be a common interest against the unmeasured aggrandisement of any Power?

It may be said, I suppose, that we might stand aside, husband our strength, and that whatever happened in the course of the war, at the end of it intervene with effect to put things right. . . . I do not believe for a moment that at the end of this war, even if we stood aside, we should be in a position to use our force decisively to undo what had happened in the course of war, to prevent the whole of the west of Europe opposite to us—if that has been the result of the war—falling under the domination of a single Power, and I am quite sure that our moral position would be such as to have lost us all respect. . . .

If we did take that line by saying, 'We will have nothing at all to do with this matter' under no conditions—the Belgian Treaty obligations, the possible position in the Mediterranean, with damage to British interests and what may happen to France from our failure to support France— if we were to say that all those things mattered nothing and to say that we should stand aside, we should, I believe, sacrifice our respect and good name and reputation before the world, and should not escape the most serious and grim economic consequences.

Speeches on Foreign Affairs, 1904–1914, by Sir Edward
Grey, ed. Paul Knaplund (1931), pp. 297-315.

---

[1] The reference is to another statement by Gladstone in August 1870 quoted by Grey earlier in this speech. Referring to the threat to Belgian independence created by the Franco-Prussian war, Gladstone dealt first with the Treaty of Guarantee of Belgian neutrality of which Great Britain was a signatory. Gladstone then added: 'There is also this further consideration, the force of which we must all feel deeply, and that is, the common interest against the unmeasured aggrandisement of any Power whatever.'

PART VI

LIBERALISM AFTER 1918

123. J. M. KEYNES: *The End of Laissez-Faire*
(1926)

Let us clear from the ground the metaphysical or general principles upon which, from time to time, laissez-faire has been founded. It is *not* true that individuals possess a prescriptive 'national liberty' in their economic activities. There is *no* 'compact' conferring perpetual rights on those who Have or on those who Acquire. The world is *not* so governed from above that private and social interest always coincide. It is *not* so managed here below that in practice they coincide. It is *not* a correct deduction from the Principles of Economics that enlightened self-interest always operates in the public interest. Nor is it true that self-interest generally *is* enlightened; more often individuals acting separately to promote their own ends are too ignorant or too weak to attain even these. Experience does *not* show that individuals, when they make up a social unit, are always less clear-sighted than when they act separately. We cannot therefore settle on abstract grounds, but must handle on its merits in detail what Burke termed 'one of the finest problems in legislation, namely, to determine what the State ought to take upon itself to direct by the public wisdom, and what it ought to leave, with as little interference as possible, to individual exertion.' We have to distinguish between what Bentham, in his forgotten but useful nomenclature, used to term *Agenda* and *Non-Agenda*, and to do this without Bentham's prior assumption that interference is, at the same time, 'generally needless' and 'generally pernicious.' Perhaps the chief task of Economists at this hour is to distinguish afresh the *Agenda* of Government from the *Non-Agenda*; and the companion task of Politics is to devise forms of Government within a Democracy which shall be capable of accomplishing the *Agenda*. I will illustrate what I have in mind by two examples.

1. I believe that in many cases the ideal size for the unit of control and organisation lies somewhere between the individual and the modern State. I suggest, therefore, that progress lies in the growth and the recognition of semi-autonomous bodies within the State—bodies whose criterion of action within their own field is solely the public good as they understand it, and from whose deliberations motives of private advantage are excluded, though some place it may still be necessary to leave, until the ambit of men's altruism grows wider, to the separate advantage of particular groups, classes, or faculties—bodies which in the ordinary course of affairs are mainly autonomous within their prescribed limitations, but are subject in the last resort to the sovereignty of the democracy expressed through Parliament. . . . But more interesting than these is the trend of Joint Stock Institutions, when they have reached a certain age and size, to approximate to the status of public corporations rather than that of individualistic private enterprise. One of the most interesting and unnoticed developments of recent decades has been the tendency of big enterprise to socialise itself. A point arrives in the growth of a big institution—particularly a big railway or big public utility enterprise, but also a big bank or a big insurance company—at which the owners of the capital, *i.e.* the shareholders, are almost entirely dissociated from the management with the result that the direct personal interest of the latter in the making of great profit becomes quite secondary. When this stage is reached, the general stability and reputation of the institution are more considered by the management than the maximum of profit for the shareholders. The shareholders must be satisfied by conventionally adequate dividends; but once this is secured, the direct interest of the management often consists in avoiding criticism from the public and from the customers of the concern. This is particularly the case if

their great size or semi-monopolistic position renders them conspicuous in the public eye and vulnerable to public attack. . . . They are, as time goes on, socialising themselves. Not that this is unmixed gain. The same causes promote conservatism and a waning of enterprise. In fact, we already have in these cases many of the faults as well as the advantages of State Socialism. Nevertheless we see here, I think, a natural line of evolution. The battle of Socialism against unlimited private profit is being won in detail hour by hour. In these particular fields—it remains acute elsewhere—this is no longer the pressing problem. There is, for instance, no so-called important political question, so really unimportant, so irrelevant to the re-organisation of the economic life of Great Britain, as the Nationalisation of the Railways. It is true that many big undertakings, particularly Public Utility enterprises and other business requiring a large fixed capital, still need to be semi-socialised. But we must keep our minds flexible regarding the forms of this semi-socialism. We must take full advantage of the tendencies of the day, and we must probably prefer semi-autonomous corporations to organs of the Central Government for which Ministers of State are directly responsible.

I criticise doctrinaire State Socialism, not because it seeks to engage men's altruistic impulses in the service of Society, or because it departs from laissez-faire, or because it takes away from man's natural liberty to make a million, or because it has courage for bold experiments. All these things I applaud. I criticise it because it misses the significance of what is actually happening; because it is, in fact, little better than a dusty survival of a plan to meet the problems of fifty years ago, based on a misunderstanding of what someone said a hundred years ago. Nineteenth-century State Socialism sprang from Bentham, free competition, etc., and is in some respects a clearer, in some respects a more muddled version of just the same philosophy as underlies nineteenth-century individualism. Both equally laid all their stress on freedom, the one negatively to avoid limitations on existing freedom, the other positively to destroy natural or acquired monopolies; they are different reactions to the same intellectual atmosphere.

2. I come next to a criterion of *Agenda* which is particularly relevant to what it is urgent and desirable to do in the near future. We must aim at separating those services which are *technically social* from those which are *technically individual*. The most important *Agenda* of the State relate not to those activities which private individuals are already fulfilling, but to those functions which fall outside the sphere of the individual, to those decisions which are made by *no one* if the State does not make them. The important thing for Government is not to do things which individuals are doing already, and to do them a little better or a little worse; but to do those things which at present are not done at all. . . . Many of the greatest economic evils of our time are the fruits of risk, uncertainty, and ignorance. . . . Yet the cure lies outside the operations of individuals; it may even be to the interest of individuals to aggravate the disease. I believe that the cure for these things is partly to be sought in the deliberate control of the currency and of credit by a central institution, and partly in the collection and dissemination on a great scale of data relating to the business situation, including the full publicity, by law if necessary, of all business facts which it is useful to know. These measures would involve Society in exercising directive intelligence through some appropriate organ of action over many of the inner intricacies of private business, yet it would leave private initiative and enterprise unhindered. Even if these measures prove insufficient, nevertheless they will furnish us with better knowledge than we have now for taking the next step.

My second example relates to Savings and Investment. I believe that some co-ordinated act of intelligent judgment is required as to the scale on which it is desirable that the community as a whole should save, the scale on which these savings should go abroad in the form of foreign investments, and whether the present organisation of the investment market distributes savings along the most nationally pro-ductive channels. I do not think that these matters should be left entirely to the chances of private judgment and private profits, as they are at present.

My third example concerns Population. The time has already come when each country needs a considered national policy about what size of Population, whether larger or smaller than at present or the same, is most expedient. And having settled this policy, we must take steps to carry it into operation. The time may arrive a little later when the community as a whole must pay attention to the innate quality as well as to the mere numbers of its future members!

J. M. Keynes, *The End of Laissez-Faire* (1926).

124. *Britain's Industrial Future*, the Report of the Liberal Industrial Inquiry (The Liberal Yellow Book) (1928)

The economic order in which the doctrine of *laissez-faire* had its origin has already in large measure passed away. The typical unit of production used to be the small firm, built up within a generation or two by its owner, and financed by his savings or those of his immediate connections. Very many such businesses, of course, still remain. But the industrial unit which is now predominant is different. The ownership of businesses has passed, and is passing in ever-increasing degree, into the hands of scattered multitudes of shareholders, who have no real opportunity of forming any judgment as to the problems or prospects of the undertakings, and no effective method of making their opinions felt were they able to form any. Management is in the hands of salaried persons; decisions of policy are left to men who are not staking their fortunes on being right, as did the founder of a one-man business. One consequence of these changes is that the inefficient producer is no longer speedily eliminated. . . .

And the increase in the scale of the producing unit has of late been very rapid. In some industries, amalgamations and absorptions have created businesses ten, twenty, or fifty times as vast, in their capital resources, in their labour force, in the dimensions of their trade, as any that would have been thought possible half a century ago.

Whole tracts of industrial enterprise, again, have already passed, by common consent, out of the sphere of purely private enterprise. We shall analyse the many intermediate

THE END OF LAISSEZ-FAIRE

forms of management which have sprung up, almost unnoticed, between the business under purely private control and the business under direct State or municipal control. . . .

A further great change, that goes far to decide the character of the modern world, is the establishment of political democracy. . . . There is now felt to be something inconsistent between the industrial status of the worker as a factory 'hand,' subject to strict discipline and holding his employment on the most precarious of tenures, and his political status as a free and equal citizen and a maker and unmaker of governments. To a certain extent this inconsistency is inherent in the necessities of industrial organisation. No good can come, as even the controllers of Soviet Russia have had to recognise, of blurring the distinction between those whose function is to conceive and to plan and those whose function is to execute their plans. Nor is there anything to be gained by applying blindly the political devices of the public meeting and the ballot box to the quite different problems of industrial life. It would, we think, be wrong and dishonest to hold out hopes to the ordinary man that he will ever be in a position to choose at each moment of the day whether he will do this thing or that, or even to take a direct part in the election or dismissal of those from whom he receives his immediate instructions. But it is not unreasonable to hope and to plan both that he shall take a direct part in framing and administering the code of discipline under which his daily work must be done and also that, through the organisation which he has built and the leaders in whom he has confidence, he shall come to exercise an increasing influence on the wider government both of the business unit and of the whole industry of which he forms part.

The State here, from the very nature of the case, can do little; but it can do something, and the nation should resolve that something shall be done. . . .

Our conclusion then is not the rough-and-ready rule that, since so much already has been done in the direction of State action, the simplest course is to do the rest and to nationalise everything. Individual management and the competition on which it is based still work reasonably well within a wide range of miscellaneous industries. They are an unrivalled method for ensuring the decentralisation of management—that is, for ensuring that power and responsibility should be exercised as near as possible to the act to be performed, and not through a long line of intermediaries. They are an excellent means for securing a variety of experiment, and for trying out the comparative efficiency both of methods and of men. They provide, though with some friction and inequality, the only practicable method which has yet been suggested of evaluating the various goods and services which it is the function of industry to supply. We regard, therefore, the direct management of industries by Departments of State, or agencies analogous to them, as *prima facie* undesirable and likely to remain the exception rather than the rule.

Faced by these conditions in modern industry, convinced that our present social order denies a real liberty to a great proportion of the population, anxious to effect the reforms that are necessary without at the same time injuring the springs of such efficiency (and it is not small) as that order retains, we have framed the constructive proposals, touching the many parts of the one great problem, which this book contains. Financial and industrial reforms, international trade and national development, the juster distribution of wealth, the worker's right to be a citizen, and not merely a subject, in the world of production—the measures we advocate in relation to all these things spring from one clear purpose. We believe with a passionate faith that the end of all political and economic action is not the perfecting or the perpetuation of this or that piece of mechanism or organisation, but that individual men and women may have life, and that they may have it more abundantly.

Britain's Industrial Future (1928), Introduction.

125. J. M. KEYNES AND H. D. HENDERSON:
Can Lloyd George Do It?
(1929)

['Can Lloyd George Do It?' referred to a pledge which Lloyd George had given that if the Liberal Party formed the Government after the general election of 1929 it would be ready with plans which would reduce the number of unemployed to normal proportions within a year. Detailed plans had been put forward in the 'Orange Book,' *We Can Conquer Unemployment*, published in March 1929.]

The Census of Production of 1924 calculated that the average value of the net annual output of a British working-man when employed is about £220. On this basis the waste through unemployment since 1921 has mounted up to approximately £2,000,000,000, a sum which would be nearly sufficient to build all the railways in the country twice over. It would pay off our debt to America twice over. It is more than the total sum that the Allies are asking from Germany for Reparations.

It is important to know and appreciate these figures, because they put the possible cost of Mr. Lloyd George's schemes into its true perspective. He calculates that a development programme of £100,000,000 a year will bring back 500,000 men into employment. This expenditure is not large in proportion to the waste and loss accruing year by year through unemployment, as can be seen by comparing it with the figures quoted above. It only represents 5 per cent of the loss already accumulated on account of unemployment since 1921. It is equal to about 2½ per cent of the national income. If the experiment were to be continued at the rate of £100,000,000 per annum for three years, and if the whole of it were to be entirely wasted, the annual interest payable on it hereafter would increase the Budget by less than 2 per cent. In short, it is a very modest programme. The idea that it represents a desperate risk to cure a moderate evil is the reverse of the truth. It is a negligible risk to cure a monstrous anomaly.

Nothing has been included in the programme which cannot be justified as worth doing for its own sake. Yet even if half of it were to be wasted, we should still be better off. Was there ever a stronger case for a little boldness, for taking a risk if there be one?

It may seem very wise to sit back and wag the head. But while we wait, the unused labour of the workless is not piling up to our credit in a bank, ready to be used at some later date. It is running irrevocably to waste; it is irretrievably lost. Every puff of Mr. Baldwin's pipe costs us thousands of pounds. . . .

So in the end we have the worst of all worlds. The country is backward in its equipment, instead of being thoroughly up to date. Business profits are poor, with the result that the yield of the income tax disappoints the Chancellor of the Exchequer, and he is unable either to relieve the taxpayer or to push forward with schemes of social reform. Unemployment is rampant. This want of prosperity actually diminishes the rate of saving and thus defeats even the original object of a lower rate of interest. So rates of interest are, after all, high.

It is not an accident that the Conservative Government have landed us in the mess where we find ourselves. It is the natural outcome of their philosophy:

'You must not press on with telephones or electricity, because this will raise the rate of interest.'

'You must not hasten with roads or housing, because this will use up opportunities for employment which we may need in later years.'

'You must not try to employ every one, because this will cause inflation.'

'You must not invest, because how can you know that it will pay?'

'You must not do anything, because this will only mean that you can't do something else.'

'Safety First! The policy of maintaining a million unemployed has now been pursued for eight years without disaster. Why risk a change?'

'We will not promise more than we can perform. We, therefore, promise nothing.'

This is what we are being fed with.

They are slogans of depression and decay—the timidities

and obstructions and stupidities of a sinking administrative vitality.

Negation, Restriction, Inactivity—these are the Government's watchwords. Under their leadership we have been forced to button up our waistcoats and compress our lungs. Fears and doubts and hypochondriac precautions are keeping us muffled up indoors. But we are not tottering to our graves. We are healthy children. We need the breath of life. There is nothing to be afraid of. On the contrary. The future holds in store for us far more wealth and economic freedom and possibilities of personal life than the past has ever offered.

There is no reason why we should not feel ourselves free to be bold, to be open, to experiment, to take action, to try the possibilities of things. And over against us, standing in the path there is nothing but a few old gentlemen tightly buttoned-up in their frock coats, who only need to be treated with a little friendly disrespect and bowled over like ninepins.

Quite likely they will enjoy it themselves, when once they have got over the shock.

J. M. Keynes, *Essays in Persuasion*
(1931), pp. 119-34.

126. SIR WILLIAM BEVERIDGE:
Full Employment in a Free Society
(1944)

In the war against unemployment, controlled location of industry and organised mobility of labour are minor measures. The main measure is the ensuring of adequate total outlay at all times. The first condition of full employment is that total outlay should always be high enough to set up a demand for products of industry which cannot be satisfied without using the whole man-power of the country; only so can the number of vacant jobs be always as high as or higher than the number of men looking for jobs. . . .

Who is to secure that the first condition, of adequate total outlay at all times, is satisfied? The answer is that this must be made a responsibility of the State. No one else has the requisite powers; the condition will not get satisfied automatically. It must be a function of the State in future to ensure adequate total outlay and by consequence to protect its citizens against mass-unemployment, as definitely as it is now the function of the State to defend the citizens against attack from abroad and against robbery and violence at home. . . .

Acceptance of this responsibility by the State does not mean that all outlay is made by the State or controlled by it. In a free society the greater part of the total outlay on which employment depends will be the spending of their personal income by private citizens. In a society which preserves a large measure of private enterprise in industry, a substantial part of the total outlay will take the form of private business investment. Acceptance by the State of responsibility for adequacy of total outlay does not settle what steps shall be taken to fulfil that responsibility. For full employment the total outlay must be equal to the output capacity of the nation, but the total can be built up in many different ways out of the different kinds of outlay. The State may seek to increase total outlay by encouraging private consumption or private investment, by undertaking additional public spending out of revenue or from loans, by developing exports, or by a combination of any or all of these methods. There are several alternative routes to full employment. The best route depends on the circumstances of the time and country in question. . . .

Attack on Want means doing not less than is proposed in my Report on Social Insurance and Allied Services to guarantee to everyone, on condition of working and contributing while he can work, an income sufficient for his subsistence and that of his family when for any reason, of sickness, accident, old age, or unemployment, he cannot work; with social insurance against interruption of earnings there is needed a system of children's allowances, paid both when the parent is earning and when he is not earning, to ensure that, however large the family, no child need ever go hungry or cold. By destroying Want we shall also strike a blow at unemployment. Social security means a redistribution of income, as between times of earning and not earning, and as between richer and poorer. It means more spending and steadier spending.

Attack on Disease requires both cure and prevention. For cure there is needed a National Health Service ensuring adequate treatment of all kinds for everybody without a charge on treatment, as proposed in my Report on Social Insurance and in the Government White Paper. But removal of economic barriers between the patient and treatment is only a minor step, even for cure of disease. The real task lies in the organisation of the health service; the building and equipping of many more and better hospitals and clinics, the recruitment and training of doctors, dentists and all their assistants. And before cure of disease comes prevention. This goes far beyond the development of what is ordinarily known as public health service, important as that is. It means taking steps to make good housing, good food and other necessary conditions of health available for all. . . . In regard to food, war experience has shown the advantage of a nutrition policy based on science. There are many converging reasons —of desire to improve the feeding of our people, of desire to make a prosperous agriculture in Britain, of desire to stabilise the cost of living—for continuing after the war, not the rationing and restrictive side of the Ministry of Food, but the bulk purchasing of supplies and their distribution at controlled prices . . . which, if necessary, may be lowered by a subsidy. The same method can be applied to coal and to other necessaries. . . .

The greatest opportunity open in this country for raising the general standard of living lies in better housing, for it is in their homes and in the surroundings of their homes that the greatest disparities between different sections of the community persist to-day. Better housing means not merely better houses, but housing in the right environment, in the right relation to places of work and recreation and communal activity. That depends in turn upon the location of industry; population goes where industry calls it. And industry depends, among other things, on transport and power. Housing, Town and Country Planning, Transport and Power all hang together in a complex of related problems which should come under the general supervision of a Minister of National Development. . . .

The policy of full employment proposed here is a policy of socialising demand rather than production. It attacks directly the central weakness of the unplanned market economy of the past—failure to generate steady effective demand for its own products. It makes possible the retention of competition in meeting social demand. It makes possible the retention of private enterprise to discover and develop the best technical methods of production, so long as private enterprise appears to be the most efficient agency for that purpose. At the same time, it does not block the way to socialisation of production in general or in any particular industry. It is a policy of doing what must be done under any economic system which aims at full employment, namely the adjustment of total outlay to the datum of man-power. . . . Nationalisation of the means of production in every industry would not be an alternative to the policy of ensuring outlay for full employment; it would only change the conditions under which that policy had to be pursued. Nationalisation of particular industries may be useful as part of this policy to help in stabilising investment, but is even less of an alternative to it; the adjustment of total outlay to total manpower is meaningless, except as a global policy, covering the whole of industry.

The policy proposed here, while suggested by economic analysis, is direct and practical and in accord with the lessons of experience. It is direct and practical, because giving employment to building operatives, coal miners, agriculturists, or any other class of persons depends on directing outlay to their products; ensuring employment up to any given amount depends on guaranteeing a market and price. It is in accord with the lesson of repeated experience of war that full employment is achieved not by socialisation of production, which even in war is still left largely in private hands, but by socialisation of effective demand, determined by a scale of priorities. That, with a different scale of priorities, to suit peace rather than war, with no limitless demand for war material requiring rationing and restrictions elsewhere, with a restoration of all essential citizen liberties, including free spending of personal incomes, is the essence of what is proposed here.

Sir William Beveridge, *Full Employment in a Free Society, A Summary* (1944), *passim.*

2. THE LEAGUE AND THE PEACE

127. VISCOUNT GREY OF FALLODON:
The League of Nations
(May 1918)

If the war does not teach mankind new lessons that will so dominate the thought and feeling of those who survive it, and those who succeed the survivors, as to make new things possible, then the war will be the greatest catastrophe as well as the most grievous trial and suffering of which mankind has any record.

Therefore it does not follow that a League of Nations to secure the peace of the world will remain impossible because it has not been possible hitherto, and I propose in this paper to consider shortly, to state rather than to examine (for it would take a long time to examine thoroughly) the conditions that have not been present before and that are present now, or may soon be present, and that are essential if the League of Nations is to become effective. These conditions appear to me to be as follows:

1. The idea must be adopted with earnestness and conviction by the Executive Heads of States. It must become an essential part of their practical policy, one of their chief reasons for being or continuing to be responsible for the policy of their States. They must not adopt it only to render lip service to other persons, whom it is inconvenient or ungracious to displease. They must lead, and not follow; they must compel if necessary, and not be compelled. . . .

2. The second condition essential to the foundation and maintenance of a League of Nations is that the Governments and Peoples of the States willing to found it understand clearly that it will impose some limitation upon the national

action of each, and may entail some inconvenient obligation. The smaller and weaker nations will have rights that must be respected and upheld by the League. The stronger nations must forego the right to make their interests prevail against the weaker by force; and all the States must forego the right in any dispute to resort to force before other methods of settlement, by conference, conciliation, or, if need be, arbitration, have been tried. This is the limitation. The obligation is that if any nation will not observe this limitation upon its national action; if it breaks the agreement which is the basis of the League, rejects all methods of peaceful settlement and resorts to force, the other nations must, one and all, use their combined force against it. The economic pressure that such a League could use would in itself be very powerful, and the action of some of the smaller States composing the League could perhaps not go beyond economic pressure, but those States that have power must be ready to use all the force, economic, military, or naval, that they possess. It must be clearly understood and accepted that defection from or violation of the agreement by one or more States does not absolve all or any of the others from the obligation to enforce the agreement. . . .

Peace can never be secured by the domination of one country securing its power and prosperity by the submission and disadvantage of others, and the German idea of a world peace secured by the power of German militarism is impracticable, as well as unfair and abhorrent to other nations. It is as intolerable and impossible in the world as despotism would be here or in the United States. In opposition to this idea of Germany, the Allies should set forth, as President Wilson has already set forth, the idea of a peace secured by mutual regard between States for the rights of each and a determination to stamp out any attempt at war, as they would a plague that threatened the destruction of all. . . .

The establishment and maintenance of a League of Nations, such as President Wilson has advocated, is more important and essential to a secure peace than any of the actual terms of peace that may conclude the war; it will transcend them all. The best of them will be worth little,

unless the future relations of States are to be on a basis that
will prevent a recurrence of militarism in any States.

Viscount Grey, *The League of Nations* (1918),

pp. 4-15.

128. GILBERT MURRAY: *The League of Nations and the Democratic Idea*

(1918)

There is no way out except co-operation. We must face
the sacrifice. We must give up some part of our freedom.
We must be prepared on occasion to allow a Congress of
Powers to settle questions which we should prefer to treat
as purely domestic. We must tame our pride a little. And
in return we shall both form a habit of friendly consultation
with other Powers instead of hostile intrigue, and shall be
saved from the deadly dilemma of either provoking war by
making preparations or inviting attack by going unprepared.
A number of nations which act together can be strong enough
to check an aggressor though no one of them alone is so
strong as to threaten its neighbours. . . .

As to machinery, what is needed in the first place is
probably a very simple thing: merely an adding together of
the present arbitration treaties, so that the various nations
which have separately agreed to arbitrate their differences
shall form a League with mutual guarantees. At present if
there are two nations bound by treaty to arbitrate and one
chooses to break the treaty the offender suffers no penalty.
He has only one enemy, and that an enemy of his own
choosing. But if there are twelve nations the offender has
eleven enemies. Again, where there is a League of many
Powers there is no danger, as there may be in a separate
arbitration, of two arbitrating Powers settling their differences
at the expense of a third. Still more important, such a League
would be a permanent organ, always ready to act, and
embodied in a permanent machinery. It would not, like
the old Concert of Europe, have to be called into action at
the last moment to deal with a trouble that is already acute.
And it would not, like the Concert, consist of diplomatists

whose normal business is to think only of their own country's interests. It would consist of men trained and accustomed to think for the common good.

G. Murray, *The League of Nations and*
the Democratic Idea (1918), *passim.*

129. *The Manchester Guardian*, Leading Article: 24 June 1919

What use have we made, what use are we making, of an unparalleled victory, an unequalled opportunity? Apart from the negative gain of dire disaster escaped, what fruit are we drawing from success, what permanent gain are we securing for the world? And it is here that rejoicing must be qualified and heavy doubts recur. We started on the waging of the war with high ideals, we entered with ideals yet higher and clearer on the making of the peace. And then—what happened? It would be hard, perhaps, fully to explain, still more to justify, but in the six or seven months of discussions and of bargaining among the victors the best fruits of victory have somehow disappeared, and the peace which emerges is not the peace we had promised ourselves or, as the enemy bitterly urges, the peace which we had promised them. The peace we had hoped for would have been one which so far as possible presented elements of finality, which had careful regard, therefore, to the deeper forces by which nations are swayed, and would enlist these on the side of peace and of permanence. It would above all have refrained from outraging the sense of nationality, that potent emotion which holds masses of men of like tradition and sentiment together and renders them capable of unlimited endurance and unlimited sacrifice. We have not done this. We have, indeed, freed more than one oppressed nationality and created new States, but at more than one point we have needlessly and flagrantly violated the national sense of existing States, and above all of Germany, the greatest of them. It is a capital error which not only violates the principle on which we professed to act but introduces an element of instability into the whole structure of the peace which goes far to destroy its value. Again, the peace was to have marked and established the triumph of democracy, but what is democracy apart from the democratic spirit? And that spirit implies the sense of common interest and of mutual good will. How much of these has gone to the making of the peace, how much of them will remain to cement it? How much thought has been bestowed on the future of the German people in the imposition of an unlimited indemnity, in the complicated system of economic restraint and isolation by which at the same time their commerce is to be ruined and their industries forbidden to expand? It may be said that to ask for any such consideration, even though the common interest of the world demanded it, from peoples who have suffered as the French and to a less extent we ourselves have suffered, is to ask too much from human nature. We do not believe it. The real democratic forces in all the countries, here, in France, in Italy, have in this matter gone far in advance of their rulers. Had they had the making of the peace it would have been far and away a better, a juster, a more stable.

The Manchester Guardian (24 June 1919).

130. J. M. KEYNES: *The Economic Consequences of the Peace* (December 1919)

I do not intend to enter here into details, or to attempt a revision of the Treaty clause by clause. I limit myself to three great changes which are necessary for the economic life of Europe, relating to Reparation, to Coal and Iron, and to Tariffs. . . .

By fixing the Reparation payments well within Germany's capacity to pay, we make possible the renewal of hope and enterprise within her territory, we avoid the perpetual friction and opportunity of improper pressure arising out of Treaty clauses which are impossible of fulfilment, and we render unnecessary the intolerable powers of the Reparation Commission.

By a moderation of the clauses relating directly or indirectly to coal, and by the exchange of iron ore, we permit the continuance of Germany's industrial life, and put limits on the loss of productivity which would be brought about otherwise by the interference of political frontiers with the natural localisation of the iron and steel industry.

By the proposed Free Trade Union some part of the loss of organisation and economic efficiency may be retrieved, which must otherwise result from the innumerable new political frontiers now created between greedy, jealous, immature, and economically incomplete nationalist States. Economic frontiers were tolerable so long as an immense territory was included in a few great Empires; but they will not be tolerable when the Empires of Germany, Austria-Hungary, Russia, and Turkey have been partitioned between some twenty independent authorities. A Free Trade Union, comprising the whole of Central, Eastern, and South-Eastern Europe, Siberia, Turkey, and (I should hope) the United Kingdom, Egypt, and India, might do as much for the peace and prosperity of the world as the League of Nations itself. Belgium, Holland, Scandinavia, and Switzerland might be expected to adhere to it shortly. And it would be greatly to be desired by their friends that France and Italy also should see their way to adhesion.

It would be objected, I suppose, by some critics that such an arrangement might go some way in effect towards realising the former German dream of Mittel-Europa. If other countries were so foolish as to remain outside the Union and to leave to Germany all its advantages, there might be some truth in this. But an economic system, to which every one had the opportunity of belonging and which gave special privileges to none, is surely absolutely free from the objections of a privileged and avowedly imperialistic scheme of exclusion and discrimination. Our attitude to these criticisms must be determined by our whole moral and emotional reaction to the future of international relations and the Peace of the World. If we take the view that for at least a generation to come Germany cannot be trusted with even a modicum of prosperity, that while our recent Allies are angels of light, all our recent enemies, Germans, Austrians, Hungarians, and the rest, are children of the devil, that year by year Germany must be kept impoverished and her children starved and crippled, and that she must be ringed round by enemies; then we shall reject all the proposals of this chapter, and particularly those which may assist Germany to regain a part of her former material prosperity and find a means of livelihood for the industrial population of her towns. But if this view of nations and of their relation to one another is adopted by the democracies of Western Europe, and is financed by the United States, heaven help us all. If we aim deliberately at the impoverishment of Central Europe, vengeance, I dare predict, will not limp. Nothing can then delay for very long that final civil war between the forces of Reaction and the despairing convulsions of Revolution, before which the horrors of the late German war will fade into nothing, and which will destroy, whoever is victor, the civilisation and the progress of our generation. Even though the result disappoint us, must we not base our actions on better expectations, and believe that the prosperity and happiness of one country promotes that of others, that the solidarity of man is not a fiction, and that nations can still afford to treat other nations as fellow-creatures?

J. M. Keynes, *The Economic Consequences*
of the Peace (1919), pp. 244-51.

131. DAVID LLOYD GEORGE:
Speech at the Aldwych Club, London,
7 November 1927

(Sir Austen Chamberlain) is disposed to imagine that Locarno was the first and the final step. Locarno was the beginning of a new world. Before Locarno, chaos. Europe, before Locarno, was without form and void, and darkness filled the earth. Then Locarno—and lo! there was light. . . . Where Locarno is concerned, Sir Austen Chamberlain is a Fundamentalist.

It is very important, if there is going to be peace in the world, that Locarno should be simply treated as one of a series of steps and that you must get along from it. When the Locarno treaty was reported to the House of Commons, I said it was essential that it should be treated as a basis for disarmament and arbitration, and that unless it was, it would be nothing better than a slobbering melodrama. That is my view at the present moment. Sir Austen made three allegations against me. First, that I talked with very little knowledge of the treaties which I helped to frame; second, that I falsely excited hopes which cannot be fulfilled; and third, that I falsely and recklessly distributed blame which had not been earned.

Those are very grave charges against any man, especially a man who has wielded vast responsibilities. . . .

He says that I am ignorant of the treaties. That is very odd. I spent six months with President Wilson, Signor Orlando, and especially M. Clemenceau, framing the treaties. We discussed every sentence of them. I discussed them in Parliament, and recently I have renewed my acquaintance more than once with these treaties. Yet I know nothing about them! Well, it is a serious reflection on my memory, if not my intelligence.

As to the second accusation, that I raised hopes which cannot be fulfilled, what are they? The first was that the Allied and conquering countries would fulfil the solemn pledge they gave at Versailles—that German, Austrian, and Bulgarian disarmament would be followed by disarmament of the conquering countries. . . .

Is that exciting a false hope? If it is, it is not a hope excited by me in a little speech at a League of Nations meeting. It is a hope excited by the greatest nations of the world, through their representatives—signed, sealed, and delivered to Germany. Is that denied?

The next hope I excited which 'cannot be fulfilled' is that disputes between nations would, if negotiations failed, be referred for settlement not to machine guns, cannon, bombs and poison gas, but to peaceful arbitration based on right, reason and judgment. Is that a false hope? If it is, God help the world. It is a hope we ventured to put in the Covenant of the League of Nations, and it is enshrined there. The third hope was that jagged ends of the treaty, which are causing irritation, disturbing the peace of the nations, would be put right and smoothed through the agency of the League.

That hope was excited by a letter written by M. Clemenceau on behalf of President Wilson, Signor Orlando, and myself to the German delegates before they ever signed the document. Does Sir Austen Chamberlain now, on behalf of the British Government, say that those are three hopes which cannot be fulfilled? If he does, all I can say is it is the most serious condemnation of his foreign policy that has ever been uttered by friend or by foe.

I have been imputing blame. I dare say I have. . . . What is the blame imputed? First, that whereas the nations had pledged themselves to follow the example we forced on Germany by disarming themselves, they have taken no steps to do so.

What are the facts? I give them and challenge anyone to deny them. They are such vital facts to the peace of the world, and the peace of the world is so vital to the life of civilisation that I am bound to repeat them. I said the conquering nations in the Great War, including the nations which came in when we were quite sure we were going to conquer, have at the present moment in the aggregate over ten millions of trained men, not merely well equipped, but better equipped for war than they were in 1914. . . . I say still it is dishonouring the solemn pledge we gave before the Germans and the rest ever signed the Treaty of Versailles. That is the blame I impute, and I stand by it.

What is the next? That territories in Europe have been annexed by force without consent of the League of Nations or of the Supreme Council. Is that denied? I say that those annexations as long as they remain will be a menace to peace in the world. Is that denied?

We put in the Treaty of Versailles provisions for the protection of minorities in the new and re-created territories. There were clauses to protect their race, religion and traditions. Those clauses have been trampled upon. Is that denied? . . .

These matters were not a question of controversy between two old friends. They were matters so important that unless they were put right, the peace of Europe would be menaced. I ask for particulars. Well, I know Sir Austen has a view that these are delicate matters not to be talked about to common people. . . . I challenge the whole attitude of our not discussing these things freely and frankly. Complete frankness in discussing these things is essential to peace. That 'hush, hush' policy which prevailed before the war, whenever you came to foreign policy, is responsible for the death of over ten millions of the young men of Europe. If we had had frank discussions of the events which led to the war, you would have had no war.

The war shattered the Olympian tradition, and rightly so. The gods had landed their worshippers in a quagmire of blood. There is an attempt to repair and to glue together the splinters of the Jovian throne. . . .

The god who is always piling incense on his own altar is a sorry spectacle. I really wish Sir Austen would cultivate a little more detachment and not take himself quite so seriously. Unless Europe advances beyond Locarno—it is a step— unless the advance be towards arbitration and disarmament, I say, from a long knowledge of the conditions in Europe, war is inevitable. Why, there is no agreement amongst the signatories themselves about Locarno.

Sir Austen, speaking here, never said a word about arbitration and not very much about disarmament. Guaranteeing an eastern frontier of France may lead to war. Arbitration can lead to nothing but peace. Arbitration is the only basis of disarmament; disarmament is the only guarantee for arbitration. And arbitration and disarmament together are the only security for peace.

Let Sir Austen face these problems. He has rested long enough at Locarno. It is no use standing on the shores of Maggiore, like a stork on one leg, looking preternaturally wise, and looking very satisfied because he has swallowed one trout. Let him lift up his wings and proceed on his pilgrimage of peace.

D. Lloyd George, *Slings and Arrows*, ed. P. Guedalla
(1929), pp. 179-86.

132. PHILIP KERR: *The Outlawry of War*,
a Paper read to the Royal Institute of International Affairs,
13 November 1928

So long as we admit that war is a rightful or inevitable method of settling the international problems of the community of nations, armaments will abound, strategic considerations will prevail, and war will continue in the future, as in the past, to be the principal plague of man. It is axiomatic that no State can long survive which tolerates the use of violence within its own borders. . . .

The inevitable end of any community which tolerates violence within its borders is anarchy and war. It is precisely the same with the world as a whole. So long as war is recognised as a rightful method of settling inter-State disputes—as it is to-day—the present-day international anarchy and ever-recurring war must inevitably continue, however passionate our longing for peace.

Let us consider for a moment what the 'legalisation' of war means and must mean in practice. In the first place, it spells competitive armaments. That is to say, every self-respecting nation will maintain those armaments which it believes to be necessary to its security and the defence of its vital interests. . . . Yet no nation can make its own vital interests secure by means of armaments except by making the vital interests of its neighbours insecure. This is becoming increasingly true in a shrinking world in which national interests in trade and property are stretching ever farther beyond their own borders. The legalisation of war, therefore, inevitably keeps the world in a ferment of suspicion and anxiety over the preparations which other nations are making for their own defence.

But its effects go even farther. It makes the settlement of the more important international problems on the basis of reason and justice practically impossible. Alterations of frontiers justifiable on racial or economic grounds, the union of peoples such as the Germans and Austrians, the acquisition of colonies to absorb surplus population, or coaling stations for commerce, and so forth, all have strategic implications.

When such questions arise, therefore, nations inevitably regard them from the standpoint of what will be the consequence of the change proposed on their own security in the event of war, and not from the standpoint of justice and reason. The fact that war—the law of the jungle—still reigns in the international sphere continually operates to provoke the fears, grievances and injustices which make its use inevitable.

The advocates of the outlawry of war, therefore, are almost certainly right in their conviction that in a world in which every nation is armed and in which the use of violence, in the ultimate resort, is admitted to be lawful, war will in fact, in every great crisis, sweep pacific process aside, just as it did in the last fatal weeks of July 1914. There is no half-way house in this question. You cannot compromise with violence within the State. You cannot compromise with violence in the international community. War must be 'outlawed' and 'delegalised' or it will master us in the future as it has always done in the past.

So much for the general principle of outlawry. How does it differ from the Covenant of the League of Nations?

The Covenant provides for regular conferences between the nations. It creates an admirable system for the investigation of international disputes, and in appropriate cases for their settlement by the Permanent Court of International Justice, by arbitration, by conciliation, and so forth. It prescribes a period of delay, enforceable through economic sanctions, during which this pacific procedure can be tried to the utmost. But it does not outlaw war. On the contrary, it specifically permits violence as the final arbiter of nations. The outlawry school believe that without the addition of the outlawry idea the League system will in practice inevitably fail, for the reasons I have already given. I think they are right. I believe that until we base all our thinking and action on the principle that reason and justice cannot be made to prevail in the international sphere until the right to use violence is entirely dethroned, we shall in practice be unable to escape war. . . .

If any progress is to be made towards the effective outlawry of war it will be necessary to draw a clear distinction between war and police force. War is the use of violence as the instrument of national policy: as the means of accomplishing some national end. Police force is the use of violence to prevent violence from accomplishing anything and to compel resort to pacific modes of settlement. The outlawry of war is not going to end the use of force in the world any more than the creation of the State ends it in the domestic sphere. What the State does is to concentrate irresistible force in its own hands, and to use it, not to impose the Government's solution, but to prevent the settlement of disputes by private violence anywhere within its borders, and to compel obedience to the decisions of reason and justice as determined by the law courts and the legislature. It will be just the same in a world in which war has been outlawed. As I see it, the essence of outlawry is not the abolition of force but the determination that international questions shall be settled by what may be called constitutional methods, and not by the dictation of the stronger or the disputants taking the law into their own hands. I think that the recognition of this vital distinction between war and police force is essential to any further progress towards the genuine outlawry of war.

League of Nations Union publication,
No. 271 (1929), passim.

133. *The Liberal Way*. A survey of Liberal Policy, published by the National Liberal Federation, 1934

[This survey was drafted by Ramsay Muir.]

India. Liberalism must desire to satisfy as completely as possible the aspirations after national freedom and self-government by which the Indian peoples are now inspired, largely through British influence; and it must sympathise with the resentment which cannot but be felt by a self-respecting people at the prospect of continued subjection to alien control. But it is indispensable that these aspirations should be satisfied in such a way as not to imperil the fundamental conditions of a free and ordered society—political unity, internal peace, and equal laws. Three hundred and twenty millions of people cannot be governed against their will; and when they, or the leaders whom they follow, have been indoctrinated with the idea of liberty, it is impossible to deny their demand. This is the spirit in which Liberalism faces the complex and fascinating problem of India.

India must not be regarded as a British 'possession'. Already she controls her own destiny to so full an extent that she can and does impose severe tariffs on British goods in order to encourage her own industries; and although Liberals (but not Protectionists) may reasonably hold that in doing so she is not serving the true interests of her own people, yet that is now her own business, and we have neither the right nor the power to prevent it. Already she is recognised as a member of the League of Nations on equal terms with other nations. And while Britain still plays a vital, though a diminishing, part in the direction of India's destiny, her function is not that of a Sovereign Power, but that of a trustee upon whom history has imposed the duty of helping India to advance with safety along the difficult and (to her) untried path of self-government. The supreme necessity is that the inevitable transition should be made in such a way as not to disorganise Indian society, and not to imperil public order, or destroy the country's credit; and that India should continue to be a member, and become an equal and willing partner, in that fellowship of peace and liberty which is the British Empire.

The Backward Peoples. In the administration of those colonies and dependencies which are predominantly inhabited by primitive peoples, two principles have been established by Liberalism during the nineteenth century. They have replaced the régime of pitiless exploitation which marked the relations of the European peoples with native races during the modern age, and which found its ugliest expression in the slave-trade. In the mandatory clauses of the Covenant, these principles have been in effect adopted by the League of Nations, as the rules which ought to govern the treatment of subject peoples by ruling races.

The first principle is that these territories must not be regarded as 'possessions' of the ruling Power, to be used solely in its interest: they must be regarded as held in trust for the simple peoples who inhabit them. It is the duty of the Government of such lands to protect the native peoples in their rights, to secure to them a sufficiency of land for their needs, to safeguard them against exploitation, to habituate them to a régime of law, to provide them with education, and to lead them gradually into a civilised way of life without any sudden or violent break-up of their traditional loyalties. On the whole, this principle has been successfully applied in most of the British colonies. . . .

The difficulty of dealing fairly with the native population is greatest in those districts, such as Kenya, which are suitable for the permanent residence of white men, and in which therefore white men and backward peoples have to live together; and in these cases some unjust exploitation has taken place which it is the duty of the ruling Power to prevent. But in other regions, such as Nigeria, the principle of trusteeship for native rights has been carried out in the spirit and the letter.

The second principle is that, since the natural resources of these territories are needed for the service of humanity, the development of these resources must be encouraged, subject always to fair dealing for the native populations. But this work must not be carried on in the sole interest of the ruling country, or made a monopoly for its citizens. Such a policy would make it intolerable that one country should control and monopolise so large a proportion of the tropical regions as Britain administers. Therefore the government of these regions must be regarded as a trust not only on behalf of the native inhabitants, but on behalf of civilisation at large. Until quite recently this principle has been systematically carried out, and the traders of all nations have been admitted to these colonies on the same terms as British traders. The result has been beneficial to the colonies, because it has enlarged their markets and increased their prosperity; it has been beneficial to the world as a whole; and it has been greatly to the advantage of Britain. It was only because Britain was known to act on these principles that the trading nations have not resented but welcomed the immense extension of the British Empire in these regions. A change of policy, and the establishment of a monopoly for British trade, might change the attitude of the world and awaken widespread hostility.

These are the principles which Liberalism established, and to which Liberalism must adhere, in the administration of dependencies not yet ripe for self-government. To-day these principles are being abandoned. They must be restored.

The Liberal Way (1934), pp. 72-5.

EPILOGUE

134. J. M. KEYNES: *Am I a Liberal?*
An Address to the Liberal Summer School at Cambridge, 1925

Civil and Religious Liberty, the Franchise, the Irish Question, Dominion Self-government, the Power of the House of Lords, steeply graduated Taxation of Incomes and of Fortunes, the lavish use of the Public Revenues for 'Social Reform,' that is to say, Social Insurance for Sickness, Unemployment and Old Age, Education, Housing and Public Health—all these causes for which the Liberal Party fought are successfully achieved or are obsolete or are the common ground of all parties alike. What remains? Some will say the Land Question. Not I—for I believe that this question, in its traditional form, has now become, by reason of a silent change in the facts, of very slight political importance. I see only two planks of the historic Liberal platform still seaworthy—the Drink Question and Free Trade. And of these two, Free Trade survives as a great and living political issue, by an accident. There were always two arguments for Free Trade—the *laissez-faire* argument which appealed and still appeals to the Liberal individualists, and the economic argument based on the benefits which flow from each country's employing its resources where it has a comparative advantage. I no longer believe in the political philosophy which the doctrine of Free Trade adorned. I believe in Free Trade because, in the long run and in general, it is the only policy which is technically sound and intellectually right. . . .

What then do I want Liberalism to be? On the one side, Conservatism is a well defined entity—with a Right of Die-Hards, to give it strength and passion, and a Left of what one may call the 'best type' of educated, humane, Conservative Free-Traders, to lend it moral and intellectual respectability. On the other side, Labour is also well defined —with a Left of Catastrophists, to give it strength and passion, and a Right of what one may call the 'best type' of educated, humane Socialistic Reformers, to lend it moral and intellectual respectability. Is there room for anything between? Should not each of us here decide whether we consider ourselves to be 'the best type' of Conservative Free-Traders or 'the best type' of Socialistic Reformers, and have done with it?

Perhaps that is how we shall end. But I still think that there is room for a party which shall be disinterested as between classes, and which shall be free in building the future both from the influences of Die-Hardism and from those of Catastrophism, which will spoil the constructions of each of the others. Let me sketch out in the briefest terms what I conceive to be the Philosophy and Practice of such a party.

To begin with, it must emancipate itself from the deadwood of the past. In my opinion there is now no place, except in the Left wing of the Conservative Party, for those whose hearts are set on old-fashioned individualism and *laissez-faire* in all their rigour—greatly though these contributed to the success of the nineteenth century. I say this, not because I think that these doctrines were wrong in the conditions which gave birth to them (I hope that I should have belonged to this party if I had been born a hundred years earlier), but because they have ceased to be applicable to modern conditions. Our programme must deal not with the historic issues of Liberalism, but with those matters—whether or not they have already become party questions—which are of living importance and urgency to-day. . . .

Half the copybook wisdom of our statesmen is based on assumptions which were at one time true, or partly true, but are now less and less true day by day. We have to invent new wisdom for a new age. And in the meantime we must, if we are to do any good, appear unorthodox, troublesome, dangerous, disobedient to them that begat us.

In the economic field this means, first of all, that we must find new policies and new instruments to adapt and control the working of the economic forces, so that they do not intolerably interfere with contemporary ideas as to what is fit and proper in the interests of social stability and social justice.

It is not an accident that the opening stage of this political struggle, which will last long and take many different forms, should centre about monetary policy. For the most violent interferences with stability and with justice, to which the nineteenth century submitted in due satisfaction of the philosophy of Abundance, were precisely those which were brought about by changes in the price level. But the consequences of these changes, particularly when the Authorities endeavour to impose them on us in a stronger dose than even the nineteenth century ever swallowed, are intolerable to modern ideas and to modern institutions.

We have changed, by insensible degrees, our philosophy of economic life, our notions of what is reasonable and what is tolerable; and we have done this without changing our technique or our copybook maxims. Hence our tears and troubles.

J. M. Keynes, *Essays in Persuasion*
(1931), pp. 323-38.

INDEX OF NAMES

(References to extracts are in heavy type)